ALSO BY PAUL RAMBALI

French Blues

In the Cities and Jungles of Brazil

Paul Rambali

HENRY HOLT AND COMPANY
NEW YORK

I would like to thank, for their help, friendship, encouragement or insight, Sue Douglas, Alan Hardman, Carlos Leon, Donata Sartorio, Pino Guidolotti, Patrice Van Eersel, André Vaisman, Noris Lisboa, Paulo Moreira and especially Carlos Nader; for inspiration and, I hope, indulgence, Eduardo Galeano; for the British title, Orson Welles. Parts of this book have appeared in *The Face*, *Arena*, *Per Lui* and *Actuel* magazines.

Henry Holt and Company, Inc.
Publishers since 1866
115 West 18th Street
New York, New York 10011

Henry Holt ® is a registered
trademark of Henry Holt and Company, Inc.

Library of Congress Cataloging-in-Publication Data
Rambali, Paul
In the cities and jungles of Brazil / Paul Rambali.
p.   cm.
Originally published: It's all true. London : Heinemann, 1993.
1. Brazil—Description and travel.   2. Brazil—Civilization—
20th century.   I. Title.
F2517.R36   1994   93-30666
981.06—dc20   CIP

ISBN 0-8050-3079-4
ISBN 0-8050-3078-6 (An Owl Book: pbk.)

Originally published in Great Britain in 1993
under the title *It's All True* by William Heinemann Ltd.

First published in the United States in 1994 by
Henry Holt and Company, Inc.

First Owl Book Edition—1995

Printed in the United States of America
All first editions are printed on acid-free paper.∞

1 3 5 7 9 10 8 6 4 2
1 3 5 7 9 10 8 6 4 2
(pbk.)

In the Cities
and Jungles
of Brazil

———

There is no magic more prodigious and delightful
than the voyage that leads through experience,
through the body, to the depths of America.
In Europe, magicians have become bureaucrats,
and wonder, exhausted, has dwindled to a conjuring
trick. But in America, the surreal is as natural
as rain or madness.

Eduardo Galeano

One

Where did you get your pacifier?

'I stole it.'

She is ashamed of this.

In her embarrassment, she forgets her curiosity about me. She lowers her head, sucking the pacifier, half hiding behind one of the other kids.

She is about seven years old, with short brown hair and moist black eyes that hide her fear. In a plastic bag, she carries all her belongings: an unopened tube of toothpaste.

She can't remember where she came from.

Her mother abandoned her somewhere on the streets of Rio de Janeiro. She doesn't know where.

The city is big.

She doesn't even know her name.

The other kids call her Pequeninha, the Little One.

The little church faces the ocean, and because it's a Sunday, the doors are open to receive the procession of worshippers who come along the beach. Kneeling at a pew, Nilson hears the roar

1

of the water behind him. The waves fall suddenly, a crescendo; in the space between them he can count the pulse of the ocean. The long triplets mean a catch is waiting.

'My friends . . .' intones the priest. The congregation settles back, but Nilson is still kneeling, his head bowed, and they are watching him with sorrowful expressions. He hears only the water, the water that drowns the sound of his sister's voice, shouting from the shore – too alarmed to be fooling – telling him to run, quickly, as he got off the boat. Their father was dying.

Sometimes, at dusk, with the nets in, Nilson wanted to stay on the boat and never return to the shore. Then he would see the little church, its doors open, releasing a small, steady light that illuminated the sand, a soft, reassuring light, ringed in orange.

Our Lady of Navigators has orange stucco walls edged in blue and a pink-tiled roof. The glass windows are tinted with oily swirls of red, blue and green. Two bare lightbulbs hang at the end of cords roped around the eaves. Candles burn on an iron stand in the corner, flickering for the dead . . .

Nilson lifts his head to stare at the candles, at the little painted statue of Jesus on the cross, at the crimson smudge on Jesus' side. He feels a wave of doubt sweeping over him, ebbing and then swelling again like the waves to bring a second emotion, disbelief, and a third, drowning him in fear. He fears that God is crueller than he had imagined. He sees again the blood from the stab-wound, dried a blackish brown on the floor and licked by flies.

His mother had taken a mop and tried to clean it. Finally it was his sister Deborah who had done the work. The stain was the last Nilson had seen of his father, until a few days later when he saw the body lying in the casket. There had been a fight, and the man carried a knife, Nilson knew. Now the man has gone. The house where he lived has been empty since the day it happened. There was no doubt that the man had done it, killed his friend, Nilson's father. The hollowness, the aching pre-emptive absence of his father, Nilson knew he would learn to support. This responsibility that is his now, he will be able to bear. But as the eldest son, he faces a danger. He knows that the man might come back, and try to kill him too.

Nilson was the head of the family: four sisters and two young brothers. They had lit candles, they had come to the beach and sobbed together. They had walked along the shore, hoping for release in the cool of the evening. Then Nilson sat up through the night, waiting. His mother had been silent afterwards for several days. When she spoke again, it was to ask Nilson how they were going to pay for the funeral.

If the man returned, Nilson would be forced to act. He would have to kill the man, and he wondered how it would feel, concluding that he could do it easily, with an emotionless satisfaction that made him ashamed of himself. If the man came back, it would be for no other reason than to kill Nilson, because if he didn't, he would live in fear of Nilson killing him.

'Vengeance belongs to the lord,' says the priest, not looking at Nilson, a boy he knows to be dutiful, attentive and kind.

This is how it began, here in the *Nordeste*, and the priest knew that it would never end, that the logic of blood justice was implacable. He knew that the war between the Cunha and Pataca families had gone on for more than a hundred years in Ceara, and that the Dante and Nobrega clans in Paraiba celebrated the birth of each other's children by setting aside a bullet.

———

Outside, there are hundreds of thousands, maybe millions of revellers dancing near-naked in the streets. Inside the office of the police captain, there is only a purposeful calm.

'If I find him, I'll take him *alive*,' promises the captain. 'And he knows it.'

As if to emphasise his generosity in this respect, he opens a locker stocked with a formidable array of guns and rifles. Some junior officers laugh at the captain's remark, but he isn't joking. His expression doesn't alter.

For two years, Captain Helio Vigio has led the manhunt. Six of his officers have died in the helicopter chases and gun battles. Now in charge of police training, he doesn't like the suggestion – repeated widely enough – that his men prefer to ignore crime unless there's a shoot-out, at which point they like nothing better than to join in. When the net closes, he promises, it will be a smooth, effective operation. Brazil is not a bandit country, after all, but the world's sixth largest nation.

Today, the nation is on holiday, embroiled in the annual carnival, a three-day festival of pagan stirrings; a traditional rite enlivened by contemporary urban violence and televised lust. As dusk falls, bringing on another carnival night, the sound of drums begins to percolate through a city writhing in tropical heat.

The drums do not distract Captain Vigio, nor does the sound of cars backfiring from the potent Gasohol fuel – a sound like the gunfire he knows very well – ricocheting between the tall, crowded buildings of Rio de Janeiro. When the three-day holiday is over, more than 150 bodies will be found in the streets, victims of inflamed passions. The causes of death: knives, bullets, alcohol, drugs. Happily, the total will be significantly lower than last year's.

Captain Vigio can take some pride in this; but he isn't thinking about the drums, the beer, the guns . . . His thoughts are on one man somewhere in a city of nine million, most likely drinking beer and talking about football, a fugitive who has become a folk hero.

———

The American is a familiar visitor at the hotel, a four-star establishment, from which they have forgotten to remove one of the stars. Seeing him again, the porters in tired uniforms laugh and slap his shoulders. They don't instantly offer him a premium black-market rate for his dollars. They simply ask if he's enjoying himself this time.

'Had one up in my room just now!' He grins.

The porters laugh politely at the shameless Gringo. His pupils are dilated and he is unsteady on his feet, though it's still early afternoon. His hands trace a figure-eight in the air and he gives a whistle. Sweat beads on his brow.

The woman is nowhere in sight. She has left through the rear exit, slipping out onto the hot, tiled sidewalk. The tiles undulate in a black and white wave pattern, subsiding and erupting with the heat.

In the streets around the hotel, she is hard to distinguish. She wears her shorts higher and tighter and brushes past men with unambiguous intimacy. In this part of Copacabana, there are many women like her who offer to exchange dollars for the always damp Cruzeiro bills and damper sheets. Like the porters, they give a premium rate; a cheap, inflationary thrill.

That's just one reason why visiting football teams choose to stay in this hotel, along with vacationing North Americans. Fortunately, they have a room for me, even in the middle of the biggest carnival in the world, when the hotel should be full up. But in these few blocks – among the most densely populated in the world – all needs can be met. And with nearly a million visitors in the city, needs escalate. To satisfy them, people follow the example set by the rulers of their country, prostrating themselves before the almighty, sexy dollar.

——

It was early afternoon on the previous New Year's Eve when José Gregorio arrived for the helicopter trip he had booked. He had hired the helicopter three times before and was a familiar face to the charter company. The pilot thought it would be a routine flight until Gregorio abruptly shifted his large frame, revealing, under his jacket, a sub-machine gun. He told the pilot to fly to Ilha Grande, a verdant island 100 miles south of Rio with a few houses and, at the far end, the Candido Mendes prison.

The helicopter landed in a visiting area in the prison forecourt. A man hurriedly climbed aboard with a woman who had been visiting the jail.

'*Obrigado*,' was all he said. Thanks. He looked pleased. His face was gaunt and bearded, his eyes alert. The woman looked afraid. Gregorio's chubby finger gripped the trigger, preparing for the worst. But, as the helicopter lifted away, the prison guards were too astonished to even open fire.

By the time the helicopter pilot was being grilled in front of television cameras about this bold jailbreak – the first time such a stunt had been pulled in Brazil – the fugitive, José Carlos dos Reis Encina, was back on his native terrain of Juramento, one of the notorious *favelas* of Rio. There was much for him to do. In a few months, it would be *Carnaval*. The tourist season would be at its peak, and with it, so too would the city's appetite for marijuana and cocaine.

And in the bars, shops and shacks that crowd the dusty paths of Juramento Hill, for different reasons, there was open rejoicing at the return of José Carlos, nicknamed Escadinha, the 'Little Climber' who, at the age of thirty, had ascended to the top of the hill's crime fraternity. Beer flowed and Samba drums played for two long nights while, at the foot of the hill, the police waited.

The Little One hides behind her friends, whose names are Luis and Pedro.

Luis is thirteen years old, with a skinny face and green woollen hat pulled down over his ears. Pedro is older, almost fifteen. His face is lined from drinking *cachaça* to kill the fear, and sniffing glue to dull the hunger. His body is thin, that of a ten-year-old. His eyes are sunk in black rings, but bright with hysteria. He laughs at everything he says, grinning manically through broken brown teeth.

'We steal because no one will give us anything! Ha!'

Pedro dances to amuse the Gringos while Luis slits the bottom of their bags. Luis opens a dirty palm to show the razor-blade.

Luis doesn't know where he comes from. Pedro says he does, but he won't say. Pedro knows where his home was, in Nova Iguaçu in Rio's *Zona Norte*, but he won't go back there. He doesn't want to see his mother. When Pedro was five, she left him with his alcoholic father, unable to stand anymore the drunken beatings. He laughs at this. Then his father died and his mother came back and, sobbing with grief, started beating Pedro.

Their home now is a tree-lined square at the end of the Avenue of *Nossa Senhora de Copacabana*, near the big tourist hotels. I've been staying in one of them, observing these kids for several days.

6

At night, they must stay awake, at least until one o'clock, when the *mendingança* passes, the van of the anti-truant brigade. Then they must wake again at six, to avoid the next patrol. The van takes children to the facilities of the FUNABEM, the National Foundation for the Wellbeing of Minors, which has 25,000 places for the seven million orphans of the streets of Brazil.

Pedro has been there. He lifts his T-shirt to show the scars. 'You suffocate in there,' he says, laughing. 'Every day you get beaten. I prefer it here. I'm used to it here on the streets.'

The Little One has fallen asleep on the park bench, sucking on her pacifier.

——————

Nilson's father owned a store in Ribamar, a little fishing town along the coast from the city of São Luis, capital of the state of Maranhao, high on the northeast rump of Brazil. Ribamar was not far from the point where Pedro Álvares Cabral, acting perhaps on secret indications from Manuel I, had anchored his fleet and claimed the Land of the True Cross for Portugal, less than a decade after the discoveries of Columbus. Here in the backwaters of colonial Brazil, the intervening centuries had passed slowly, almost unnoticed.

The shop sold *farofa* and beans, tins of cooking oil, rope and batteries. Vicente Lima Jesus da Silva was thirty-eight when he died. He joked that he couldn't remember how long he had been married to Adalgisa, Nilson's mother. He tallied the children instead, all seven of them, though sometimes, when he was drunk, he lost count.

He had given Nilson an English name, because he liked the sound of English names. And Deborah too. Those were all the English names he knew, other than Washington, and he already knew several Washingtons. The other children had Portuguese names, except the last girl, Quiani. That was an Indian name. The baby boy Zozimo had named himself, trying to say Vicentinho, the name of the middle boy.

Vicente only drank when things were not going well. Sometimes these periods lasted for several years; when the droughts hit and trade slackened, though there on the coast, near the state capital, they were never really hungry like the people in the interior. Vicente's cousin had a boat and there were always sardines to grill, and *corvina* when the catch was good.

'Why don't you let Nilson come out on the boat with me?' his father's cousin had offered.

That was how Nilson learnt to fish.

He was fourteen years old when he started going out on the boat. His father was glad to forgo the help he got delivering to the farms to let the boy learn to fish. When there were no sacks to unload, Nilson played football in the street and his father preferred to see him learning something. He made Nilson go to the church school in the evenings. He was proud that his son could read the letters about promotional offers they received from suppliers and that he knew where to sign the bank forms.

Nilson was frightened at first, out where he could no longer see the shore, not even the little church, in the company of sweating, joking men. But soon he came to prefer being at sea. He found he didn't want to come back to the shore. He learnt of the dangers – the narrow, treacherous channels at the mouth of the Itapicuru river next to São Luis, the stories of flood tides to the north, on the Amazon delta, that came in like a solid wall of water four yards high, smashing boats and jetties. He heard of the legends: the friendly dolphins and manitous that nudged sailors to safety; the song of the siren, Iemanjá, who lured them to their deaths. And he took pride in his new skills, mending the nets and sorting the catch. He liked to slip his fingers into the gills of a fat *corvina* and carry it home down the street.

Two

I had come across a short item about Escadinha in a newspaper in February of 1986. It described the helicopter prison break, and mentioned the popularity of the 'Little Climber' among the slum dwellers, adding that the people of Juramento had no water or electricity, no schools or hospitals, like millions of others in Latin America. They were looking forward, however, to being part of Brazil's fragile new democracy.

These were clichés, only partly true. The conditions of life for the people of Juramento hill were inadequate – medical care, education and diet were insufficient – but a struggle was going on to improve them. Church and neighbourhood groups were fighting on their behalf and the authorities of the state of Rio de Janeiro, governed by the veteran left-winger Leonel Brizola, didn't entirely disdain them. In the meantime, according to the report, they had ample distraction in the antics of their bandit hero and the forthcoming carnival.

The brevity of the report and the assumptions it contained were revealing of attitudes about life in the Third World in general, a muddle of concern and ignorance which I shared. I knew very little about Brazil when I arrived for the first time, a few months later, in the middle of *Carnaval*; into what, without a hotel reservation,

I was assured would be a tourist nightmare. I had been sent by an editor to write a story about Escadinha, which I hoped would combine romance and lawlessness in an exotic setting. To make the story work, I had promised he would show his face in the carnival parades. I think she knew this was a vain promise when she sent me. 'Have you ever been to Rio?' she asked with a sigh. 'You should see it.'

I puzzled about Escadinha's motives, and about the context that might explain them. I was excited at the prospect of setting foot on the southern part of the American continent, a land of sombre dictatorships, stunning riches and sensual festivities. This was before the great political shift of the late Eighties, when the world came to be divided, not into East and West, but North and South. It was before forest fires in the Amazon began to appear on the satellite photos, before anyone detected a hole in the ozone layer. It was before a Brazilian Indian named Raoni appeared on TV chat shows with a large, defiantly native lip implant. His plea to save the rain forest and its people from destruction became the rallying cry of the world-wide Green movement. The Amazon, symbol of ecological rupture, began to haunt the imagination, and the conscience of the North, the developed world. If it had been feasible to hold a rock concert there, it would have been the Woodstock of the Eighties.

But then, Brazil remained the province of a few specialists; mineralogists attached to international mining companies for the most part, plus a few anthropologists following in the footsteps described by Claude Levi-Strauss in his classic *Tristes Tropiques*, and a breed of North American liberal academics who came often as not to the *Nordeste*, Brazil's Dixie, drawn by the literature of Jorge Amado, to investigate another, apparently kinder fate of African slaves in the New World. Like everyone who comes to Brazil, they became fascinated by the shadowplay of a half-recognisable reality. They in turn became familiar to Brazilians, who refer to them as Brazilianists.

Apart from them, and from the tourists coming for the carnivals or for Amazon cruises, those who came to Brazil were still propelled by impulses that hadn't changed over the centuries: fortune-seekers, fugitives, orchid-chasers, connoisseurs of exoticism, fascists and free-thinkers, beachcombers and vagabonds. Fleeing themselves or their history, they came to a place without history, where the past sleeps with the present, the booming present of São Paulo, the imperial past in Rio, the colonial past of Bahia, and further north, in the equatorial forest, a primeval past . . .

It was rare at that time to even come across much news from Brazil. News itself had been suspended during the years of the military dictatorship that began in 1964, when a US battleship anchored in Rio's Guanabara Bay to prevent Brazil becoming a second and vastly more dangerous Cuba. History in Brazil had been frozen in caricature: a happy, dancing people; a bitter Marxist exile; a singer of florid, torrid, love-tortured lyrics. Twenty years of solitude were coming to an end and 1986 was a turbulent time. To bring down the dictatorship, every Friday evening at 7 p.m., in the cities and the towns, beside rural highways named after presidents nominated by an electoral college of the military elite, people came out on their balconies to bang pots and pans or leaned from cars and sounded their horns, clamouring for direct elections: *Diretas-já!* If the political traditions of the Brazilian elite were a parody of European ones, two decades of military rule had left the Brazilian people with only this carnival expression of political need.

As the dark days grew to a close, General Figueiredo, the last president under the military dictatorship, was asked what he would do if he was a worker earning the minimum wage.

'I would put a bullet through my head,' he replied.

My first, overwhelming impression, as I took my bearings in the streets of Copacabana, a few hours after I had been deposited by first a plane, then a taxi, was the smell. I am hoping now to keep wonder and curiosity alive, in the age of armchair and video travel, by recalling the smell, the one thing that you can never write down, film or bring back, that will always remind you of a place or a person. Because it can never be recorded except in the mind, smell is most intimate and the most mnemonic of the senses, linked to appetite and, through that, sex.

The smell of Africa and the Caribbean is that of palm oil,

11

used for cooking, a cloying, soapy odour to me, like stale boiled washing, though appetising to many. North America smells like the inside of an empty refrigerator, because of the air-conditioning, or the upholstery of a new car. The smell of Brazil is composed of sugar molecules – the hot, sweet smell of baking sugar that wafts from the *padarias*, the bakeries and coffee shops; and the smell of Gasohol, the potent mix of sugar-derived alcohol and gasoline that powers many of the cars. Atomised in nickel carburettors, the highly volatile alcohol fuel breaks down completely in combustion, leaving only carbon dioxide and water in the air and no poisonous carbon monoxide. Instead of the usual smell of big-city pollution, there is the smell of burnt sugar in the air, as though Rio was not merely decadent and unserious, but secretly made of candy floss.

It's my first taste of the innocent sensual lure of Brazil, my first glimpse of an Indian standing unclothed in the forest. It triggered a jet-lagged rapture in me – as the sight of the natives, naked in their opulent lands, had produced reports of a delightful Eden to the Portuguese crown. As well as their interest to covetous naval powers, these accounts held other temptations. Pêro Vaz de Caminha, who sailed with Cabral, described the natives displaying their 'shameful parts' with the same innocence with which they showed their faces – faces he found handsome, with fine noses. His letter was 'lost' for more than three centuries.

The history of Brazil is riddled with dissemination and littered with mistakes. The Indians hid in the forest, laying false trails and jaguar traps; the soil was sandy and soon grew barren. The bay of Guanabara was thought to be the mouth of a great river, named after the month of January, but inland from the magnificent bay lay only a swampy, disappointing basin, ringed by the *Serra do Mar*, the coastal range that runs the length of Brazil, covered in rich vegetation in the 500-mile stretch that shoulders the coast between Rio and São Paulo. In his *Flora Fluminense* of 1790, José Mariano da Conceciao Veloso gave vivid details of 1640 plants in the Captaincy of Rio. To find the equal, you have to go thousands of miles north, to the Amazon.

Rio de Janeiro nestles in the lush bosom of nature, suckled by the heady aromas of the *Mata Atlântica*, the tropical forest that covers mountains rising over 3000 feet. From the high-rises squeezed in beneath, you can reach out and touch the rain forest. In the middle of the city, in the middle of a hot afternoon, in a sweet-smelling traffic jam, you are still close to the mountains and the ocean. If there are other cities with beaches, Rio *is* the beach. The beaches sweep in great lugubrious arcs, sweeping away contradictions; a democratic space dissolving urban tension.

Travellers approaching the bay of Guanabara by ship, after traversing the silent, mossy penumbra of the Sargasso Sea, saw a landfall in the New World unlike any other: the mountains of Rio rising like the teeth of a giant shark out of the ocean; the Corcovado – on which a statue of Christ the Redeemer was raised in 1931, arms open in embrace of the city's contradictions, paid for by donations in the city's churches – and the Sugarloaf, jutting into the ocean, with a name full of childish delight.

To the east, across the mouth of the bay, is the town of Niteroi, linked by a new $4 billion bridge, one of the projects that incurred the huge foreign debt. To the north, spreading out along the flat shoreline of the bay, are the working-class suburbs. Rio's infamous *Zona Norte* resembles North American cities: tract bungalows and telegraph poles, freeways swooping and lacing through the unkempt miles of garages, motels and supermarkets. People stand at bars and coffee shops wide open to the street or wait at the bus stops, hot and weary. They are the janitors, cleaners, shopgirls and clerks who must travel for hours to work, waiting for economic surges that, like the buses, have no more room for them by the time they arrive.

Between the lowly, tired-looking neighbourhoods are wide sprawls of anonymous warehouses and factories. Like everything in America, the buildings seem to have been new for a day – or as long as the last boom lasted – and then abandoned in the rush to build again, further on, the next day. Twenty or fifty years later, they still look as if they were built yesterday, and cleaned only by the rain that leaves thick black streaks. In the evenings, they shake off their weariness and put on bright neon signs, becoming new and colourful again.

To the south are the lush, moneyed suburbs, the postcards of Rio, where the girl from Ipanema – warm and tender and soft and sensual – strolled between the cafés and the beach. A road leaves the city heading west along the coast through a tunnel that burrows under the *favela* of Rocinha, at one time the biggest shanty in the world. Shacks hang over the tunnel exit, a few feet above the commuters speeding home to the new beachfront developments that extend along the coast. This is the modern Brazil: condos and apartment blocks thrown up in clumps, dizzily high, in a vain bid to defy the vast American spaces. Residences of twenty storeys stand next to empty, unfenced terrain that waits, like the people at the bus stops, for another surge of growth. The buildings don't look old yet, so, I surmise, they must have been built today, and sure enough, the local edition of *Veja* magazine runs a supplement about the real-estate boom along this part of the coast. *Leave the crime and grime, come out where the air is fair*, bleats the editorial, the advertising refrain of modern American cities.

———

The police weren't inclined to go looking for Escadinha up the muddy slopes of Juramento, one of the shanty towns that cling like lopsided shrub to the steep mountainsides surrounding the city. Once, half a century ago, these places were thought colourful, full of music and folklore, a reminder of Brazil's rural past in the soaring new metropolis. The insalubrity, crime and prostitution were else-where, nearer the downtown customer, where they largely still are.

The shanties multiplied as industry and poverty worked their grinding miracle, until the folklore – the Samba Schools and the *Macumba* priests – became hard to find amid the squalor, like the villas of old imperial Rio, crowded now by the skyscrapers. These shanties have been characterised as Informal Cities, without sewage or civic representation, improvised from the detritus of the Formal City. But for the 200,000 denizens of Rocinha, at least, there is the compensation of one of the best views in the world, across the beaches of Ipanema and Leblon. One rural tradition remains, and has acquired big-city dimensions. The denizens of these Informal Cities

14

invade the Formal City at Lent, dressed in a parody of wealthy finery, with drums, masks and dancing feet, turning this tropical part of the world temporarily upside down. In Rio, there is an official policy of integration, gradually incorporating the shanties into the city plan, and an unofficial plan of containment. These people don't pay taxes; some of them steal watches, cars, televisions, even the electricity to watch them. When they burst into the city at *Carnaval*, it's like a fever, the rash of a recurring infection.

The unique geography of Rio places the rich and poor on each other's doorsteps; if you want to steal a television, or just go to work cleaning an office or an apartment, you don't have to ride a bus for three hours, as in São Paulo. It takes fifteen minutes to descend the slum hillsides into the wealthy neighbourhoods.

Born in a better part of these slums – for even slums have their better and worse parts – Escadinha led a gang that ruled the impoverished neighbourhood of Juramento. They rose to power in the late Seventies via a series of bloody gunfights with rival gangs that had been preying on locals with protection and loan rackets. Turning to wealthy districts like Copacabana and Ipanema for their income, Escadinha's gang used some of the proceeds to benefit the people of the Juramento. Perhaps he had no good motive other than richer pickings. If it was true, there was a mystery: living outside the law, Escadinha was free to make up his own rules. Why didn't his morality end with his own self-interest? Instead, he had become a saviour of the slums, friend of the urchin children.

If someone needed clothes, a bed, a new roof, they came to him. For the recipients of his generosity – more accustomed to being the victims of crime – Escadinha became a hero and benefactor, Rio's Robin Hood. It wasn't long before the sheriff – in this case, federal agents – put an end to this. Escadinha was sentenced to twenty-two years in prison for the armed robbery of a Brinks security van. He denied guilt in this affair, but admitted to the charges of drug trafficking that netted him a further eight years.

This was the first that the public outside of Juramento had heard of the Little Climber. In the police photos, he appeared bearded and downcast, apparently cowed by his fate. It seemed to be the end of another stick-up kid from the slums.

———————

To reach these slums, I cross a frontier beside a highway. The wooden shacks border the fast-moving cars, shacks separated by dusty paths without names. Though I pass easily for Brazilian, being swarthy and black-haired – and I am wearing only a T-shirt, shorts, plastic sandals and no watch – I quickly become the object of intense scrutiny. No one comes to Juramento without a purpose, nobody crosses the unofficial frontier without business.

I try to walk as though this was the case and I know where I'm going, but I am soon lost and out of breath from the steep turns. I pause to look back at the highway below and some boys call out to me from a yard. My Portuguese is poor.

'*Turista*,' I tell them, jabbing at myself with a thumb.

They stare at me, confused, and then at each other. So now there are tourists here too!

They grin and raise their thumbs, the Brazilian national gesture.

In the shanties, things are looking up.

Beyond the frontier with the highway, I was in the kingdom of Escadinha. The fact that social justice depended on a gangster in Rio was evidence of institutional collapse. In fact, the institutions of the new, democratic Brazil were struggling to become a reality, shining words describing a fiction that few, in any case, could read.

'It's the Third World,' I was told with a shrug by several of its more cosmopolitan citizens. 'It's Brazil.' Beyond the Latin fatalism, there was a sense of weary astonishment.

Once, it was clear where the Third World was. Fly south to reach it, get used to the heat and the beggars with bent limbs or bare stumps; the dirt and fear ground into the faces of the children. The way one can get used to these things, both on TV and in real life, is part of the mechanism of despair. Before long, I began to find my way in the dusty streets without names. I noticed that sometimes the refuse was piled in municipal containers. From the shacks, I heard people cooking, arguing, laughing and the TV blaring.

It was the Third World. Yet a similar pattern of collapse could already be discerned in the First World, in the no-go zones of Southcentral Los Angeles or Liverpool 8, lit by Nightsun lamps from police helicopters.

Rio was full of contradictions. In Rio, I found the First and Third Worlds co-existing, as later I would find throughout Brazil the past and the present co-existing. Rio was a nervous tropical New York alongside a quaint, impoverished, pre-war Naples; a mix of the charm and manners of southern Europe – which have disappeared or become Americanised in the US – with New World liberty and violence.

I rode the buses just to discover what the destinations written on the front looked like, lured by the innocence in place-names like Botafogo and Flamengo. I found suburban bungalows in greying stucco lining cracked sidewalks, and endless apartment blocks rising between palm fronds. I became immersed in the corrupt bathos of Rio's politics. The city was ruled for many years by governor Leonel Brizola in uneasy alliance with racketeers and drug lords such as Escadinha, a bargain struck between crime, poverty, ambition and power.

I was soon lost amid vertiginous contrasts, along the streets where seven million urchins sleep at the feet of luxury towers; where television is king and a kitsch, hot-coloured sensuality is its *Macumba* queen. I was haunted by the immensity of Brazil, and by the sense that, behind the modern façades built with surges of foolhardy ambition, lies a raw, wild and still unsettled territory. I was moved by the melancholy truth behind the façades; by the schizophrenic optimism of a people who languish – despite huge resources – in poverty and shame. Brazil was a nation on the brink: gazing up at dizzying perspectives of rapid development across an abyss of debt; a people who strive in hope as they revel in distraction.

Slums, Skyscrapers, Samba. Between the tall white apartment blocks and the wooden shacks of Rio, I begin to see there is an awkward truce, a deferred conflict. The natural drama of the mountainous backdrop dwarfs the high-rise aspirations of the middle-class; the opulence of Rio's setting makes the poverty seem less harsh. It's a pact made in the sun, at the beach and over three nights of *Carnaval*.

It links places like Juramento to the north and the affluent districts of the south, like the crowded buses that pass along the borders of the mountains, the lake and the bay, criss-crossing the constricted urban growth. In the buses, maids and workers sit counting their ever-dwindling Cruzeiros, folding the inflation-racked bills over with a practised flick to keep track of ever-multiplying zeros.

Replacing the clammy wads in their pockets, they gaze heavily from the windows as the bus speeds on, rolling and heaving. It's the movement of Samba, a rhythm shared by the women walking by.

Others, shaded by tall buildings and swollen bank accounts, stroll to and from the beaches, pausing at corner bars for sandwiches and *vitaminas*, fortifying milk and fruit cocktails. As they stand eating at the counters of the *lanchonetes*, children shuffle behind them, begging scraps of food. Passing them crusts, the lunchers eye one another resignedly. Along the beachfront there are $500,000 penthouses and, below, barefoot children living in the streets.

Three

_____

How does the world become immune to the suffering of children? What mechanism allows compassion to harden into unconcern, and unconcern to become irritation, so that finally the shopkeepers club together to pay a man in black sunglasses $70 to put a gun to the head of a nine-year-old? *Bang.*

The man in black sunglasses smiles a *loco* smile . . .

Keep your money, he says.

He is Commissioner Sivuca, sixty years old, an ex-member of a special police unit established under the dictatorship and given summary powers to deal with crime in Rio de Janeiro. Commissioner Sivuca boasts of having executed 'more than two hundred marginals' in his career. He feels the death squads are doing a necessary job, and he is seeking election as a state deputy to represent this view.

The roots of the death squads lie in the doctrine of national security imposed by the military government for twenty-one years, a doctrine that presupposes that the people are the enemy of the state. For twenty-one years, the Military Police acted with impunity. The civilian government has drawn up a new constitution, the most noble in the world, but they are powerless to draw up the reality. Instead, crime bosses like Escadinha offer unconstitutional guarantees.

They are known as *pivetes*, 'little farts'. Execution with guns, knives or stones is an increasingly common solution to the plague of homeless, delinquent infants. The number suspected to be the victims of death squads – private militias formed by members or ex-members of the Military Police, by security guards and hired killers – is growing. In the five years up to 1989, nearly 1400 minors met a violent death in Brazil. A third of these deaths occurred in 1989 alone, when 379 *pivetes* were found dead in gutters or under flyovers. The majority were aged fourteen to eighteen, but there were fifty-nine under the age of ten.

It costs $250 dollars to have an adult assassinated, but just $70 to rid the world of a *pivete*. This is not cheap, however, being roughly equal to the minimum wage, the monthly salary of most Brazilians.

'There is a clean-up campaign going on in the large urban centres,' according to the sociologist Luis Sergio Machado. 'It's considered almost normal to see them disappear from the streets in certain areas, notably the tourist zones, where the street kids, potential bandits, are very present.'

The minor is protected under Brazilian law. If they don't go to an early grave, they go to the overcrowded dormitories of the FUNABEM. Whatever the infraction – vagrancy or armed robbery – they end up together, and then, if they haven't already escaped, they're released on the day they reach their majority.

'We never saw Tarciso again,' says Pedro, giving a nervous, diabolical laugh.

There are a dozen or so children living in the square in Copacabana, near the luxury hotels. They come and go depending on the day's possibilities, and the night's terrors. They live in a frightening child's world of bravado and rumour. They survive from petty theft, washing windscreens, surveying parked cars, running errands and making grocery deliveries.

There are some older girls in soiled mini-skirts, who giggle when I ask where they live. One of them waves at a man passing on a motor-bike.

'He's a policeman. But he's nice. The police take what the *pivetes* steal. Sometimes they even tell them where there's something to steal. He takes his share too but he gives us money to eat. He protects us.'

To survive the *pivetes* must form alliances, with drug dealers if they stay in the *favelas*, who employ them as *aviõezinhos*, 'little airplanes', to make deliveries, and, if they prove reliable, might one day give them a gun to stuff in their shorts. But this is a popular stereotype, the stuff of headlines. The *pivetes* are just as likely to end up staring at the barrel of a gun, especially if they choose to come into the city. At best, they face being racketed, becoming pickpockets and prostitutes, and can depend only on each other.

The half-built, abandoned building looks like nothing: an iron superstructure, planted in rubble, supporting empty floors. The building in Parque Guinle, overlooking the *favela* of Tavares Baixo, holds terror for the *pivetes*. Some of them told social workers they were dragged here and tortured with electric prods by members of the Military Police.

Since then, the building has been guarded day and night by two officers. They have orders to prevent a recurrence and keep the press away.

Wagner knows the building well, but shrugs at the allegations of the social workers. Wagner has been an officer in the Military Police for twenty years. For the last fifteen years, he has been on duty in Rio's *Zona Norte*. A legal commission reveals that in the first six months of 1989, there were more killings in the Baixada Fluminense (1044) than in the civil war in the Lebanon (850). This statistic Wagner takes with the exhausted stoicism of someone used to figures that rise, always rise.

'There is a civil war going on in Brazil,' he says. 'What you have to understand is that the violence against the *pivetes* is happening in the context of a social war in which all the classes and ages are involved.'

He is a lean, muscular man with a thick grey moustache and a bald head. He denies nothing, neither the executions, the beatings, nor the racketeering. He considers these just details of the generalised chaos.

'Corrupt, violent officers?' He snorts. 'Of course they exist . . . There isn't the space to lock up all the young delinquents. So they get a beating and get thrown back on the streets.' He confirms what the girl had told me in the square. Some officers take a share in passing, or even encourage the *pivetes* to steal for them.

'But I'm sure the professional killers in the police are just a tiny minority. The problem is that even the police no longer believe in the justice of this country. So some of them think they have to make a stand as patriots, as vigilantes. They assassinate the bandits because in the culture of the police the only good bandit is a dead bandit. And a *pivete* is a bandit before he's a child. But in the death squads there are a lot of ordinary citizens too: shopowners who are fed up with being stolen from, workers who are fed up with being mugged. The murder of teenage delinquents is a problem of lynchage.

'And you have to understand that a lot of the kids, who are sometimes very young, have firearms . . . A child doesn't have the same notion of murder and death as an adult. They think a gun is a toy. You can't take too many risks . . . '

Wagner speaks from experience. He has used his gun against a teenager cornered after a hold-up.

'You don't go looking for those situations,' he says evenly. 'I've been in the police a long time. We all know about officers who took risks.'

Brazil is the only country where the death penalty is applicable to children, bemoans a newspaper editorial.

Among proposals put to President Sarney for the new constitution was an idea from business groups to alleviate the plight of the orphans. They suggested a law forcing firms to employ 5 per cent of their workforce between the ages of twelve and eighteen, at the minimum salary, but with half deducted for food and training. The statutory dragooning of children might have been an improvement. According to the National Institute of Statistics, two million adolescents of between ten and seventeen years of age work without pay in Brazil. A further 1.7 million earn half the minimum wage.

The problem of abandoned children goes back to the colonial period, and the names of the institutions that were meant to cope with them reveal the official prescription: correctional schools, disciplinary institutes, preventive institutes. Yet the minor is protected under Brazilian law, a law that mocks the reality of children who go from selling chewing-gum to selling themselves, from running errands to running drugs, from stealing watches to holding up buses as their childhood is stolen from them, and they are no longer children, but just a nuisance and an eyesore.

Article 227 of the new constitution states that *children must be protected against all forms of negligence, violence, cruelty and oppression.*

The minor is protected under Brazilian law, but in Rio, the Association of Hoteliers went to court and won a legal injunction on the city to act to remove abandoned minors 'from tourist zones'. At the same time, an independent legal association set up to protect the legal rights of minors dealt, in its first ninety days, with 250 cases of children who had been the victims of violence.

Brazil is the only country in the world to have instituted a Children's Day, a national holiday on 12 October preceded by a huge commercial bazaar during which the TV channels are crammed with ads for toys. Everywhere, there are images of delighted children and contented parents.

On this Children's Day, 2000 *pivetes* are assembled in the centre of Rio. They have been brought together by church organisations, charities and welfare groups, with the support of the UN and UNICEF.

A solemn look engraved on her face, a girl of twelve in bare feet and rags holds a banner announcing that there is *No Children's Day for the children of the street.*

A middle-aged woman looks on in tears. 'I'm ashamed,' she weeps.

From the balconies of the tall apartment blocks, streams of paper float down, a tickertape salute to this parade of misery.

23

Some of the children, drunk with the attention they are receiving today instead of the habitual unconcern, wave their banners wildly, smashing them against the trees, dancing with joy, screaming and shouting.

On the steps of the town hall, there are huge piles of oranges waiting to be given away. The distribution of the oranges turns into a rout. The *pivetes* charge at the mountain of fruit, stuffing their pockets, snatching up armfuls of the oranges and running away down the side streets.

In Brazil, Father Christmas comes not to give presents, but to steal children. Papai Figo used to roam the streets of Recife collecting errant infants and putting them in his sack; a Brazilian bogeyman. But now there are so many children with nowhere to go when night falls that he comes in a van. The next day, he sells their organs for transplants.

Pixote is rounded up in the suburbs of São Paulo and slammed into the back of a police van. Through the windowless louvred doors, he sees his childhood receding fast: a nagging grandmother or aunt, from whom he ran away as soon as he could.

He is given a blanket and thrown into the dormitories of the FUNABEM, where, the first night, he witnesses another boy being gang-raped. 'Keep your mouth shut,' he is told. 'One hand washes the other.'

He has his head shaved for lice, smokes a joint in the exercise yard. He is nine years old, locked up with juvenile killers and teenage queens.

Someone spits in his milk. 'Drink up now,' he is advised. 'You'll only have to tomorrow . . .'

Pixote has a pug face and a scar down his right cheek, an adult face on a kid.

There are classes, and he learns to write.

'The . . . earth . . . is . . . round . . . like . . . an . . . orange.'

In the yard, he learns to play at armed stick-up with a piece of wood for a machine gun. He smiles with relief, looking into the bottom of a can of glue, drinking the vapours as though from a cup of hot chocolate, and surrendering to helpless, hysterical laughter.

He dreams he is running naked in front of a crawling police car . . .

His best friend Fumaca, who wore a Superman T-shirt, disappears, dead from internal haemorrhaging after a beating. With Dito and his boyfriend Lilica, Pixote escapes, out of a window and across downtown São Paulo, to an uncertain freedom.

'What can a queen expect from life?' asks Lilica, feeling sorry for himself.

'Nothing,' says Pixote, wondering why he asked.

One of Lilica's boyfriends gives them an address in Rio to sell some coke they have stolen, but they get burned. A pimp sells them a woman, Sueli, for the little money they have left.

'You know how it works?' she asks. 'Fifty-fifty.' They agree.

Sueli is pregnant, but aborts herself with a knitting needle. 'What are you staring at?' she snaps at Pixote in the bathroom. 'It's you.'

Sueli lures men for the gang to mug while they have their trousers down. When one of the muggings goes wrong, Pixote shoots, killing his friend Dito.

Hector Babenco's film, based on the book by José Louzeiro, ended with Pixote sucking at Sueli's breast. Unable to bear both their pain, she threw him out.

Pixote was played by eleven-year-old Fernando da Silva Ramos. He was chosen from 1300 auditions, one of the nine children of a widow from an impoverished suburb of greater São Paulo. 'It was very easy to play Pixote,' he told the press. 'I knew that life very well.'

Fernando had been to school. An intelligent boy who liked to play pinball, he had already appeared in a small dramatic role, thanks to his haunting, already mature face, and wanted to be an actor. For a few years, Fernando was a celebrity. The film won the New York Critics Award for best foreign film and Fernando's incarnation of the vagrant youth was celebrated for its grim veracity and emotional force. He went on promotional tours abroad and appeared in two more films over the next two years and in a television soap opera.

But the role of Pixote wouldn't go away. Fernando was accused of a burglary in 1984, and pleaded in tears with reporters, 'I want someone to take away this image of Pixote that clings to me. I want to be able to live like everybody else, and not be forever harassed.'

All the delinquents of Brazil had come to resemble Pixote. In August of '87, Fernando was again accused of a crime, identified by someone who claimed to have seen 'Pixote' committing a robbery in a nearby suburb. The Military Police raided his house. Fernando was there, shirtless, and before he even knew he had been accused, he was dead. The police had fired eight bullets into him. They thought they saw a gun, but witnesses said Fernando was unarmed. He was nineteen years old. The whole world knew Pixote, but his baby daughter Jacqueline, eighteen months old when Fernando died, will never know her father.

———

The thin, scampering children of Juramento, who wear only well-washed football shorts, will do anything for Escadinha, the bandit hero. They describe him with the awe usually reserved for soccer stars, mixed with proud familiarity. His audacious helicopter escape from the Candido Mendes prison was no surprise to them. Escadinha had done it once before, cutting short his thirty-year sentence by scaling the wall of a less secure prison to flee in a waiting car.

During his first jail spell, Escadinha had found himself sharing cells with political offenders imprisoned under the dictatorship: Maoists, Castrists, anarchists and Marxists. From them, he learned the strategies of the urban guerrilla. He bought the children toys, clothes, milk and books for school. His VW van would arrive laden with these goods, a miraculous bounty. In return, they formed a clandestine network to protect Escadinha.

Like the eleven other *favelas* of Rio, Juramento is a self-contained kingdom of the poor, with 30,000 inhabitants and a dozen or so entry points. There is no glass in the windows of the shacks, no electricity or water other than that which can be tapped off the city, and when it rains, the gutters run with mud and refuse. The hill is riddled with alleys and passages and the children, like children everywhere, know all the secret routes. They warn Escadinha of strangers in the area or police approaching by flying homemade kites. There are kites swooping above as I make my way up the hill, and I wonder if they are being flown because of me.

Their parents, too, owe a debt to Escadinha for the clothing and medicine he distributed and for the favours he bestowed. It may have been the mafia-style tactic of any shrewd, rising crime baron, but whatever his motives, Escadinha was repaid with an obstinacy that frustrated the authorities. The denizens of Juramento hindered access by the police and helped the Little Climber make good a number of spectacular escapes from his sanctuary on the *morro*.

On the run for two years after his first jailbreak, Escadinha fashioned for himself the myth of a compassionate mobster, controlling a 100-strong gang with the help of his brother, nicknamed Paulo Maluco, 'Mad Paul'. As the gang pursued their activities, he remained hidden. Almost cornered in August '84, he escaped a cordon around a nearby farm and then another, twelve hours later, when police swooped on Juramento with helicopters and forty men. They netted 100 kilos of marijuana, three kilos of cocaine, rifles, revolvers, grenades, dynamite, police uniforms and stolen goods along with four gang members. But no bandit leader.

Unable to approach the hill from below, the police made more raids by helicopter, resulting in gun battles that caused one woman resident to complain that 'the place only turns into a hell hole when the police arrive!'

When, in November '84, a police helicopter crashed on the hill, killing the pilot and three officers, they opted to change tactics and wait for Escadinha to come out. Just a few days later, he obliged.

A green Chevy Opala was seen speeding away from the hill. Catching up, police tattooed the car with machine-gun fire as the two occupants tried to flee down a side street, wounding Escadinha but not his passenger, a pregnant fourteen-year-old he was ferrying to hospital.

'He won't stop helping people,' promised one *morro* resident afterwards.

'Here, he is king,' said another woman, describing how Escadinha had run back to the hill to avoid capture. 'There isn't a mayor or president to equal him. He protects us and we count on him. He doesn't sell bananas,' she reasoned, 'he sells drugs. But he doesn't kill people and he isn't guilty of the crimes he's accused of in the press.'

She was referring to armed robbery, extortion, dealing in stolen goods – and murder.

'He knows a lot,' added a neighbour. She was impressed by his good shoes, fine clothes and evidently charmed existence. 'He won't be caught.'

A few months later, in the spring of 1985, a stolen car was identified by a police patrol in a nearby suburb. A man got out, but froze as police approached, brandishing machine guns. He didn't put up a struggle, just raised his arms and gave himself up. In the car were a number of firearms and his girlfriend, Rosimar Mateus. The police had recaptured Escadinha at last. They fired shots in the air, as much in triumph as to ward off the jeering crowd that had gathered.

A few hours later, Escadinha was sitting in police headquarters, handcuffed behind his back, grinning. He almost seemed to be enjoying the attention. Shorn of beard and moustache and wearing spectacles, he appeared a mild villain, unexpectedly self-assured according to the prosecutor who questioned him. Thin and animated, he showed signs of protracted cocaine use.

He said, 'I don't know anything. I'm not ready to give an interview. If there is anything, it's for the police to say. But everything that has gone out in the newspapers accusing me is lies and sensationalism! It hurts me when people say I'm a thief or a murderer. I never robbed, in spite of being accused of armed robbery and being sentenced. And I've never killed anyone nor ordered anyone killed.'

On the table in front of him, meanwhile, lay the contents of the car boot, a small arsenal. The police captain shrugged.

Escadinha was transferred to Ilha Grande this time, where he was surrounded by flies and water, and apparently forgotten until the helicopter came to get him.

On the TV news that evening in 1985, Escadinha's recapture,

like his subsequent helicopter escape, was scarcely distinguishable from an episode of *Falange Vermelha*, the daily saga of a terrorist gang trying to reconcile crime with social concern.

In custody Escadinha had shown no hint of remorse at his chosen lifestyle. He too was oblivious to the contradictions. He boasted that he had several times watched from nearby the confused police raids on Juramento and had even danced in the previous year's carnival.

'I was in the Salgueiro parade wearing a white suit, red shirt and yellow scarf. I plan to go again too!'

Back in jail, his bravado didn't desert him. Protesting at conditions on Ilha Grande – there was no sink or toilet in his cell, no ventilation and swarms of mosquitoes and cockroaches – he went on hunger strike. He wrote a letter to the prison governor demanding to be transferred to a jail that met with the rules of the constitution. 'Or is there a law that denies me the right to breathe? I'd rather die in a hunger strike than die from these conditions.'

The prison governor was unmoved. 'Every day there's a hunger strike here. If he is on one, it's not going to get him anywhere.'

Two days into his campaign, fourteen other prisoners had joined him. By the fifth day, Escadinha was moved to the prison hospital.

'My sacrifice has been worth the effort,' he concluded from his new, more salubrious hospital bed. 'I got out of the hole I was in.'

Now he is on the run again, a fugitive back on the *morro*. There is little chance of me coming across him, despite the attention I draw on the hill. By identifying myself as a tourist, I hoped I wouldn't be mistaken for a plainclothes policeman. But I begin to feel the stares, and behind them, the suspicion that I'm either a liar or a fool. I decide to head back down the hill, to follow up the only lead I have, the address of Escadinha's father.

I find the two-room house on the fringes of Juramento, a suburb where the streets have lighting and names. A striking figure with a bushy white beard, seventy-four-year-old Manuel Encina isn't sure if he is pleased or dismayed with his son. 'I feel sad but also proud,' he says. 'The police will try to kill him to stop him. But he's not a bandit; he helps people. I worked hard to ensure his education.'

Manuel Encina was once involved in politics. He was an anarchist, he explains, who came to Brazil fifty years ago, a refugee from repression in Chile. His son is hardly typical of the other crime bosses who run the slums of Rio: Silvio Maldicião on the Morro de Rebu, Pena on the Morro da Providência, Pedro Ribeiro on the Morro de Santa Marta. According to his father, Escadinha grew up not in the bars or back alleys but behind a school desk. He didn't leave until the age of eighteen. Indeed, Escadinha's advice to his admirers is, 'Study to be someone in your life.'

Their father blames drugs for luring José and his brother Paulo into the underworld, though, he insists, 'the real problem in Brazil is not drugs but corruption, white-collar crime.'

It's a familiar tale, written over the decades of military rule. The campaign to be rid of the old regime was peaceful, if noisy and colourful in the Brazilian way. For two years it grew, pressured by spiralling inflation. At set times, whole cities would halt – people would sound car horns, emerge on balconies and in the streets to bang pots and pans. The organised, persistent clamour was unassailable. So too was the debt problem. The Brazilian foreign debt had spiralled to $120 billion, the highest of any country in the developing world. It was much easier, finally, after the huge rallies in '83 and '84 calling for direct elections – *Diretas-já* – to hand the whole mess over to a civilian government.

The civilians celebrated politically by abandoning all censorship; emotionally, they abandoned themselves to the wildest carnival in decades.

More importantly, writers, ex-student and union activists, and others who had been in exile since the early Seventies, began to return, no longer so raw but with the maturity and resolve to change the country. It's an optimistic tide that swelled before in Brazil; in the Twenties, when the Samba Schools were formed; in the Fifties, when the dictatorship of Getulio Vargas came to an end and the nation's administration was transplanted from Rio to Brasilia, architect Oscar Niemeyer's brand-new future city high on the inland plains, with free public transport for civil servants but nowhere for anyone to go.

Since the exaltation of '84, however, the slums have grown worse. Monthly rent and price rises drive people out of even their lowly shacks. They eat, sleep and make love in the streets. In this chaos, where to turn for help? In such an environment, distinctions blur between crime and politics. The governor of the state of Rio needs the votes of the middle-class and the slum dwellers – the Formal and Informal citizens – who only have to be able to sign their name on the electoral roll.

It's regalia rather than rhetoric that wins the loyalties of the poor. Their allegiances to the local Samba Schools – not schools but community groups that came together initially to produce the carnival floats – are transferred *en bloc* on polling day. Funds for the lavish parades come from the *Bicheiros*, the big bosses of the *Jogo do Bicho*, a street lottery based on animal characters that, though illegal, is allowed to flourish.

Four

'Want to make a little wish?' the man asks me. He is seated at a table near the doorway of the bar.

He shrugs when I register only confusion. '*Ta legal*,' he says, giving me the Brazilian national gesture, a thumbs-up. That's fine. No problem. Here comes another one now . . .

'*Mil* on the dog,' he says, a construction worker in a lopsided hard-hat who quickly drinks his glass of hot, sweet Brazilian coffee.

'You're barking up the wrong tree,' someone jokes, and everybody laughs.

The man jots with a pencil on a slip of paper and gives it to the construction worker, who leaves a bill on the table. It's midday. By 3 p.m., the result will be out . . .

The *Jogo do Bicho* is a numbers racket based on animal characters, a system of signification that appeals to the Brazilian psyche. The Indians believe in the spirits of animals, and the *orixás*, the African saints, have characteristics associated with the animals they demand as sacrifices. There are other, official lotteries, including a weekly one based on the results of soccer matches. But the *Bicho* is an obsession, combining aspects dear to the Brazilian heart of criminality, innocence and folly.

Perhaps because it's illegal, people prefer the *Bicho*. They distrust officialdom, but they know they can trust a crook to be honest. As well as handling more cash each week than some banks, the *Bicho* is more reliable too. A winning animal always pays out. Otherwise, who *can* you trust? In every neighbourhood, there's a game. If it isn't in the bar on the corner, it's in the barber shop or the store.

'It's difficult to understand, to feel, to respect, to know Rio without the *Bicho*,' writes the author João Antonio. 'Of all our institutions, it's the one that best reveals the soul of Brazil.'

In Rio alone, the *Jogo do Bicho*, the 'Animal Game', is reckoned to have a turnover of $10 million a week and employ 50,000 people; as many as Autolatina, the automotive giant formed by Ford and Volkswagen in the late Fifties to build cars in Brazil and Argentina. You can tell the employees of the *Bicho* by their nice clean shoes, because this isn't working. They are agents, lookouts, runners, tellers, bagmen and maybe one day they might get to be bosses, *Bicheiros*. You can tell the bosses by their heavy gold jewellery; stout, nervous types, you can see them in the private boxes at the *Sambadromo*, alongside various civic notables, watching the parades of the Samba Schools that they've bought – along with the villas, yachts and football clubs – with *their* winnings.

It all started, innocently enough, in 1892, at the zoo. The zoological park was the endeavour of Baron de Drummond, on his land at Villa Isabel, and, at first, it was generously endowed by the Imperial treasury. The Republicans, coming to power in 1889, saw no need to continue this largesse towards the cronies of Emperor Dom Pedro II, and left the Baron and his animals to fend for themselves. Having spent a great deal of money to acquire species from around the world, Baron de Drummond was in dire financial straits by the time a Mexican named Zevada proposed a scheme to run a lottery in the zoo.

Drawings of different animals were printed on the entrance tickets and, at the end of the afternoon, a placard was hoisted above the exit with the winning drawing. The lucky tickets were worth up to twenty times what they cost. This simple diversion rapidly caught on. Instead of tickets, families would ask for a lion, a monkey, a snake and a cat at the ticket booths, which had to be enlarged for the flood of visitors. The tram company didn't have enough cars to cope at the weekends.

Promenading in his zoo on crowded Sundays, amid the flags and laughter, the music and the cries of the animals, the Baron laughed at his good fortune.

The animal lottery became a daily diversion. It began to spread beyond the gates of the zoo – at which point, it was outlawed by the government. Driven underground, the *Bicho* ceased to be a mere fad and acquired a fatal, illicit thrill for punters – many of them poor blacks, the descendants of slaves accustomed to sharing in secret rituals. For upwardly mobile mulattos not yet admitted to the Jockey Club, it provided a substitute for the pleasures of the turf. In the free and easy city, every shopkeeper became a bookmaker, taking orders for beans, onions and tigers on the side. By the end of the month some households had run up bills for the *Bicho* equivalent to those for their groceries. The lucky ones paid for their groceries from the *Bicho*. There was no longer any need for extra tramcars to the zoo, the animals of the *Bicho* roamed the city. Rio was one huge bestiary, and inside each animal was potential jackpot!

The animals lurked everywhere, on illustrated signboards, in the configurations of words, and especially in dreams, providing much amusement for the urbane, superstitious Rio public. The backs of laundry tickets were printed with advice on how to divine the *Bichos* from dreams. After lunch, a ruminative calm settled on the city, as the animals ran their secret race. The result of the lottery was announced – in secret – at 3 p.m. and, by a process of urban magic, was at once known by all. What is magic but a kind of contagion, an obscure or ill-read cause and effect? Even today, bets on football matches in Brazil are made not only out of loyalty or the evaluation of skills but by the accumulation of scattered portents. In the same way, the disparate ingredients of a *Macumba* ritual – stones, hairs, ointments, broken toys – combine in mysterious, irresistible formulae.

There are academic studies of the *Jogo do Bicho*, including one, from the University of Pernambuco, analysing the mathematics of a game that has spread to all the major cities, typically consisting of twenty-five animals and over a dozen types of bet. The multiplications involved are a daily test for Brazilians, who, even if many of them can't read, are inflation-trained in street numeracy and have little trouble keeping up.

During the first half of the century, the *Bicho* became established in Rio, in factories, banks, insurance companies, department stores, even in the pages of a newspaper, *Mascotte*, which had a double language devoted to the game. Rings of bookies and runners were dismantled by the police. When they caught the bankers, the draw was divided in two; a disappointment for the punters, but an incentive for the police.

Today, the game has changed. The stakes are higher. The *Bicheiro* on the corner has become the big shot in the *Sambadromo*.

One of these was Natalino José do Nascimento, who had only one arm, which made him no less fearful. There was menace in his eyes, appropriate for a son of Ogun, and his repute as a gangster was confirmed by sojourns on Ilha Grande and Pig Island. He found time nevertheless to become the godfather to 250 children. He was, in effect, an honourable member of the community of Portela, the president of the local Samba School – renowned in the Seventies for its lavish, no-expense-spared carnival parades – and the owner of a professional football club.

Even as the manacles snapped around his remaining wrist once again, and he was led away, aged seventy, to a retirement in the pen, he looked back with pride at his achievements.

'Here, there are forty-one paved streets and thanks to me all these hills have running water,' he said. 'In this *favela*, of which I was the founder, more than two hundred homes have been built thanks to me. I gave them the land and, what's more, the materials! All for the poor, for the people! The Samba owes a lot to my profession and if I wanted to, I could have been a senator!' He paused to consider the irony of this. 'But it wouldn't have been long before they stripped me of office for some little infraction!' he joked.

Samba, football, *Bicho*; here is the power nexus, delivering dreams and payoffs to the poor and votes to their smart new friends. The politicians give away beer and T-shirts and the *Bicheiro*s give away spectacle. João Antonio complains that they exploit paternalism, their good deeds mask bad deeds. And what was once quaint, with overcrowding, has become murderous. The easy Cariocan values have been warped by the rural influx, by the dictatorship and inflation. Bodies in the bay now testify to deadly disputes over a lucrative pitch.

And then there is the power hex: supposedly clandestine, the *Bicheiro*s like display, flirt with notoriety, want to be part of the legend. Since the example of Natalino in the Seventies, they've all been spending on *ad hoc* social programmes and Samba Schools. The sums have reached millions of dollars, causing purists to complain they're perverting the popular spirit of the Samba parades. It's unfair competition for schools without a big-time *Bicheiro* behind them.

Carnaval fulfils its function of turning the world upside down: beggars become princes, the law-abiding become lawless and the lawless become upstanding. You can see them in the private boxes:

Castor Goncalves de Andrade Silva, sixty-six-year-old boss of Mocidade Independente. Dares to wear a Rolex in Rio and a white suit at the head of the Mocidade parades. Condemned for illegal casino operations: running a warehouse full of slot machines. Accused of being behind the death of an ex-associate.

Valdemiro Garcia, better known as Miro, sixty-three-year-old president of the Salgueiro School. Considered the top banker of the Rio *Bicho*. Convicted for his involvement in illegal casino operations with Castor de Andrade. Like Castor, he favours white suits, with matching white ties. Homicide proceedings are pending against him.

Luiz Pacheco Drummond, or Luizinho, fifty-two, president of Imperatriz Leopoldinense. Suspected involvement in arms trafficking. Rumoured to have ordered the killing of an assailant and an ex-employee. He too wears a Rolex in Rio. Works out a little at the gym but that tummy is hard to hold in.

Aniz Abrahao David, fifty-four, president of Beija Flor. Cited in an army report as a drug trafficker. His ex-wife Eliana has accused him of organising assassinations. Of Lebanese origin, he also wears a Rolex, and, as a mark of casual seriousness, no socks.

Ailton Guimarães Jorge, or Captain Guimarães, fifty-year-old president of the League of Samba Schools. Active in the schools of Niteroi and Espirito Santo. Former member of the DOI-Codi brigade that tortured political suspects under the military regime. Suspected of involvement in the death of a police officer linked with the *Bicho*. Cited in an army report on drug trafficking and organised crime. Rolex, large belly, double-chin, needs a haircut.

José Petrus, or Zinho, sixty-two, ex-president of Mangueira, one of the biggest schools, and today the boss of Estacio de Sa. Controls the bookies of downtown Rio. Described as the official spokesman of Cariocan crime, he has a relatively clean record with the Feds as, until 1990, he was known as Luciano Pereira. Rolex, double chin.

José Carlos Monassa, fifty, president of Unidos do Viradouro. A rising star of the *Bicho*-Samba connection. In two years he has transformed his school into one of the crowd favourites, with ostentatious and expensive parades. Gold Rolex, gold chain, jazzy shirt.

Carlos Texeira Martins, or Carlinhos, sixty-seven, president of Portela. An out-of-town *Bicheiro*, he has taken over the Samba School made famous by Natalino in the Seventies. Floral shirt and clean white bucks but as yet no Rolex. Suspected involvement in the deaths of his ex-associate Nelinho and a competitor, Paulo Cesar Correia.

Want to make a wish?

———

The helicopter landed on an empty road, 50 miles southwest of the city. Escadinha, José Gregorio and the woman transferred to a waiting car and sped away. It felt good to be back in Rio, to smell again the air sweet with Gasohol fumes.

Within an hour they were at the home of Manuel Encina, Escadinha's father. 'He kissed me, then his mother. But I told him to get away from here. It was the first place they would look.'

Half an hour later they drove to a nearby hill, where Escadinha spent New Year's Eve with Gregorio and his brother Mad Paul. They drank a lot of beer and talked about football and *Carnaval*, six weeks away. The next day, Escadinha left for the Bolivian border to meet with suppliers. A few miles away on Juramento, news of his escape brought people out for a huge barbecue, paid for by the gang, and two nights of Samba.

In the weeks that followed, all that was heard of the Little Climber were rumours. At *Carnaval*, in the *Sambadromo* and at the dozens of street parties that went on for three long nights, police had the hopeless task of unmasking one disguise in a city full of temporarily hidden and jumbled identities.

———

A Samba parade starts with the sound of 200 drums – deep *surdos*, rattling *tamburins* and *pandeiros* – not loud but all-enveloping, an insidious throb. The drummers chase the same rhythm, relentlessly, for nearly an hour, as the costumed dancers find their loose formations for the parade. In the concrete stands of the huge *Sambadromo*, an elongated stadium, like a runway with spectator stands, that stretches across several blocks in midtown Rio – built by Oscar Niemeyer and transformed into public schools during the rest of the year – a hundred thousand spectators begin to stamp their feet and rock their hips.

It's the movement of Samba; the start of *Carnaval* '86. At the entrance to the *Sambadromo* track, the parade amasses, a profusion of colour and glitter. There are more than 3000 dancers in each parade, dressed in satin and tulle, adorned with sequins and feathers, the assorted ingredients of a gigantic human cocktail that will spill, wave upon wave, for two hours. A hundred in crimson, a hundred in yellow, then gold and silver, pink and green, edged on by the ferocious drums.

Under their head-dresses and capes, the dancers seem out of place in the modern arena, members of sham urban tribes. But the scale takes the spectacle out of tradition and into the present. The all-night parades are a cross between ancient ritual and TV spectacular, broadcast live for three nights from cameras poking tirelessly at drunken, laughing faces and bare, ribald backsides. In the stands, the atmosphere resembles that of a football match – with whole suburbs turning out to cheer their Schools – consecrated to carnal pleasure.

The centrepieces of this gaudy pageant are the giant floats illustrating the themes chosen by the Samba School committees. Imaginative feats of cardboard-and-wire engineering, they tower four storeys high and are painstakingly constructed over several months outside the buildings of the Samba Schools. Functioning as community centres in the various districts of the city, the Schools rally local efforts to produce the most striking and topical display. Local pride is at stake and there is an annual contest between the fourteen schools of Rio. This year, the Portela School chooses to present Brazil's nightmares (the foreign debt) and dreams (to live freely in the forest like an Indian). The ever-popular Mangueira School opts to dramatise Brazil's hopes of winning the next World Cup. Ominously, a tropical downpour falls on their floats of football teams made up of five-year-olds surrounded by cheering showgirls.

The girls shake their bared breasts – an innovation of the Beija Flor School in 1979 – improvising a lewd, loose shimmy. I can't help but wonder who they are, the thousands of women flaunting themselves with such abandon. As well as choosing the themes, the School committees decide who can dance in the parades: nurses, maids, secretaries from the neighbourhood. The men carousing with them in make-up are clerks, employers, husbands. Men and women, bosses and workers are rendered equal by the charade and the merry profanity.

It's a contagion that easily spreads to the stands, where strangers laugh and embrace, and outside to the streets, where the people of the *favelas*, unable to afford a ticket, cling to the railings, enveloped in the darkness by the sound of the drums, eyes bright with glimpses of costume finery.

Samba is the urban blues of Brazil, a country idiom amplified in the slums. It's not to be confused with Salsa, the more steady, syncopated dance-band music of the Spanish Caribbean and New York. Samba stirs the feet, not the hips. It comes from African rites, dances meant to scare up spirits. Tribal rather than allegorical, it has no Iberian elegance other than in the Portuguese lyrics, and these too can be crude as a witchdoctor's mask. It's very different from the soft and sensual, stereotypically Brazilian Bossa Nova, a guitar-based style, influenced by the cool jazz of the Fifties. The most famous of the Bossa Novas is 'The Girl from Ipanema', composed by Antonio Carlos Jobim and Vinicius de Moraes and sung, in English, by Astrud Gilberto, a lullaby as warm as the breeze that blows between the skyscrapers along the Ipanema beachfront, the hippest address in Rio around 1956, when the song was written, offering cheap rents and a Brazilian Beat lifestyle under tropical skies.

Bossa Nova is the music of the apartments, Samba the music of the streets, hectic as a rush-hour; a fury of drums, wood-blocks and oil cans. It was this fury that drove the *babalorixás* into trances that summoned the Gods from Angola and Guinea. The African chants became tunes that acquired Portuguese words; the same chants that, suppressed by fearful slavemasters, became the call-and-response verses of the cottonfields in North America. Angolan rhythms and melodic patterns borrowed from European ballads produced the blues. But the Samba, born of the free, written by the proud, with crafty African Gods at their elbow, was never mournful but mocking. It mocked the pretensions of the Brazilian bourgeoisie, who disdained this music of sex and slums; music that was loud, black and poor.

But they were eager to hear it in Paris, where the Tango – that sleazy fandango from the waterfronts of Buenos Aires – had been a wild success. A French promoter booked The Batons, a jazz orchestra led by the flautist Pixinguinha, the *little songbird*, to appear at the Scheherazade nightclub. The Parisians danced to *maxixes, lundus, cortajacas, batuques, cateretes, modinhas* and a new dance, the Samba. Far from taking pride in this success, Brazilian newspapers called it a national disgrace. A few years later, the editorialists were shamed again, when Heitor Villa-Lobos presented his jazzy adaptations of Brazilian folk airs to Parisian audiences who praised their freshness and 'national character'.

Villa-Lobos liked big cigars and 'vagabond' tunes. At a party in

Paris, a woman asked if he had eaten people, and what they tasted like. She was perhaps recalling the tales of Norman interpreters who jumped ship and went native in the sixteenth century, marrying Indian women and joining in cannibal festivities. Eating people was not a question of gourmandise, but of faith, in which the valour of the eaten was absorbed by a process of sympathetic magic. It was a gesture of respect, like the Indian custom noted by Hans Staden, a German traveller who was nearly eaten himself in the sixteenth century, of allowing an important prisoner to sleep with your wife and daughters before putting him to death.

The French were always susceptible to the tropical joys, especially those of the Bay of Guanabara, where they were the first European settlers. The daughter of Gonneville, who accompanied her father on an expedition to the Brazilian coast, a few years after Cabral, in 1503, returned with an Indian husband. In 1531, the Tupi furnished a French frigate with 3000 leopard skins, 600 parrots and 300 monkeys. Villegaignon founded a religious colony on an island in the bay and Jean de Lery came there in 1556, moving to the mainland to live with Indians and write his anthropological masterpiece. The colony was for a few years the heart of Atlantic France and there is a legend in Normandy that Brazil – and, indeed, America – was discovered by a certain Jean Cousin, four years before Columbus' first voyage. Cousin's crew members later sailed with Columbus. But the naval records were destroyed during the English bombardment of Dieppe in the seventeenth century.

The French benefited from an *entente cordiale* with the Tupi, who preferred trading with them than with the Portuguese, whom they liked to eat. Perhaps it was that, tiring of the religious quarrels that racked Villegaignon's 4000-strong camp, free-thinking Frenchmen like De Lery were more inclined to go native; or that the Tupi were not so innocently playing off one coloniser against the other.

The Portuguese founded their colony of São Sebastião da Rio de Janiero in 1565, on the shores of the bay, and four years later took over Villegaignon's island fort, abandoned by the wretched troupe that remained from the arguing Catholics and Protestants. By 1600, the population consisted of 750 whites, 3000 Indians and a hundred black slaves.

41

The first black slaves had arrived in the capital of Bahia sixty years earlier. By the eighteenth century, 25,000 were arriving annually in Bahia alone. By the nineteenth century, a traveller visiting Brazil reported that of the country's 3,116,000 inhabitants, 2,936,000 were black. After the abolition of slavery in 1888, all documents giving the demographic picture of Brazil's black past were burned by Ruy Barbosa, who said he was burning 'the traces of shame'.

———————

Where is Escadinha? An intelligent youth, he had put his wits to work in the fast track of drug peddling. By operating outside of Juramento, he earned the tolerance of its inhabitants. Maybe he thought he was adjusting the ledger, or just assuaging his conscience, when he began to make gifts of food and medicines.

Drawn into a life outside of the law, Escadinha was free to make his own rules. His morality could have ended with his own self-interest, like that of any petty hood. But by his late twenties, Escadinha began to find that being a benefactor, far from discharging obligation, brought more responsibility. People owed him favours and others asked for favours. With nowhere else to turn, they turned to him.

And behind his headline-grabbing antics lay increasing influence and power. He is said to have helped deliver the local vote for the election of the new mayor, a member of the Democratic Workers Party.

One day they might erect a public monument to his memory, or just a common tombstone. For now, the people of Juramento have more pressing concerns.

'Last year he paid for all the materials,' said one young mother. 'How are we going to send the kids to school now?'

Nearly three months have passed since Escadinha's escape from the island prison when a man stumbles into a midtown hospital, bleeding profusely from a wound in the chest.

He tells the nurses he has been mugged. They want to call the police but he shakes his head. He wouldn't be able to describe his assailants.

Earlier that day, police had raided a hideout in Juramento, wounding two suspected gang members in the ensuing gun battle. The two men had fled through the alleyways. By the time the police arrives at the hospital, the injured man is already in surgery. He had a bullet-wound in the chest and has lost a lot of blood.

The anaesthetist lifts the mask from the patient's face for a few seconds. Captain Vigio recognises Escadinha at once.

Five

Waking up from a long carnival night, I go to the beach, to roll in the pounding surf of Copacabana and see the city skyline from the water. I had begun to feel that Escadinha's life, which had seemed like the stuff of fable, the ballad of an American frontier, was simply one more existence that, as Gabriel Garcia Marquez put it to the Nobel jury when he received his prize for literature, lacked conventional means to render it believeable. 'Our crucial problem', he called it. 'We have had to ask little of our imagination,' he explained. 'This, my friends, is the crux of our solitude . . . ' And he chided those who could imagine no other fate than to be caught between 'the two great masters of the world'. Three months later, reading of Escadinha's recapture, I will barely be stirred by the cliffhangers of politics and crime in Rio.

My loss of bearings, my surrender to the fatal drifts of libido and sentiment, begins that day, contemplating, from a few yards out in the ocean, the green, virgin frontier looming up behind the skyscrapers. I begin to realise there are, as Marquez said, other fates than to be caught between the two great masters of the world, by which the old buddy of Fidel meant the then still ominous East and still cocksure West.

It's at the beach, that day, that I meet Marly, buying frozen green coconuts to suck through a straw. She has brown hair that tumbles down her back and a brown body pinched by her bikini, which seems to be all strings and triangles and several seasons too small, though I realise from comparison with her brown beach baby friends that it's this year's style.

She warns me about the *pivetes* who steal from tourists on the beach. It seems to confirm something awful for her. Marly is ashamed of the poverty of Brazil. She is a rich girl – which is how she puts it, a little self-consciously – who has learnt English at a private school in Rio.

She has just returned from a trip to Europe, where she went to Czechoslovakia. Her father wanted her to see a Communist country, a real one. Cuba is closer but she couldn't imagine going there. Marly's father was a Communist but he has never seen a Communist country, and wanted his daughter to discover the reality of his youthful ideals. She had to report that it was depressing. She remembers the queues and the rain, and she shudders, tossing her hair and leaning back on her elbows, lifting her face to the sun. Cuba must be better, she surmises, though I wonder about this as it has no tradition of middle-European pessimism to fortify the Cubans for the queues, and has the distinction of being the only sad Latin American nation, though also the only one with enough hospitals and schools.

Marly's father owns a soya farm in Mato Grosso. In the Sixties, he was an admirer of Che and Castro. But he was an anti-imperialist more than an idealogue, who never really saw eye-to-eye with the beachfront Communists of Rio. Slowly, though he wouldn't admit as much, he came to realise that a Communist revolution would deprive him of his privileges. So he sided with reform rather than revolution. At least that would have been his route, were it not for the radical effect of the 1964 coup. He was forced on the one hand to present a façade of conformity, studying at the University in Rio, while he secretly joined an underground group and acted as a contact for leftist plotters linked to Leonel Brizola.

It's something Marly's father doesn't like to talk about now, out of old habits of caution and also a sense of disappointment. He admired Fidel for humiliating the Gringos while Brazil knelt

45

down to them during the coup. News of Che Guevara's murder in '67 left him in a sombre mood. He returned from college in Rio to run the farm and the duty to his family was like a penance for the failure of his revolutionary ardour.

He sometimes spoke darkly to Marly of others he knew who paid a higher price. A few years later, Marly was born and then three more children, all boys. The baby girl was like a renewal of innocence in the world for him. She had fulfilled his hopes as she grew beautiful and strong and then surprised him by deciding to enroll in engineering school.

'When I tell people here I'm studying to be an engineer they aren't surprised but when I tell people in Europe they all say, oh! They think there is something strange . . . ' She knew that anything she wanted to do was OK by her father.

We arrange to meet again that evening. Marly has offered to drive me around the city. She knows the best views, she says. 'You have to see Rio at night, from the hills.'

It will be another carnival night.

Her bed is hard, with just a thin cover, and a copy of the Kama Sutra on the shelf beside it, next to a book of photographs of Macumba rituals.

'I used to believe in it, very strongly, but I don't so much anymore . . . My *orixa* is Yansan. Everyone has an *orixa*. I was told this by a Father of the Saints who looked at the shells. Yansan is a very strong goddess, the third wife of Shango, the god of war. Shango was married first to Oba, a kind of secondary goddess, then married to Ochun, a very beautiful goddess of the rivers.'

When Shango went to war, he wanted his wife to come with him. Oba didn't want to go. So she arranged the marriage between Shango and Yansan, her younger sister, who became a goddess of war. In Brazil, strong women are called daughters of Yansan.

'Yansan is the only god who isn't afraid of death. The Macumba of death is very secret, very beautiful. It's Yansan who officiates over the funerals.'

The daughter of Yansan is not afraid of dying.

46

She brings the storm clouds, thunder and lightning, and leaves calm . . .

I want to see if the pages of the Kama Sutra are marked.

I lie on her bed, and the days turn into weeks. The windows are open but the air refuses to come in unless we turn the fan on. And the fan makes too much noise but it drowns out the noises we make so the maid can't hear; and then we sleep. When the fan isn't on, we listen to Caetano Veloso, who sings a version of 'Billie Jean' with his acoustic guitar, a slow, sensual version that turns the song around, taking Michael Jackson's paranoia about being seduced by a woman and turning it into an ironic apology for his helplessness at being seduced by her.

Gradually, I learn the words to the songs Marly loves, songs about love, about Caetano's foolish entanglements and forlorn trials. And songs about politics. Not urgent, protest songs but songs that treat politics as though it were the subject of as much pleasure and pain and confusion as love.

'It's because of censorship. They talked in metaphors, allusions. Our generation is cynical about politics; now even here in Brazil they are cynical, where politics matters despite the corruption, which is why we are cynical. But for those who grew up in the Sixties, like my father, it was a passion . . . '

———

A woman walks by, near naked, in the streets of Copacabana. A housewife, she is walking in her bikini the few blocks to the beach. Squeezed by the angular perspectives of the avenues, surrounded by office workers lunching in the restaurants, she stops to shake off her towel.

It's not the easy sensuality that surprises me, the uninhibited grace to which I have no immunity – but, again and again, the scale and the contrast: the abundant curves of the woman, like the curves of the mountains behind, and the tall, erect buildings of this tropical Manhattan.

I am having lunch with an old friend of Marly's father, but I've

47

lost track of what he is telling me. My attention has shifted to the woman. Her lemon-coloured bikini top is several sizes too small, pushing her breasts up. There is a slender piece of fabric covering her crotch, and her bottom is almost bare.

The woman bends over to place her beach bag in the trunk of her car. João senses that he has lost my attention. He tells me instead that this is the new style of bathing suit, all the rage this year.

'It's nick-named the Dental Floss . . . '

He gives the helpless grin of the mature, happily married man. His wife, who is with us, makes a face.

João had fled the repression of the military years, afraid that he would be next for jail or torture. The worst thing about it, he says, was the insidious sort of self-repression, 'what the singer Chico Barque called a worm in the stomach', bred by the climate of censorship. João ran a small magazine, a student publication. They courted censorship, sailing close to the revolutionary wind that was blowing across universities in North America, Europe and Japan at that time, the late Sixties, by publishing issues full of blank spaces.

Now, more than fifteen years later, he has returned from exile in Europe, with the ideals of his generation tempered. He has returned to form an Ecology Party in Brazil, eager to throw himself into the new democratic struggle. But he has doubts. In Brazil, he knows, there is one of the key environmental issues, the destruction of the tropical rain forest. But João's fervour has cooled in the year or two that he's been back. 'I wouldn't speak of compromise, or cowardice, but waking people up is going to take time.' There was a certain lassitude that had come to infect him too.

'The Brazilians don't care about the forest. It takes hours even to fly over it.' What was a certitude in Europe is no longer. 'It goes on forever, like an ocean . . . '

Instead of telling me about the rain forest, João tells me about the Tanga bikini. These were first seen on the beaches of Rio in the early Eighties. They quickly earned their nickname, an example of Brazilian humour, sardonic and direct. The Dental Floss was popularised by Monique Evans, a fashion model who wore one on the beach at Copacabana and in a carnival parade. Pictures of Monique in *Veja* magazine in '82 clinched it and soon the Tanga was everywhere.

João's wife, who is North American, says the women work out to have the right curves, but that doesn't stop those who don't. 'Anyway, what I realised is they suit bigger women.'

She was dismayed, when she arrived in Brazil, at the Portuguese cuisine, rich in sugar, starch and cholesterol and, for some, protein. 'She started to worry about her cellulite,' jokes her husband. 'I told her it wasn't a problem. Brazilian women don't worry. Look at the way they walk. Anyway, Samba is the cure.'

'Right, you can wiggle away the excess. *Rebolado!* Right . . . Brazilian men like it. That's what I realised. They *like* big asses!'

'It's a Latin culture . . . '

'I don't know if it's the culture or the crazy hormones.'

'We *are* in the Southern hemisphere,' João apologises.

'Americans are obsessed with tits, Brazilians are obsessed with ass. Look at the map of the continent, it's like a woman with a huge ass! That's Brazil,' she says.

Her husband laughs loudly. He says breasts obsess Brazilian men too, because they're rarely displayed, except recently, in *Carnaval*. 'We are Catholics, don't forget. We were breast-fed by the Madonna. As for asses . . . Catholics have a cult of anal sex, because of contraception. But we don't talk about it, except as a joke, or in bed . . . '

He explains that although sodomy is a sin, you can be absolved in confession. 'This is the advantage of Catholicism over Calvinism. Protestants have a much harder time. They must carry in their conscience their prurient guilt.'

Later, I joke with Marly, asking if it's true what João had said about Catholics.

'I'm a lapsed Catholic,' she says. 'So I wouldn't know.'

———

Ivo Pitanguy prides himself on the part he plays in the cultural life of Rio. For a decade, he was president of the Modern Art Museum.

He lends his comments to tasteful photo books about the bay of Guanabara and the southern littoral, expensive tourist souvenirs that show the lascivious curves of the bays, the protuberant mountains, the warm, brown faces of the people, the bulging bodies on the beach, in a fine grain and high-contrast light.

He finds Rio exceptionally beautiful, a magical encounter with nature; so magical, one hardly feels the interference of man. 'No matter how hard men try, building in a multitude of styles, they can't equal all her sallies, all her sinuosities, all the ways the sea has found to penetrate the vegetation along this coast.' Pitanguy came here in the Thirties from the state of Minas to study medicine, and he has been in love with the city ever since.

'The city of Rio is nothing but nature and beauty, splendid nature,' he says. It's a natural park that man didn't create, that he has been unable thus far to ruin, in which he is privileged to live.

Dr Pitanguy speaks from a unique perspective: he is a specialist on beauty, the world's greatest plastic surgeon.

Women and men from all over the world, whom splendid nature has failed; from California, New York, from the Gulf states, the European capitals, from Caracas and Buenos Aires, anywhere beauty is prized and priced, they come – to the most beautiful city in the world.

He is vague about what constitutes physical beauty, and he entertains anyone who asks to some curious, diverting physiological facts instead – such as that, in youth, the growth periods of the sexual organs coincide with those of the nose. His evasiveness is partly due to the difficulties of rendering in English an aestheticism learnt from the French – all educated Brazilians over a certain age possess French language and culture – and to his wiles as a consultant. Before you can satisfy someone's desire to be beautiful, you must know what it is that makes them ugly. A chin lift might mean that age is wearing on them. Perhaps the delicate incision and fine stitching to tighten the skin about the eyes will make them feel young – but for how long? A woman who asks for higher cheekbones or firmer breasts may really want to be reconciled with her dead father. A man who asks for a *retroussé* nose is really asking for a sex change.

50

The doctor acknowledges that the skills of man pale beside those of nature. Arriving in Rio for a consultation with him, it must be disconcerting to be overwhelmed by the natural beauty of the city – and its women, women with bad skin and bulging thighs often enough, and depending on class, with hard lives that wear on their faces; but incomparable in their frank comportment. They know that the city too is a woman. They are surrounded by sinuous curves and the secret sustenance of the powerful, pervasive aromas of nature, as though in some giant perfumed sauna. This is hard on the men of Rio, but I never heard them complain.

The doctor's secret is really the ravishing city itself, which effects a change in one's self-perception. He feels that the generosity of the natural environment has rubbed off on the Cariocans, who are liberals, without petty envy or provincial snobbery, 'for whoever arrives in Rio is welcome. Whoever arrives brings with them, in our eyes, a natural beauty, and all those who profit unconsciously finish by being marked by this grandeur that is nature's.'

But Pitanguy rues the fact that the citizens of Rio nowadays look more and more like *Nordestinos* – poor people – even those who can afford not to; though at the General Hospital, where he is still a consultant, he notes a certain rude Brazilian elegance in the simplicity of jeans and sneakers. He learnt his craft at the emergency door of the public hospital in Rio, cutting and saving what he could; terrible cases: cheap limbs caught in the maw of a remorseless industrial machine.

As well as the victims of work accidents, across his table passed some of the notorious figures of the *favelas*, victims of disputes settled with jagged glass and cabbage knives. Pitanguy admits to a nostalgia for this sort of violence. Personalities like Madame Satan, whom he first encountered bleeding from stab wounds at the hospital, wouldn't survive the automatic weapons of today, their hair-triggers in the hands of crazed adolescents.

Madame Satan was the 'Queen' of the Lapa slum, between the port and the *Morro da Providência*, at the old downtown intersection of crime and poverty. 'He was a very interesting figure, a homosexual, an artist, very creative,' according to Pitanguy. He was also the most feared rogue in Rio, according to the newspapers of 1939, a Panama-hatted black diamond who strolled the streets of Lapa whistling a Samba tune. The lyrics might even have been about him.

At the age of seven, his mother had sold him in exchange for a horse. He was sold again, and again, until he was bought by a brothel, where – among other initiations – he learnt to cook. Food was his solace. He grew strong and became the doorman. From there, he took over the *favela*, where he became Madame Satan, protector of whores, a compassionate pimp who was loved and feared, who remembered how he too had been bought and sold. Madame Satan had a large, redoubtable frame, and in the carnival wore a golden cape and huge rings on her fingers, shaking her hips with showbiz friends like Carmen Miranda.

Born in Portugal, the daughter of a barber, Carmen became Brazil's biggest star and came to Hollywood. She didn't have much of a voice but she had the gesticulating hands and flashing eyes of a Latin temptress. She sashayed heroically under an improbable hat of tropical fruit, like the basket carried on the heads of Bahian mammies, of which it was a parody, a hat heavy with sexual and cultural prejudices that the gorgeous mulatto bore with happy deference. Her reward for this indignity was ten houses and eight oil wells, according to her press agent; but Senator Joe McCarthy, in the moral chill of the Fifties, labelled her obscene and Fox decided not to renew her contract. New York gays came by charter-flight in the Seventies to lay tributes on her grave in the public cemetery, bringing with them flowers and death.

Madame Satan wound up in the prison on Ilha Grande, where she continued to receive tributes and, sometimes, the attention of rivals. Severely beaten in a prison brawl at the age of seventy, she was put on limited release. She almost died, but recovered, thanks to her ferocious resolve. To her band of aggressors, she dished out as good as she got, killing six of them with an iron bar, such was the ferocity that life had taught her. Her plea of self-defence was accepted, and she retired to a *Terreiro de Macumba*, a cult house, across the Bay of Guanabara in the suburb of Niteroi, under the benevolent protection of Senhora, the greatest of the *Mães de*

Santos, Mothers of the Saints, whom no one would dare to cross lest a modern-day devil step from the shadows.

———

On Friday night, I take a bus to the park, the downtown area of shops and cinemas. I am supposed to meet Marly there, in a bar. From Ipanema, the bus bounces along at a ridiculous gait, rolling and pitching like a woman, the movement of Samba. *Rebolado*, says Marly. Shake your hips, she commands.

At one stop, a dwarf in full carnival regalia gets on. She sits on one of the high seats behind the driver, her feet swinging, shod in silver high-heels. Her costume is silver too, with a high, flared skirt of tulle. She has silver ribbons tied in her hair. No one pays any notice to the dwarf – except a drunk who tries to engage her in a conversation about who will win the Samba contest. The tiny *Sambista* replies cheerfully but soon grows weary of the drunk, who is oblivious as he tries to make his long-lost point.

The bus lurches to a stop again. A tall woman gets on, moving awkwardly in a tight orange dress. I notice she has large, hirsute hands; a thirty-year-old, she is coiffured and made-up with all the zeal of a teenage girl. No woman of her age would still be experimenting with make-up . . . Perhaps guessing my thoughts, the transvestite turns to gaze out of the window. The other passengers seem not to notice anything unusual about her and it strikes me that, of all places, she has chosen to compete for attention in a city that boasts such beautiful women. Perhaps the transvestites were inspired by them – or by the tall and voluptuous city itself, like the clients of Ivo Pitanguy. They seem to court display and at the same time want to go unremarked. In Rio they have it both ways.

They are such a familiar sight that the Friday evening downtown crowd hardly pay them a second glance. Groups of teenagers and couples from the suburbs queue for cinemas, and after the show mingle in bars nearby that host the decadent cabaret of the transvestite society, seemingly tolerated and enjoyed. Brazilians relish spectacle. No display is too large in a country of such abundance, no bauble too bright. They like the garish posturing of Anglo-American rock. They think Freddie Mercury had style. I, however, can't avoid staring at the transvestites. I am puzzled, at first, by their bone structure, larger and more strongly defined than that of most women. It gives them the stature of strange Amazons, and can lend their faces a pronounced and overwhelming beauty. Sitting at bar stools, standing on corners, they are like a new race of meta-women, the result of patient, fastidious transformations. Their faces belong to posters or movie screens, or to carnival mirrors; faces of leering, outsized perfection. In some, an underlying sensitivity has found expression – too aching and tremulous to bear as a man. But they can be garish faces too, ugly and over-painted, hiding hideous emotional scars; the past of ugly, sensitive men. And there is something about their body proportions that is wrong, or *too* right.

The incredible, pneumatic figures, straight out of horny male fantasy, are a projection of male desire moulded by hormone therapy and brought off with buttock implants. They have perfected their walks in the glare of the headlamps of kerb-crawling cars and their bitchy retorts to the insults of cat-calling kids. Lately in Brazil, they've taken to injecting cheap silicone themselves, and after a few years, or months or even days, it hardens, the skin crumples and the curves turn to lumps.

The implications of this larger-than-life beauty are uncomfortable at first – implications they are aware of in their direct eye-contact with other men, eye-contact that most women would avoid. As men, they have the advantage of understanding male sexuality. But this understanding means they are sentenced to cater to men in the way that women, with an imperfect understanding, cannot; and no surgery can remove the memory of men from them. Their relationships must be doomed to failure, except in a pantomime of desire, acted out in the arts, the clubs and, in Brazil, the streets. But they have found no place even here, these newly public if not new meta-women, except as prostitutes.

In a bar with dim lights and music, Marly introduces me to her friend Helio, a winsome youth with a tender face. He wears jeans, sneakers and a loose shirt, open to show a smooth chest. Marly met him at a party and she was smitten for a while, crazy about him till she realised his flirting, his easy intimacy with her, was a friendly game he played with girls.

'It was hopeless. He only followed me around because he wanted to copy me. When I brought him home, he stole my make-up!'

'No! It's not true. I idolised her. I worshipped her. She's marvellous, isn't she? Those eyes . . . '

Marly threw her head back to laugh this off. She tossed her brown hair and blushed. Helio's flattery, having no ulterior motive, was sincere. Marly had told me about Helio's past. 'He's very intelligent, very smart. I thought he was so mature, but it's just that he grew up too fast in some ways. He was an orphan. For a while, there was an old woman who took care of him. She died and they put him in a home, a very bad place, and he ran away.' Helio was fifteen and living on the street when he was lured to the home of a man who kept him for a while as a kind of maid in his apartment, for whom he learnt to play a coquettish role that suited his teenage impetuousness. When the man started bringing other boys back, Helio reacted with the jealous scheming of a *telenovela* star. He denied the man his affection, and teased him, until finally Helio was thrown out.

'We're still friends. He was kind to me. He taught me a lot of things, took me to the cinema and the museums and he gave me books to read. He came from a very good family.'

But Helio is not a prostitute. He affirms this to me without being asked. 'I don't like anyone touching me,' he says. 'And with this new disease . . .' He shudders.

At the airport, visitors are asked to declare if they are HIV-positive. Soccer stars appear on TV warning of the dangers of AIDS with an innocent enthusiasm, as though they were endorsing something. I remark that Brazil is socially backward and forward at once: liberated and naive, repressed and knowing. Helio knew Markito, the Brazilian fashion designer who died in 1983, becoming the country's first AIDS martyr. The town hall of Uberaba, where he was born, and from which he fled as soon as he could, nevertheless paid for his body to be flown back from New York. They had a funeral parade with thousands of people and the police band. His corpse was blessed by the bishop and – a detail that must have comforted his spirit – by the Carmelite sisters.

'It was *barroco*. It was pathetic, hypocritical – his family hated him and so did the whole town – but beautiful.'

Helio is eager to tell me the origin of the term *baroque*. 'It used to mean in Portuguese a misshapen pearl.'

By 1984, only seventy people had died officially of AIDS in Brazil – mostly homosexual, poor or middle-class. The health authorities added the disease to a long list of priorities and asked risk groups to refrain voluntarily from giving blood. It was another stigma, another trial of faith, not only for the sufferers, but for Brazil. Droughts, poverty, inflation, disease – there is a joke that God envied the Brazilians their earthly paradise.

Helio is taking acting classes. Like all actors, he works nights in a bar. There, he has a cabaret performance as a woman. A nervous soap star, worried about everything, according to Marly. 'It's a parody of the *telenovelas*,' Helio laughs.

'It's an excuse for him to dress up in women's clothes – and make fun of us,' says Marly.

'Nonsense,' says Helio. 'I love women. I should have been born a woman.'

'You should have been born a man!'

Helio sucks his cheeks. Realising what she has said, Marly kisses him, and this time Helio blushes.

He explains the Brazilian fascination with what he calls 'transformation'.

The first Brazilians, the Indians, were bisexual, he says, citing anthropologists like Darcy Ribeiro and Levi-Strauss. 'The Indians are so delicate. And they're always touching each other.' For Helio, this affirms their liberated sensibility. In certain circumstances, Indians did swap sex roles, though this would not have had the same meaning for them. Some Indians were also thought 'amoral' because they believed that conception required a combination of sperm from different men.

'Another reason,' says Helio, 'is that there weren't enough women for the theatre in Brazil.'

Women had been banned from theatres in Portugal under the reign of Dona Maria I, to spare them from the attention of 'the worst of the vulgar crowd'. They couldn't even enter as spectators, and the use of curtains in boxes was forbidden in the eighteenth century. The decree was revoked in 1800 but well-to-do women still stayed at home, especially in the colonies, setting the stage for mulattos – female or male – to entertain with parodies of such women, and for visiting European actresses (who had to furnish a medical certificate affirming they were disease-free) to enjoy an instant notoriety.

There are other reasons for the flowering of transvestism in the exotic hot-house of Brazil, ignored by historians until lately, because they belonged to the little-understood rituals of Africa: the *Macumba* and its off-shoot, *Carnaval*; ceremonies of trance and transformation.

The man I had seen on the bus was probably not a transvestite, Helio explains, but someone on his way to *Carnaval*.

'Have you ever been before?' He asks. '. . . You know, everyone in Brazil is homosexual,' he says extravagantly. 'As long as *you* are doing the fucking, you're not a homosexual. You're *machista*!'

In 1846, the Portuguese Consul encouraged the immigration of prostitutes from the Azores, who were followed by Polish and French women. His motive, according to the historian Gilberto Freyre, was to stamp out male prostitution from the Portuguese districts of Rio. By the turn of the century, Pires de Almeida was able to confirm that 'male prostitution has notably declined, for the sole reason that female prostitution has dramatically increased.'

The transvestite prostitutes are not a new phenomenon in Brazil, then, but their circumstances have changed. Like similar figures who once served to ease the pressures of society, bearing its woes or serving its vices, they are pressured themselves now by anxiety, by the weight of all those millions of woes, the sordid shame of all those vices: the jester has become the high-paid comedian heading for an overdose, the balladeer a pop star who thinks he must save the world. So the transvestite has been depersonalised by the impersonal city, and made familiar by TV, a fetish and a commodity. If their role in some Indian societies was as the village prostitute, the village has become a dangerous, distended nightmare. Arrested in Brazil, they are gang-raped by *machista* police before being thrown in jail, where they resort to disfiguring themselves to ward off other inmates, or so as to get moved to hospital beds from which it's easier to escape. This was the common enough plot of *Kiss of the Spider Woman*, Manual Puig's allegorical story of a jailed Brazilian transvestite, a bird caged and brutalised. In recent years, they have discovered a level of tolerance, even a demand for their services in Paris and Milan, and have arrived there in large numbers, to be racketed by pimps and police where no Madame Satan will come to defend them.

'You want to know what guys do with a transvestite?' asks Helio. I suppose he can tell from my expression that I'm curious.

'She fucks them! Not the other way around.'

He gives a delicate shudder.

———

In the evenings, Marly waters her orchids, terrestrial varieties like Cypripedium and Neottia – potted outside the window of her bedroom.

These flowers, in their sensual, infinite beauty – there are thousands of varieties – fascinate her. 'They are like women,' she says, 'the sex of women.'

Winding vines that explode in exuberant flowers; varieties like Vanda and Oncidium that cling to rocks, branches and trunks, sending their roots out through the air to find water; species so odorous a single flower will fill a room with its scent.

Like other marvels brought back from the New World – emeralds and diamonds, tomatoes and tobacco, talking coloured-birds and animal-people – the orchid haunted the imagination of the Old World, which glimpsed in the newly discovered varieties of these flowers the naked, profuse beauty of a world far older than itself. Today, this profusion is called biodiversity, the subject of international conferences, pending treaties and research grants from drug companies.

Warscewicz was the most determined and methodical of the orchid chasers; the brothers Lobb fought over the blooms; Hartweg was driven mad by them; Veitch, O'Reilly and Colonel Benson endured the tropical jungle to bring back just a few plants. Carefully tended, most of these nevertheless wilted or stubbornly refused to flower. But what splendour! What rarity! Orchids, like diamonds, were previously found only in India. It wasn't until the nineteenth century that horticultural skills evolved enough to preserve them in European and North American climates, where the obsession proved contagious. In 1894, Benjamin Williams, a fellow of the Royal Horticultural Society, wrote the *Orchid Grower's Manual*, a hefty and still definitive tome, the flowering of a lifetime's experience of growing orchids at the Victorian and Paradise Nurseries in London's Holloway Road. Williams had never been to either India or Brazil, but imagined the flowers in their natural habitat, 'throwing off their sweet perfume to the breeze'. Such is the strange spell of these flowers that open like the sex of women, like laughing faces, the secret laughter of the jungle.

Soon Marly will be leaving for São Paulo, to go back to college, and I must leave too, wishing I could take her, my orchid, with me.

Six

I have become accustomed to much that was exotic at first, but one sensation has not left me; that I could reach out and touch the rain forest, the *Mata Atlantica* that covers the mountains. The scents of Marly's orchids invade the room each morning, mingling with the din from the street.

In scents lies the intoxication of the forest, the essences of which – spices – were coveted and fought over with a frenzy that is impossible to imagine today, unless it be for the illicit white crystals refined from the coca bush. Cocaine still sustains at least one Andean economy, as refined sugarcane was once the mainstay of the Atlantic colonies. Coffee and sugar stimulated equally strong addictions; cocoa mixed with milk produced chocolate – imagine a world without chocolate, or indeed, without tomatoes, known when they first revealed themselves in the New World as Love Apples. Ginger and nutmeg, cinnamon and chilli: for barrels full of these essences, as well as the lure of other, more glittering hoards, sailors like those who accompanied Magellan on the first voyage around the world – laying anchor in the Bay of Guanabara in 1519 – ate worm-ridden crumbs that smelled of rat's piss, and gave up their dreams on unknown seas with a bravery evoked in the old Portuguese sailor's proverb, 'Sailing is necessary, life is not.'

In Rio, the seduction of the tropical forest is enhanced by its unexpected proximity to the city, against which, and with little effort, it's able to preserve an equal footing on the steep, virtually unbuildable mountainsides.

The enchantment of this forest is unfamiliar to me. It's the first time I have seen such abundant, exotic growth and I have the instinctive reaction that its vigour is excessive, indecent even. The year-round lushness seems uncanny to me, a suspension of the order of temperate zones. The hillsides burst with trees, their leaves a deep, dense green, studded with dazzling yellow or dripping with purple and magenta; large, strange and magnificent blooms. In the struggle of tropical vegetation to grow, there is an overwhelming violence and sexuality, which seems to permit an equivalent abandon in anyone who breathes its scents, a subtle olfactory hint that, as the early missionaries ruefully observed, there is no sin south of the equator. The Tropics are carnal: the humidity, the heavy aromas of ripe fruits, sweet and sensual. The skin secretes; the very air is favourable to secretions. That's why tropical vegetation is so luxuriant, why there are so many insects. It's favourable to reproduction. From comportment, a psychology is born. The cognitive mind is lulled, and the reptile mind wants to make love.

To savour this, I visit the Botanical Gardens, located at the feet of the mountains behind the beachfront district of Leblon, in what for two hundred years were the swampy fields of a sugar plantation.

In 1808, Dom João VI arrived from Lisbon in an English ship, fleeing Napoleon with 20,000 members of the court and as much wealth as they could carry. It was an expeditious bit of British politicking, which would lead to more than a century of trade and banking prerogatives. As the new capital of the Portuguese empire, meanwhile, Rio enjoyed an increase in the quality of its entertainments. Dom João VI bought the sugar mill to set up a gunpowder factory. At the same time, he established a royal kitchen garden to cultivate spices from the East Indies.

The front wall bordering what is now a busy main road and the avenue leading into this garden are lined with stately palms, ten storeys high. The palms were brought to Brazil by Luiz de Abreu Vieira é Silva, who was captured by the French on his way from

Portuguese Goa and imprisoned on Mauritius, where the famous Gabrielle gardens were located. He escaped with species that he presented to Dom João VI: nutmeg, cinnamon, avocado, lychee and grapefruit. He also brought seeds for sago and breadfruit trees and for the palm *Roystonea oleracea*. At the top of the avenue of palms – their bare, Doric trunks lending elegance to the gardens – is a plaque commemorating the oldest and tallest of these, known as the Palma Mater, planted in 1809, and struck down by lightning in 1972. Dom João awarded prizes and medals to encourage the adaptation of foreign species, and he liked palms so much he gave tax concessions to anyone who planted them. They still surround the big plantation houses in the countryside, marking oases of past splendour amid the newer growths of electric pylons and Golden Arches.

On ascending the throne of the United Kingdom of Portugal and Brazil, Dom João changed the name of the gardens to the Royal Botanical Garden and allowed accompanied visits by the public. The afternoon I pass in contemplation here is my first encounter with the interior. From the garden, sitting by jackfruit and rambutan trees that throw down aerial roots entwined with orchids, watching the heat wreathing clouds around the top of the Corcovado mountain, I resolve to discover what lies behind the coastal ranges.

The first Amazonian hardwoods were planted here in 1859, the beginning of an awareness of the region's value. In the haphazard arrangement of architectural pieces such as the gates of the old gunpowder factory and the statues of Greek gods, fashioned by a bastard mulatto, Maestre Valentim, in the last century, are traces of the eccentric, orphan history of Brazil. At one time, a part of the gardens was given over to tea plantations, and supplied the whole of Rio. In the Daisy Valley, the Panama Hat Factory was located, and the breeding of silkworms was tried and abandoned.

It was to the Botanical Gardens that Oscar Niemeyer came as a student to draw plants that he tried to stylise for his architectural perspectives. He loved to walk at twilight through the shaded alleys, under the imperial palms, and stop full of curiosity in front of a species he didn't recognise, or in front of the giant water lilies, or the joyous immortals that, everywhere, spurted their colours. And so it was from here that a gracious, exuberant tropical nature lent its forms to the monumental architecture of modern Brazil.

———

Oscar Niemeyer says that in Rio 'misery always existed and was always overlooked.' But never as today when 'our brothers the *favelados* regard the city as an enemy camp of luxury and corruption.'

He complains of the rich, including liberals who talk of democracy, 'as though misery were democratic.' Life smiles at them. 'For meals in restaurants they pay the equivalent of a worker's monthly salary, while the poor wait for a miracle, the miracle that will happen the day we realise that misery isn't inevitable, but a huge injustice that must end!'

This miracle, Rio resists with infinite, seductive guile. Not even the miserable are immune to her beauty. For why else would they endure her scorn?

Earlier, Niemeyer had raised a city, Brasilia, from barren scrub. It succeeded Rio as the federal capital in 1960, a triumph of planning, a city safe for public officials, in which, when the boom finally sputtered out, the president lined up the official cars and asked for bids. But Niemeyer's design was flawed. He had overlooked the construction workers, who were left to construct from spare and broken materials their own city on the outskirts.

The *favelas* of Rio number more than 400 and more than a million people – 14 per cent of the population – live in them, places very different from each other, but all of which, in the words of Licia Valladares, a sociologist at Rio university, have a reputation for Cariocans and visitors alike of 'poverty, criminality, lawlessness, creativity and exoticism'.

In the Seventies, attempts were made to raze the *favelas* of the *Zona Sul*, the wealthy southern part of the city. Near the Pria do Pinto, fires blazed. The firemen failed to arrive, but the next day the bulldozers came promptly. More than eighty *favelas* were destroyed; the hillsides were in flames. But the former inhabitants – 'cheap hands and dancing feet', Eduardo Galeano calls them – refused to remain in the public housing far from the centre to which they were transferred, and returned. Unable to squat again the land from which they had been evicted, they joined their former neighbours in nearby *favelas*, who constructed additional floors to cater to the demand of even the poorest of the poor to enjoy the view of the mountains and below, the great leveller, the beach.

In the *favelas*, migrants from all over Brazil have re-created a semi-rural way of life, with its social relations. The frictions of the big city erode these relations, but the occupants have banded together to confront local bodies and landowners. The names of houses and neighbourhoods are marked by bittersweet Brazilian humour: *Nova Brasilia; Morro do Faz Depressa*, Hurry-up Hill; *Chácara do Céu*, Sky Gardens; *Morro da Esperança*, Hill of Hope.

There is a kind of organic, natural beauty in the haphazard human-scale architecture of the *favelas*; the overcrowding a community-building answer to the lack of space, the recuperated materials a solution to the problem of finite resources. The shanties that exist on the periphery of the urban surge the world over have at least this virtue, that they are unplanned, born of nobody's paternal designs, but built on hope and need. Their residents in Asia, India, Africa and Latin America have come from an unchanging rural past to give birth to orphans with the television on.

The *favelas* of Rio came into being after the *Guerra da Canudos* in 1896, the bitter repression of a rural rebellion in the *Nordeste* led by Antonio Conselheiro, a quasi-religious leader or *beato*. As a pretext, the government accused him of being a monarchist, a threat to the ten-year-old republic, and sent in the army. A journalist named Euclides da Cunha went with them, recording the events in *Os Sertões*, a gripping novelisation that paints the characteristics of the peasants of the *Nordeste*. 'The core of our nationality, the bedrock of our race,' according to da Cunha, who admired their astuteness, courage and stamina, but, influenced by current European theories of racial purity, blamed their faults on mixed blood.

At the end of the war, the surviving soldiers descended from the interior of Bahia to the capital to ask for their pensions. They camped on the *Morro da Providência*, near the army headquarters in the old centre of town. On the slopes, they found *favela* bushes, a plant of their native *Nordeste* that produces a spice for cooking and a hard, heavy wood for furnishings. The hill became known as the *Morro da Favela*, while the soldiers were gradually forgotten.

The ex-soldiers were black or mulatto. Before taking up arms, they had been slaves, and it was against other ex-slaves that they had fought. The *Guerra da Canudos* was a battle to ensure the loyalties of slaves liberated in 1888, a year before the birth of the Republic. Coming from the 'backward' *Nordeste*, where they had been battling land reformers, the black soldiers must have been bemused to find that the former slaves in Rio had, in the intervening decade, much improved their lot, and were doing almost as well as the mulattos.

Out of the camp on the *Morro da Favela* grew tumbledown shacks, made of old planks and clay, and oil drums from the nearby port, where there was work to be found too. The soldiers were joined by ex-slaves from other parts of Brazil, especially the *Nordeste*, who drifted towards Rio, and eventually by Cariocan blacks, expelled from the *cortiços* and *cabeças de porco* – literally pig-sties – the large, old, dilapidated and subdivided buildings of the centre, inhabited by entire families in small rooms, most of which were demolished in a drive to civic improvement inspired by the public hygiene movement at the turn of the century.

With their believers, the African Gods of Bahia came to reside in the *favelas* of Rio, where their beliefs became known as *Macumba*. It's at places of cult worship that the *umbanda* is practised. Women who live in apartments and their maids from the *favelas* join in asking the *babalorixás* – 'Fathers of the Saints' in Portuguese – to invoke the assistance of Pomba Gira or Exú.

Exú was a messenger in Bahia, a mercurial but unimportant figure who beseeched more powerful deities. In Rio, his wily ways came in handy; country craft became city cunning. He found work delivering not messages but curses, employed by other fallen angels of the slums. He is invoked by drums and smoke, and enters through the soles of unshod, dancing feet. Possessed by him, believers roll on the ground laughing at the revenge they will have on their masters, a cathartic laughter, with, at the end, salvation or expiry, the mock release of a mock death.

Maria Padilha can deliver curses too, and beg favours of more potent Gods, but she must be invoked with flattery and rewarded with foreign whisky before she will use her influence.

In the confusion and improvisation of the Fathers of the Saints, she can take the guise of Exú too, Exú in drag. She pants and screams, as though making love with Exú, for Maria is a whore who enters only the bodies of whores. Devalued bodies, bought cheap by drunken dockworkers and furtive clerks, they become, in the shadow world of *Macumba*, temporary shrines, the Mothers of Saints.

The slum-dwellers are a source of amusement and anxiety for the middle-class of Rio but above all a source of cheap labour. They are maids, drivers, cleaners, doormen, seamstresses. But even with the low minimum wage, they don't all find work, especially in times of economic crisis. The Cariocans debate what to do with the *favelas*, pull them down or encourage them. This is the current tendency. The *favela* is the cheapest, quickest solution to the housing crisis, and offers several advantages to its denizens: no long journeys to work, no spending on transport and no rent. Urban planners have stopped thinking of rehousing and now look for ways to improve the existing. Nearly all the *favelas* of Rio now have running water. All of them have televisions and whereas before they often stole electricity, they can mostly now be connected if they pay the charge. The water jug carried, African-style, up the hill by women, child at the hip, has disappeared. This has encouraged the *favelados* to invest some of their meagre income. The wooden shacks have acquired brick walls, the tin roofing has been replaced by tiles, and some of the squatters have become owners.

The problem is land, the root of all strife in this nation with so much territory. Who owns the land? Will they sell, or wait for values to rise and then get an eviction notice? In Mangueira and Cabritos, local associations supported by church groups succeeded in buying the land on which their mostly brick-built houses stood. At the end of the Eighties, the government gave out 20,000 deeds.

The new owners paid the registry charges, and built another floor when the children married, and then a third floor, divided into small rooms and rented, producing income. Four- and five-storey buildings have appeared in the largest *favelas* – Rocinha and Jacarezinho – divided into rooms rented by agencies. One third of the occupants of *favelas* are tenants of other *favelados*.

These houses change hands, part of the Rio property boom. But few families arriving in Rio now could build their own house and see it become capital. If so, it will be far from the centre, in a crowded, distended space where they will be joined by established *favelados* who have been squeezed out of their old homes or, for reasons of poverty or otherwise, decided to sell. They can no longer afford to live in the centre. When they leave, others come, changing the social profile of the *favelas*. The new *favelados* are not cheap hands but semi-skilled workers, clerks, drivers, small shopkeepers – forced by rising rents and inflation-racked incomes to move to a room in a *favela*. They might have a better view – even if it's into the kitchen of a penthouse – but they will have to put up with other nuisances such as the helicopter raids by police as ruthless as the bandits they chase, and to whom all *favelados* are criminals. The supermarkets, bars and boutiques that thrive in the *favelas* close when the helicopters begin to buzz the hills. The mothers snatch their kids indoors. 'Words are replaced by exchanged looks,' writes the sociologist Licia Valladares. 'Doors normally open are closed. The *favela* isn't what it was . . . '

And neither are bandit heroes. The daily heroism of the *favelados* was a courageous struggle that would go on without the uncertain patronage of Escadinha. In the history of Brazil, I learnt of the exploits of other Robin Hoods, like Lampiao, a contemporary of Sandino who rode into towns in the *Nordeste* at the head of a ragged cavalry, and reduced his ransom demands in times of drought.

And in a newspaper, I read much later of the execution by a gang reportedly controlled by Escadinha, who was back on Ilha Grande, of fourteen prisoners. They were murdered at the same time, on the same day, but in different prisons, as a show of strength by the gang.

At the same time, in the crowded cells of a São Paulo jail, they were drawing lots to decide who would be the next to commit suicide as a means of drawing attention to their conditions. Five prisoners died before the authorities acknowledged anything out of the ordinary was going on.

Seven

Nestling in the hills beside the Botanical Gardens, a giant satellite dish points skywards. The dish sends up to the Brazilsat the signal from the world's fourth-largest TV network, but the most powerful. There are 160 million people in Brazil – more than two-thirds of them regularly tuned to Tele Globo.

In the land of the illiterate, television is king. The Globo signal is more than just a buzz of shows, dramas, news and advertising. The Globo signal *is* Brazil: defining problems, promoting ideals and providing distraction in the meantime. From this dish comes a colourful blueprint from which modern Brazilian society is knit, the 'Global Quality Standard'.

'We have a standard of quality,' explains Professor Poyares, assistant to Globo's president. 'We call it the Global Quality Standard.' He smiles, turning his palms upwards. 'People *like* us. We can't help it!'

Like the president of Globo, Dr Roberto Marinho, Professor Poyares is a doctor of communications. In the semi-literate society, communication is power. Globo is the heart of a communications empire that was estimated to be worth $1.3 billion a quarter of a century after the TV station was launched, and it is controlled entirely by Dr Roberto Marinho.

At the age of twenty-two, Roberto Marinho inherited a news-paper, *O Globo*, from his father. Expanding first into radio, then TV, he now has interests ranging from property to manufacturing, and employs 12,000 people. He lives in a hillside villa south of Rio and divides his twelve-hour working days between the newspaper, where he still occasionally writes editorials, and the TV channel.

'Don't call it an empire, I don't like the word *empire*. Call it an ensemble,' he says. He is a short, spry, white-haired man. He apologises that he is too busy to give me much of his time, and he is circumspect about what he says, declining to comment on the forthcoming presidential elections. He describes the gallery he is setting up to display his art collection of 500 pieces – and the activities of his educational foundation, which sponsored the first International Ecology Festival.

There are many who say simply that, as the man who owns the Globo signal, Dr Marinho owns Brazil.

It has been three years since my first visit to Rio, and I've returned this time in the midst of a political carnival, the presidential race, an exciting novelty to most Brazilians who have never before voted for a president.

The race is being run on prime-time. Television will deliver the winner to a zealous electorate, half of whom can't read. There aren't enough schools for the *favelados*, but there are adequate TV sets. And they have only to be able to sign their name to vote.

I have an invitation to visit the most influential TV channel in Brazil. The Globo signal emits from studios inside a compound of modern buildings. As the network grew, so the studios have expanded. A huddle of new buildings houses the most up-to-date TV facilities in Latin America, beside some of the oldest palm trees in the Botanical Gardens.

Globo is the world's biggest producer of TV programming. Though larger than Globo in terms of audience, the big three US networks are prohibited by law from producing more than 10 per cent of what they broadcast; laws designed to avoid concentrating power and profits. Brazil has no such laws. Globo produces four hours of *telenovelas* a its origins'.

The *telenovelas* are daily visits to other people's lives. The message is simple, says the celebrated *telenovela* director Jorge Fernando. 'The poor struggle to survive against the wickedness of the rich.' It's a message for Brazil, with international appeal: $20 million worth of exports in 1987. *Telenovelas* like *A Escrava Isaura* and *Dancin' Days* have emptied the streets of Portugal, Poland and even China during their daily broadcast. One of the best, *Malu Mulher*, was seen throughout the world in the early Eighties. Depicting the struggles of an independent woman, it began with Malu throwing her husband out of the apartment and her furniture out of the window. The hand-held cameras and saturated lighting added to the Latin heat. Unsurprisingly, Italy is one of Globo's biggest customers and they have moved into Europe with the purchase of Tele Monte Carlo.

Globo broadcasts three *novelas* every evening. The 6 p.m. one is domestic and uncomplicated; the 7 p.m. one spicy and glamorous; the 10 p.m. one more realistic and tougher in its treatments of social problems. After 10 p.m. characters like Malu have to deal with corrupt officials as well as love rivals, they get mugged as well as divorced – for the Globo transmitter is also an antenna, sensitive to shifts of concern in society, even as it shapes those concerns.

'We try to reflect society,' explains Professor Poyares. 'The social fabric is woven from all the strands of communication. Globo is neither above nor below society, it's part of the fabric.'

Currently, the 7 p.m. *telenovela* is *Top Model*. Be assured there are plenty of glamorous women in it. It is mid-afternoon and, in one of four studios the size of a small theatre, next week's episodes of *Top Model* are being recorded in a hectic, concentrated rush of set and

71

a week, completing in two hours scenes that would take weeks for the cinema.

'The visual language of the *telenovela* is more difficult than the cinema because I'm constricted to a view of a hundred and eighty degrees,' he explains, seated by the cameras lined in a row. 'I can't do a counterpoint shot. It's the economic logic of an industrial TV. I shoot six times forty-two minutes a week, for six months at least.'

The *telenovelas* resemble life in that you never know what tomorrow holds. To find out, in TV, you have to look to the ratings. 'If a programme sinks below fifty per cent of the audience, we ask questions,' says Professor Poyares. Globo works closely with the market research firm IBOPE. When a *telenovela* begins, no one – writer, director, viewers, chiefs of Globo – knows how it will end, six months or two years later, depending on its success. The episodes are written and filmed about a week ahead of transmission. Secondary characters can take over from the main ones if the public prefers them.

The key to the *telenovela* is the close-up. The camera invades the actor's personal space, creating intimacy to keep the viewer involved. Rapid editing between close-ups creates emotional crescendoes. 'For each episode, we have to have three climaxes,' says Bandara. 'We have to score three goals, like in football! These are for the three ad breaks.'

A *telenovela* costs $50,000 an episode to produce. Over six months it will cost $6 million – and bring in to Globo some $60 million worth of advertising. Being a private, family-owned company,

Globo is not obliged to disclose financial secrets – like how much additional money it makes from 'merchandising', placing products in the *novelas*. A company called Apoio – 'Support' – was formed by Globo to exploit this lucrative area. But the *telenovelas* are not the only source of revenue for Globo. One second of advertising during the 8 p.m. news costs $1000. The eight to ten minutes of ads each evening bring in over half a million dollars.

On the set of *Top Model*, the lighting is exceptionally bright. 'There must be no shadowy corners. It's one of the demands of the Global Quality Standard,' explains Bandara. 'If I use shadows and contrast for expression, the signal in the Sierra or the Amazon will be poor. There is a technical imperative to capture the largest audience over the whole of the territory.'

From the start of TV in Brazil, this imperative was political as well. When the military seized power in '64, education, the humanities and social sciences – potential agents of unrest – lost out in funding to the science of communications, a means of social control. Brazil counted fifty-three faculties of communications by 1975, unequalled in the world. Launched in '65, Globo developed under the eye of the military, who saw it as a means to unite and shape the country in the image of a modern, docile consumer realm.

'There is a special relationship between TV and the home,' says Anna-Maria Roiter, Globo's director of corporate communications. 'The velocity of TV is exceptional in Brazil – because of the illiteracy. It's one of the factors. Also, newspapers are expensive and limited to the professional class.'

Globo likes to pretend that it has no competition, and it's true that its signal is the clearest and most widely received. Of the fifty-five stations in Brazil, twenty-four are affiliated to the Globo network. The rest are divided between TVS – owned by Silvio Santos, whose real name is Abravanel, a Jew of Greek origin who began selling newspapers in the street and still appears on screen to present his programmes every Sunday – and Manchete, founded by Russian émigré Adolfo Bloch with the profits of a large magazine group. But neither can match the Global Quality Standard. There is a level of professional sophistication at Globo that rivals the

North American networks, with none of the fudged cuts or sloppy camera angles of Third World TV. And Globo is seemingly able to dazzle Brazil with its bright, incessant visual self-promotion.

'Globo's only source of income is advertising and it must do everything it can to lure the public,' explains Anna-Maria Roiter. 'The videographics are part of that. It's important to seduce people.'

There is an Indian word – *miçanga* – for mirrors and jewels, anything that shines. The settlers offered *miçanga* to seduce the Indians, and the Indians revealed for them the *miçanga* of Brazil: shoals of diamonds lying on riverbeds and seams of gold squeezed under hills. The fascination with *miçanga* remains strong in Brazilian culture. The TV is *miçanga*, a bright, gaudy jewel flashing its hypnotic light. It's also the *miçanga* from which latterday fortunes are made. The Indians, though, had no word for kitsch.

Globo is very proud of its visual hooks: striking logos and title sequences like the one for *Top Model* of women walking an Escher-like structure, precipitous and foxy. These are created by the Austrian Hans Donner, who has been with Globo since the mid-Seventies. 'He has done much to establish the reputation of Globo,' says Anna-Maria Roiter. 'I don't think there is a channel in the world that puts such emphasis on the visual identity. It's part of the reason for our success. The preoccupation with the visual is very strong in Brazil, again perhaps because of the level of illiteracy. From the European perspective it might look kitsch but Brazil is a tropical country and it has a different aesthetic. It's part of the climate, like *Carnaval*. There is a preoccupation with entertainment here.'

A flamboyant country, Brazil gets the television is deserves.

The studio of the *Jornal Nacional* is frayed with use. Old lights hang from the ceiling invisible to the camera pointing at the red and blue desk and the faces of the newsreaders. Every morning, the editor of the national news speaks to the other twenty-four stations in the Globo network. Globo centralises the material from São Paulo, Bahia and elsewhere. From this studio goes out the network's only live broadcast, the 8 p.m. news, regularly reaching over 70 per cent of Brazilian viewers, more than 100 million people.

'I don't think of the number of viewers,' says Sergio Chapelin, a newsreader for fifteen years. 'I'm part of the family.' His was the face that announced the military stepdown after the People Power campaign for direct elections. Yet, as the campaign grew, the editors of the *Jornal Nacional* somehow failed to notice such events as the rally in '85 of nearly a million people in the Cinelandia district of downtown Rio, calling for *Diretas-já*. Consequently, the station is seen as the instrument of conservative power. 'People who don't like Globo try to take it out on me. Globo represents the centre-right and there are people who don't like that.'

The news imparted each night by Sergio Chapelin from this small studio can change the mood of the country. But Globo can't afford to be too far from the mood of the public. When the military was evidently doing nothing against the demands for direct elections, Globo began to report on the campaign. *Diretas-já* swept the country.

The newsroom upstairs, where the editorial decisions are taken, is the only unmodern part of the enterprise: a crowded office, with old typewriters on scuffed desks and a water-cooler in the corner. It's where Henrique Coutinho works, deciding which events merit Brazil's attention.

He has been with Globo for fifteen years. Before that, he was a journalist with *Jornal do Brasil* and with *Abril*, publishers of the country's best-selling newsmagazine, *Veja*.

I ask him if it's true that Globo represents the centre-right and whether this is the policy of Dr Marinho.

'Yes, if it concerns Brazilian politics, it's true. Dr Roberto Marinho has a certain influence. Not a very close control but a certain influence.'

In the build-up to the elections, Globo has been perceived as lending its powerful transmitters to Fernando Collor do Mello, the youthful, charismatic figure who came out of the backwoods to galvanise the campaign with grand promises and pious gestures. He too has a background in communications. His family owns a TV station in his home state of Alagoas, affiliated to the Globo network.

'What will happen if Collor doesn't win?' I ask.

'Dr Roberto has an incredible facility for accommodating the power. He has always done it, for more than sixty years. But there's no real liberty for doing interviews. We're obliged by the legislation to show two hours a day of political messages from the candidates. It's absurd. Each candidate has time allotted based on their representation in parliament. There are parties with ten to fifteen minutes and others with fifteen seconds.'

Globo routinely announces the poll results on Fridays. When Collor began to fall in the polls, Globo didn't wait until Friday, but broadcast on Wednesday, to show that Collor was still leading.

'That was manipulation,' says Coutinho. 'Why not wait until Friday? Because it would allow the rumours to develop. The Friday thing was very subtle. Like Collor always wears a shirt and tie, while the others are in open-neck shirts. But Dr Roberto isn't naive, he isn't stupid. He insists on showing Brizola and the other candidates from the left at the same time as Collor.'

In the final weeks, Globo will play an artful game of promoting the leftist candidate Lula at the expense of the more moderate Leonel Brizola, Collor's main opponent. Collor's victory will also be a victory for Globo, but one favour he won't need to repay the number one network.

'He will let that continue,' says Coutinho. 'That's already something. Brizola said the first thing he would do if he came to power was shut Tele Globo. But it's impossible, the law won't allow it. The president no longer has the right to give the concession. Now it's the congress. And in the congress Globo has a large influence too. Anyway, with Collor there's no risk. His brother worked for Globo for many years, and his younger brother is the boss of the station in Alagoas. But I don't think the viewers see the relation between Collor and Globo.'

'Brazil is a country with a high level of illiteracy,' I remind him. 'Television has an awesome responsibility here.'

'Incredible. Very much. First, there's a minimum level of thirty per cent illiteracy. Second, the only news which is really national is the TV. The press is limited. Globo has seventy per cent of the audience. It's a power. I'm responsible for the entire news programme at

76

the weekend. Sometimes I feel a terrible responsibility. To choose one headline or another subject; that's heavy at times.'

'How much can you explain to a semi-literate country? Aren't you obliged to cater to emotion rather than reason?'

'It's normal that things should be like that. We can't show at times the most important subject or choose the most interesting angle. People don't know at times that they are being tricked. It's a certain way to pose a question . . . '

'Are there any taboos for the news?'

'*Não.* I don't remember. Drugs, sometimes, problems with the police. It's not a taboo exactly. Drugs we try not to show to avoid encouraging abuse. But the fight against drugs we show.'

'And corruption?'

'It's supposed to exist but it's hard to prove. When there is a specific case of someone important, yes. Except when it's an enemy of Dr Roberto, then we show it. Like Ibrahim Abi-Ackel, an ex-minister of justice. We had a campaign against him. He was depicted as a bandit, a smuggler, because he censured a Globo *telenovela*, *Roque Santeiro*. Dr Roberto came down hard on him.'

'Don't you feel an obligation to separate the interests of Globo from those of the public?'

'Of course. Especially because my political interests don't coincide with the television station.'

Coutinho is silent for a moment, then he tells me that in the forthcoming elections, he will vote for a Communist candidate. It's a gesture he has waited his whole life to make.

'What I do here is what the boss wants. I can't do what I would like to do. Globo belongs to Dr Roberto Marinho and it's him who decides. But I have my own ideas.'

The contradiction that Henrique Coutinho admits to reveals not hypocrisy but the woeful daily compromises of life under the regime. He plans to retire soon, and with the military gone and the possibility of political pluralism, he can now openly mark his distance. But in my youthful idealism, and with my taken-for-granted constitutional liberties, I am disappointed by his dereliction of personal duty. 'TV should reflect society, no?' I argue. 'It was used to unify the country.'

'That was a decision by the military – which was very important I feel for the nation. But I think that the *telenovelas* serve that function: reflecting society. If we don't do it in journalism, we do it there. The *telenovelas* are very important cultural products.'

'Do they have a specific political message?'

'The *telenovelas*, sometimes, yes. Corruption, for instance. Things that happen in Brazilian society can appear in them a few days later. It's surprising that in the *telenovelas* the ideas are often very much to the left. Dr Marinho doesn't use his influence there too much.'

'Does he watch them?'

'I doubt it. The problem is that one must be interesting to have the audience. One year, we didn't show *Carnaval*. It was a scandal! Manchete showed it and won 85 per cent. It was very bad for Globo. Why didn't we show it? Because Dr Marinho thinks *Carnaval* is something very vulgar, not very nice. Little prejudices like that. People watched Manchete that year – and the year after, Dr Marinho tried to buy the carnival outright. Even during the *Diretas-já* campaign, Globo kept a certain distance, but the public pressure for elections was so enormous that, to have an audience, Globo had to join in the campaign. We have to be democratic to have the audience.'

'Dr Marinho's aim is to make money, then. But behind that, isn't he also a kind of conservative counterweight in Brazil?'

'He will do everything possible to hold society back. But if that isn't possible, he will accommodate the change.'

'Would he provide the same counterweight if the power swung to the right?'

'Up to a certain point, yes. He's very intelligent, the old man. If a right-wing *coup d'état* began here now, he knows that it would have no real chance of success in the long term. I doubt that he would support that. I think not. It's interesting. Sometimes the newspapers have a different position to the TV. The newspaper says one thing and the TV shows another. And he owns both. Sometimes he writes the editorial himself. It's a question of competition. If we don't show it, we lose the audience – so we have to show things. The audience creates the politics of Globo, because it's through them that we make money. Advertising is our only income.'

In an office nearby, Jorge Fernando, director of *Que Rei Sou Eu?* is preparing his next *telenovela*. His last series, an allegory of contemporary politics set in the Middle Ages, finished this summer after a six-month run in the less restrictive late-evening slot.

'It was a satirical story, a parody of medieval dramas, but above all a way of criticising the political class,' he explains. 'All the people who mattered in Brazil were depicted each night through symbolic characters. What's surprising is that the public didn't understand the satire until the thirtieth episode. It was the week that the government decreed free TV time for all the candidates. We hung signs on all the horses in the *telenovela*. It was clear to everybody after that.'

But maybe Globo's viewers are more sophisticated than both Fernando and Coutinho think – for the language of the tele-literate is the language of TV itself. To Globo's surprise, a new show called *TV Pirata* is running fourth in the almighty IBOPE ratings. A weekly satire of Brazilian TV, it features a parody of the *telenovelas* set in a slum.

Globo is selling a modern image of the country back to itself. The discrepancy between the scenarios of the *telenovelas* and the scrabbling of many of Brazil's citizens is inescapable. But in the skyscrapers and the slums alike there is Globo, the ultimate pop television. A kind of TV Motown, they have their equivalent of the Motown Sound: the Global Quality Standard. They have absorbed all the intellectual talent in Brazil, according to Regina Casé, a comedienne who has become a star through *TV Pirata*. 'The most original messages pass through the *telenovelas*,' she says. 'Already, themes like the Amazon and pollution appear. It's a safety valve.'

Outside another studio, the Teatro Fenix, a few blocks from the main Globo compound, dozens of families queue for Globo's star attraction. Every Tuesday and Wednesday morning it's the same. The streets are blocked with cars and buses disgorging excited children. They have been invited to the *Xou da Xuxa*, pronounced 'Show da Shusha'. Xuxa is an ex-model who went from the fashion pages to the soft-porn magazines, before finding her way into the hearts of millions of Brazilian children – and into the arms of the footballer Pelé. Her name is an easy sussuration for Brazilian babies: *Shusha!* It means caress. Her dolls – little golden girls – fill the toy shops. Her daily morning TV show is a social and marketing phenomenon, Globo's greatest success. Her records top the charts, selling millions of copies. The title of one of them was '*Todo o Mundo esta Feliz*', the whole world is happy. The Xuxa Show is a two-hour televised circus for kids and its star is a blonde-haired, fair-skinned big sister to a nation of mulatto children.

'I've thought about that,' says Xuxa, observing herself in the dressing-room mirror as the make-up girl, who is brown-skinned, does her work, 'and dolls are supposed to be blonde, aren't they?'

In the studio, under the bright lights, the children are agog, overwhelmed by the polystyrene reality of a world where everything is colour and music and everybody is happy. The floor managers shepherd them about, talking into headsets. Their party costumes have been lovingly run up at home by aunts and maids. Many are wearing white ankle-boots, a kiddie fashion-craze launched by the *paquitas*, Xuxa's chorus of teen showgirls, who are already on the set and dancing in white shorts and red majorette tunics.

Every little girl in Brazil wants to grow up to be Xuxa, who once revealed that she and Pelé liked to make love while they listened to Marvin Gaye's 'Sexual Healing'. But the spell wore off, and she left Pelé for the second most famous living Brazilian, the racing driver Ayrton Senna.

In knee-high black suede boots, mini-skirt and a gold satin shirt cut high at the front to reveal her midriff – an obscure hint of Catholic sexuality that intrigues me as much as her belly button itself – Xuxa will soon be joining her *paquitas* to tape her show. Politely, she offers a moment of her time.

Xuxa means caress in Portuguese. 'A little too sensual to be your real name, surely?'

'Oh yes! Maria de Graca Xuxa Meneghel ... When I was born

my mother said to my brother, who is two years older than me, I've brought you a little doll for you to play with!'

"So what do you want to be when you grow up?"

'A vet,' she laughs.

She considers the reasons for her success. 'At first I thought it was my fine hair that the kids remembered. But blind children love my voice. So I thought it was my voice. But deaf-and-dumb children love my look . . . I think it's charisma, quite simply!'

Bravo Xuxa! 'Today there's nothing about you in the newspapers, does it worry you?'

'Ah but yes! Look' – she picks up a TV guide – 'Look: "Xuxa; I've thought a lot about having kids!" See!'

'You don't have any children?'

'I would like to very much but it's impossible with my career.'

'Blonde or brunette?' I want to know if Xuxa feels any unease about being a Caucasian role-model for a brown nation.

She grins. 'I think Brazilian children prefer blondes. Barbie is a blonde, she has blue eyes. They play with the doll and suddenly they see a replica in flesh-and-blood on the TV.' Xuxa is referring to herself. 'It fascinates them because they all identify with their dolls. In their imagination, the children would like to look like me. Like me, when I was small, I dreamed I was Snow White, that I was playing with the little deer and the birds. That's why I wanted to be a vet.'

As well as singing songs in her shows, Xuxa talks to her public about the unhappy world: about drugs, deforestation, the noble Indian and the need for proper nutrition. She takes her role as child idol seriously, but in a country with seven million children sleeping on the streets, what can a TV star do?

'I've inaugurated the Xuxa Meneghel Foundation. It's a large house where fifty orphans can sleep and two hundred and fifty more can come to play, learn about music and do practical things. There's even a swimming pool.'

This is just part of the Xuxa enterprise. 'I hope I can remember it all . . . I record albums, I make films, I have a line of clothes, dolls, dictionaries, furry animals, beauty products for little girls, boots, sandals, bicycles . . . '

81

'How much do you earn?'

'I don't know because I'm paid by Xuxa Productions.'

Xuxa was ranked among the thirty richest people in showbiz by *Fortune*. 'What's the turnover of Xuxa Productions?' I ask.

'I don't know.' She turns to her press assistant, who shrugs. The interview will soon be over.

'Are you rich?'

'I work every day,' she says, not the little girl any more. 'In Brazil, that's already something . . . '

It's showtime for Xuxa! The screams of millions of children fill the cities of Brazil. And her imitators are catching up. *Clube da Criança* on Manchete, which is where Xuxa started before she was bought by Globo, features Angelica, a cheerleading blonde out of the same mould who bounces in every afternoon and kisses the camera – *smack!* – on the lens. Among Angelica's retinue there is a man inside a large plastic bottle of cough syrup with flashing lights.

There are flashing lights everywhere, as at a fairground game. Behind Angelica, groups of kids wander and jig around trying to decipher the cues of the floor manager. It's a crazy rah-rah circus piped with toy ads. Angelica has recorded a version of 'Joe le Taxi' that knocked Xuxa off the number one spot.

But Xuxa has faced bigger dangers . . .

Douglas and his brother Alberto were fans of the *Xou da Xuxa*. Their father had lost his job at the cementation plant after an accident, and their mother worked at São Paulo airport to support the family. Quiet and well-behaved boys, they had good school records, they never stole from their parents, they weren't marginalised. And they liked Xuxa.

Alberto, the eldest of the two, also liked guns. He and some friends often went to a waste ground near the family house in a modest suburb to fire off arms they had made themselves, or found and repaired. Douglas spent his free time with his Atari videogame. They kept their admiration for Xuxa to themselves.

One day, the two brothers checked into a hotel in Rio. Alberto used the name Humberto Lococo. They had driven from São Paulo in Douglas' Chevette. The car, which looked like a wreck, had been transformed into a mobile arsenal. Home-made bombs were attached underneath, ready to be released by a switch on the dash. They had rigged a half-inch steel plate behind the front seat, with a lever to lift it into place.

Three days after they arrived in Rio, they pulled up in their James Bond Chevette near the entrance of the Teatro Fenix. There is a Military Police cabin at the corner, and from it, a twenty-four-year-old cadet approached the car to tell them they were parked in a restricted zone. Alberto shot at him with a .38 revolver. A second officer rushed out and Alberto fired again, injuring him. By the time an armoured car had caught up with the Chevette, speeding wildly through the streets of Rio, the young police cadet was dead.

Pursued by the armoured car, the Chevette crashed into a wall. Douglas, aged eighteen, died on the way to the hospital, his back broken. Alberto, aged twenty-three, had a severe neck wound, and died a few days later, having regained consciousness only briefly. According to the officer who was with him, Alberto was lucid. He said they wanted to save Xuxa and the Paquitas, because they were being 'explored . . . '

'Explored?' asked the officer. 'You mean sexually?'

Alberto made a positive gesture. He said, 'I love Leticia.'

Leticia Spiller, aged eighteen, was one of Xuxa's showgirls.

The arms found in the Chevette were all broken, apart from the one that Alberto had fired. The bombs had failed to work. If they had, the car would have exploded as the brothers had moved the petrol tank to make space and it was leaking. Despite their elaborate preparations, they had forgotten to repair the brakes, which failed in the fatal crash.

Interviews with family and friends, with teachers and psychiatrists, gave no clues to their actions. They were kind, shy, ordinary boys, who left no trace of the film that was playing in their heads, full of sexy, pubescent showgirls, automotive violence and bursts of gunfire; an average night on American TV, in which they were the stars.

The kidnap attempt prompted Xuxa to cancel her engagements

and take a vacation in Argentina, where she told reporters she was
thinking of leaving Brazil for a while, to concentrate on her career
in the United States.

Eight

Luis stands with his shirt open and his belly protruding comfortably, full of beans from the *feijoada* earlier that day. He hasn't been to a match in over two years. He has been neglecting his communion. Now his face is transfixed and radiant. 'Fluminense!' he intones, almost to himself, as though it were the name of an old girlfriend.

His seven-year-old son jumps excitedly at his side. Fluminense are on the offensive.

Luis has moved to the outskirts of Rio to take a job as an electrical engineer. Usually he is too tired to make the journey to the Maracana on a Sunday, and sits in his two-room house, with the front door open, watching the matches on TV and drinking beer with his neighbour. Today he has brought his son for a treat.

'Fluminense ...' cries Luis. The boy looks up at his father with pride.

The match between Fluminense and visitors Cruzeiro from Belo Horizonte, the capital of the state of Minas Gerais, started at 5 p.m., by which time the temperature had descended to a comfortable 22 degrees. It was early in the season and the stadium was nearly empty. Only 20,000 supporters had turned out, barely filling vast terraces that can hold ten times as many. But they make their presence felt by beating Samba drums, a profane voodoo thunder that reverberates under the concrete canopy.

The Maracana stadium in the suburbs of Rio de Janeiro is the cathedral of soccer, its kick-off line the altar on which the most solemn prayers of Latin American men are offered. At either end, strung with white nylon cord, are the gates of heaven or hell, glory or shame. The final whistle signals the end of ninety minutes of soccer purgatory.

On the terraces, huge flags stream from bamboo poles, bearing the names of the *torcida*, the supporters' clubs: The Blue Rebels (Cruzeiro's colour is blue), *Influente!, Flumania!, Superflu!* Banners hang from the terraces with the Rio team's logo, a carnival skull with a parrot, the Brazilian national bird. Cruzeiro's chances of beating the local team are slim. Fluminense are one of the great clubs of Rio. Despite the violence of the city, there are no barriers to keep the supporters apart. Police in blue overalls patrol the stands. A can thrown on to the pitch means a rough exit, and nobody wants to squander their day off in this way. The justice of the game will be enough.

Luis promised me it would be a good match. Cruzeiro are on better form than he expected. When the referee awards a free kick against Fluminense, Luis scowls and calls him a drunk. In this rude country, there is a touching politeness to the fans' cries. 'Everyone gets the minimum wage here,' someone shouts at Fluminense's manager. 'Put them to work!'

The supporters wear shorts and T-shirts, and soccer shirts if they can afford them. Luis' son is wearing a Fluminense shirt. Team shirts are the most expensive thing you can find in Brazil. The nylon shirt cost Luis half his weekly wage.

Before the match, I had taken Luis and his son down into the vestry of the cathedral, into the changing rooms. At the end of a long series of low tunnels, their concrete walls dulled with sweat, a handwritten list of the Fluminense team was pinned to a door. Inside, the players sat on wooden benches or lay on the floor doing warm-up exercises. They signed autographs for the boy while Luis stood respectfully at the door. There was a strange silence, a ritual of genuflection. None of the players spoke. I wondered if these footballers were conversing with the spirits of the *Macumba*.

That week in the newspaper, there had been an interview with Bebeto, star of the national team. He was laid up with an injury after a Rio derby in which he had led his new team, Vasco de Gama, against his old team of Flamengo. 'They used *Macumba* on me!' lamented Bebeto. He believes in Jesus, he affirmed, but fears the Orixas, the African Gods that flourish in his native Salvador. Luis thinks the explanation is more simple. 'If *Macumba* worked, the Bahia team would be the national champions every year!' he laughs. The manager of Flamengo had told his players to 'mark' Bebeto. At twenty-five, he is probably the fastest centre-forward on earth. Brazil is pinning its World Cup hopes on this graceful, sensitive giant, nicknamed *Bebe Chorao*, 'the Cry-Baby', for his tearful displays on the field.

'It's better now,' says Luis. 'Before he used to cry all the time: when he missed a shot, he would cry; when he lost a tackle, he would cry.' Vasco de Gama matched an offer of $3 million from Bayern of Munich to snatch Bebeto, who had joined Flamengo at eighteen. He is the highest-paid player in Brazil, earning $8000 a month. 'The salary of a myth,' says Luis. The Cry-Baby lives in the wealthy Barra di Tijuca with his wife, a professional volley-ball player, in a house with seashell-shaped couches and a room full of trophies. Bebeto has built himself a small zoo at his parents' home, where he goes to relax.

We were allowed twenty minutes in the dressing room. Reporters, photographers and TV crews crowded around the star players while others dribbled balls distractedly in a corner, curious and envious of the aura surrounding the top professionals. Another match was playing on the TV in the lounge, as the players made their way down the final tunnel, followed by the photographers. Trotting out to the middle of the field, they fell into three straight rows, holding the pose for just a few moments as the photographers' flashes burst simultaneously, before spreading away to take their positions.

At half time, I walk through the same tunnel on to the pitch, to stand on the spot that, for more than a billion people, might as well be the centre of the world. From here, the stadium seems much smaller. Hidden by the dazzle of the floodlights, the crowds recede, their presence sensed only by the noise. With the score at nil–nil, the ball flies for the start of the second half and the tempo of the drums accelerates: *boom-boom-boom-boom!*

I squat by the Cruzeiro goal, next to the radio commentators with old microphones in one hand and soggy, curled notebooks in the other. They half-sing their lyrical commentaries and are capable, Luis told me, of crying '*Goooooooolllll!*' for up to a minute! When a plane crashed in the Amazon region in 1989, killing seventy people, it was found that the pilot had been listening to a match report on the radio.

I have my nose to the turf where Pelé first displayed the soccer artistry that turned him into the game's most enduring myth. The Maracana was also the showcase for Zico, transferred to Udine in '83 for £3 million but back with Flamengo two years later after problems with his muscles and Italian tax inspectors. The stadium was constructed for the World Cup in 1950, on a scale that only Brazil would contemplate. The fate of the national team that year was a symbol of the foiled aspirations of this struggling giant. Brazil beat Sweden 7–1 and Spain 6–1 to reach the final with Uruguay. Twenty minutes from the whistle, they were 1–0 up. Then Uruguay scored twice. Two hundred thousand faces peered into the abyss; a sinister national memory that prefigures all the dashed hopes of transamazonian highways and unworkable nuclear power stations.

A boy at the time, Luis remembers the event as though it were a family funeral. 'My father didn't speak. There was nobody on the street the next day. We had offended God and the world was going to end.'

It was eight years before Brazil returned, having digested the lesson of their defeat, with a new defensive strategy. In the quarter final against Wales, seventy minutes passed without a goal. Then a nineteen-year-old Pelé, the youngest player on the team, scored the winning goal. Led by Pelé, Brazil effaced the memory of failure and won the World Cup. Four years later, as the team boarded the plane for Chile, President João Goulart told them, 'If you win, my people will complain of nothing for the next four years. Your victory will be all the rice and beans they need!'

They won again but the president was wrong. His people complained about poverty and low wages and the military took over. In 1966 Brazil lost to England, but four years later went to Mexico with the best side ever. Brilliant individuals – Gerson, Tostão, Pelé – and perfect teamwork produced no draws, nothing but wins.

'That was our greatest moment. We didn't deserve to win in '86,' rues Luis. 'Maybe next year with Bebeto . . . He's good – but you can't compare him to Pelé. They have a different temperament, but some of the same genius in their feet.' Bebeto will not get the chance to show off his. He will be kept in reserve for the semi-finals, because of his fragility, but Brazil will fail to reach them.

The memory of Brazil's greatest soccer-player, the 'Man of a 1000 Goals', is invoked nowadays in TV ads for canned sardines. Pelé has interests in media, haulage, construction and dairy farming. 'My ambition,' he avers, 'is to become the first black president of Brazil!'

Back in the twenties, players like Artur Freidenreich, a mulatto of German stock who scored the winning goal in the South American championship of 1921, and Carlos Alberto, a mulatto player with Fluminense, would iron their curls in the dressing room before the match. The crowds taunted them with cries of 'Rice powder!' – which they used to whiten their faces. President Pessoa recommended that no black players be sent to the next championship, for reasons of national prestige. Now Pelé wants to be president.

Luis says he would vote for him.

'Pelé was my hero.'

And then, with ten minutes to go, Fluminense score!

In the cathedral of soccer, Luis joins in uttering the holy communion.

'GOOOOOOOOOOLLLLLL!!'

Nine

I ring Marly in São Paulo, where she is at college. I can't come to see her there, as I have to go north to Bahia. I am hoping to meet the leading candidate in the presidential elections, three weeks away. After his victory – which is virtually certain – it will be much harder to get an interview. This is my excuse for not coming to São Paulo, as I had promised one day I would.

Marly tells me she has just returned from the *Nordeste*. She tells me about a trip, a crazy trip. 'We wanted to do it. To see what it was like . . .' She rode the bus for fifty-two hours to Ceara, 'a town of ten thousand people with no proper sanitation.' She gives a technical description, almost conscientiously, of the daily privations faced by the people of Ceara. At first, I assume this is because she is practising her English, and wants to get it right. Then I realise it's as though the proper technical nomenclature will bring with it the appropriate solution.

Then she says, revealing her own indignity, the sense of a hoped-for civility that I always liked about her, 'I had to walk across town and back every morning, to get water to wash.'

There were young men on the bus returning home, having made some money; eager, strong, rough, their country softness rubbed hard and calloused by the city. They joked with the girls but paid them respect, surprised to see women with such fine hands on the bus.

Families got on loaded with parcels tied with string, parcels so heavy, so dense, so important, they couldn't be left in the luggage hold. Marly wondered what they contained. She knew she would be dismayed at the answers, so she didn't ask.

In the city, she had often seen people with no home, squatters evicted at the roadside, and what surprised her about them was always the goods piled up around them. The old sofas they sat on, as though the street had become their living room, and the sacks and bundles around them. It all had a worn, broken, discarded look; it had already been thrown away.

To someone used to new things, or old things with warmth and charm, it was an embarrassment to find herself wondering what people would want to preserve such tired objects for.

Marly's father, when he heard of her trip to Ceara, was only a little surprised. His daughter had ridden the bus for 100 hours, to Ceara and back. She had seen the roadside shacks that would have to be torn down, felt the jolts from the bumps and potholes in roads that would have to be resurfaced, walked for three miles each morning to fetch water in a town that would have to be dug up and plumbed if it was to grow. 'There are so many questions,' she says, 'but what are the solutions?'

Soon she would have her engineering qualifications. Then she could work on finding them.

———

Nilson had been on the bus for nine hours when Marly and her friends boarded it in Ceara for the journey south, back to São Paulo. She sat in the empty seat beside him and, after a few hours, began to talk to the soft-spoken boy who was afraid to cross her gaze.

Nilson told her how, as he ran back to the house with his sister, a friend had come hurrying towards him, confirming what his sister had said. 'They've killed your father!' Nilson could still hear the words. All he felt was disbelief, crazy disbelief, until he

91

got home and found it was true. Then he couldn't understand it. He wanted to go back to the day before, but he knew he couldn't.

The death of his father set in chain a dangerous destiny. Nilson would be expected to avenge the murder. The man, knowing this, would be faced with two choices, either to flee or to face Nilson, and be forced to kill him too.

The man had come to stay with Nilson's family from somewhere in the *sertão*. He had worked on the ranches to the northwest, in the state of Pará, but said there was no more work now – they had stopped burning and clearing – and there were too many mouths. Some of these mouths were his responsibility, it seemed, from the melancholy way he said this. He had cut sugarcane on the plantations but the work was seasonal and the hands were cheap. He wanted to get a job in a factory in São Luis. He had heard that in the canning factories, you could earn good money for steady work, to buy a TV or a refrigerator. Nilson's father laughed at this. And the man told Nilson and the other children about the *onça-preta*, the black cat as big as a dog who prowls the edges of the forest, and the flies as big as your hand, and the alligators who lay in wait at the river's edge to snap at a man's heels, wrestling him down under the water until the life had bubbled out of him, so as to be able to eat him in peace.

The man was a friend of Nilson's father, and they drank often together and joked about old times. He helped at the store while Nilson was out working on his uncle's fishing boat and Vicentinho, his younger brother, was at school. Afterwards, Nilson learnt from his mother that the man had borrowed money from his father. The man had said how much he liked the life in Ribamar, as they sat outside the store enjoying the breezes that came in at night from the ocean. He bought a parcel of land down the road and built himself a two-room house. Nilson believed it was because of the loan that the man killed his father. Vicente had asked for the money back. The police said his father had been drinking, and there must have been a row over something. They had looked for the man but he wasn't at his house and no one had seen him in the town since that afternoon. Maybe he has gone to São Luis, the police suggested. They could do nothing. There was no proof.

92

The store had not been doing well, and Nilson wondered if that was the reason his father needed the money back. To pay for the funeral, Nilson had been forced to sell most of the remaining stock, the pigs and the chickens too.

Every night he sat outside the house and watched the road in the direction of São Luis, wondering if the man would come back, walking casually, as though nothing had happened. Nilson tried to decide how he would react. A few months had gone by, and he wondered if he could summon again the hatred he would need in his heart to do away with his father's murderer. He was nagged by the knowledge that the man would fear his act of vengeance, and might try to kill him.

Once, he even went to the bus terminal, to watch the people getting off, convinced that the man would return that day. He planned to follow him, to try to discern his motives for returning. All day, he searched the faces of people getting off the buses, weary from their long, hot journeys, and he saw the people boarding the buses, fresh and excited, in Sunday clothes, the women patting their babies, the men guarding heavy parcels tied with string.

In the garden that led down to the beach outside the church were stone benches and a stone statue of Our Lady of the Navigators, three feet tall, standing in a small fishing boat. Nilson had waited for the people to pass. They gave him long looks of concern, and some came and touched him on the shoulder, repeating how sorry they were. The church was one storey high with, above the entrance, a cross made of deep-brown *jacarandá*, as were the pews and the simple altar table inside. There were only a dozen pews, no longer enough for the growing congregation on this part of the beach. But more, newer churches were opening along the road. Nilson's father's store had been bought by a Pentecostal sect who were busy repainting before they opened for business.

New apartment blocks had been going up on the hillsides of the bay, and over the hill, to the north, lay the big port in São Luis that was growing too. These new landmarks were unmissable now but somehow immaterial to Nilson, too new, lacking a history, though he was glad enough to navigate by their outlines when he was far out and the seas grew rough.

It was in the garden of the church that Nilson had made up his mind. 'Justice comes from heaven. I'm not going to run after him and kill him,' he told the priest, who had come out to talk to Nilson, and was relieved to hear this. He asked Nilson what his plans were, because he knew that for Nilson to stay would be perilous. He knew that what had happened to Nilson was not uncommon. There were plenty of boys of thirteen who went around with knives in their pockets and bitterness in their hearts.

One of Nilson's older sisters had gone to São Paulo to work as a maid. His mother had asked her to send money for the ticket and Nilson told the priest he would soon be boarding the bus for the long journey south. His sister worked for a guy called Tony, who had an agency sending out cleaners, people from the *Nordeste*. She said she thought that Tony would be able to find work for Nilson.

It wasn't an economic problem, now that the store had been sold and the bills paid. Two years ago, Nilson had left his uncle's boat, and had become the boss of another boat. The boat was owned by the Rancho da Pesca. Nilson fished for *cururú* and caught 2000 kilos a week, a *quinhão*. The owner of the boat kept three parts, Nilson earned two and the crew earned one part. The owner of the boat made the count at the end of the week, after the crew had taken what they wanted to eat.

Nilson didn't understand mathematics very well. He was twelve when he stopped going to school, though he didn't go to work straight away. He hung around, helping at the store and playing football. He studied a little at night at the mission school, but that finished when he was sixteen. Then his uncle invited him out on the boat. He had wanted to save enough money to buy a boat himself. Then he wouldn't have to give half of his catch to the owner. That much he knew. He would no longer see the light from the church on the beach at dusk.

He stared out at the passing scrubland that he had never seen before, that stretched on through endless little towns like the one he had left, the half-familiar look of their streets an empty comfort.

He had joined the people at the bus station, eager people in their best clothes, but these were scant protection against the indignities that the city ahead had in store for them.

Ten

The bankers have gathered in New York to receive the atonements of the Brazilian delegation. Owed some $68 billion, the bankers were uneasy. Three weeks earlier, on 19 October 1987, known as Black Monday, the Dow Jones had made its biggest plunge since the Great Depression. Eight months earlier, Brazil had defiantly suspended debt repayments, and the value of the titles held by the banks has fallen by $30 billion. But Brazil is now on its knees with insufficient foreign reserves to finance imports of machinery and raw materials. The $4 billion gained by not paying the debt has all been spent.

Dilson Funaro, the minister of finance who took the initiative, is not with the Brazilian delegation, however. He is wondering whether to stand for president, after opinion polls show he is the most popular politician in the country.

Funaro was at an earlier meeting in April, though, the first time the bankers had sat at a table with their clients since the Brazilian debt crisis began. 'For five years, the banks had denied that there even was a crisis,' says Funaro. 'They insisted the IMF had the solution. But the increase in bank interest rates since 1980 alone has added some $25 billion to the debt.'

What is euphemistically known as the IMF 'medicine' Brazil had stubbornly refused. 'We will not pay for the debt with recession and

96

unemployment,' President Sarney had declared on TV the day the moratorium was declared. With a debt of $120 billion, the largest of any country in the developing world – though Mexico was not far behind – Brazil felt it was being strangled.

Fifteen years earlier, the nation was on development highway. Its economy was growing by a phenomenal 13 per cent a year and there was even money for new social programmes. But import costs increased 120 per cent with the first oil shock and Brazil found itself running on empty. To keep the juggernaut rolling, Mario Henrique Simonsen, the new finance minister, went borrowing. Banks in North America, Europe and Japan – flush with the gains deposited by the oil-producers – were happy to see him, and approved the National Development Plan that he showed them. The amount Brazil borrowed in 1974 alone was equal to all the money it had borrowed over the previous two hundred years! More than $40 billion flowed into the country over the next five years, on floating interest rates that, to begin with, were low.

The return on the projects in the Plan was a comfortable 15 per cent and, to an extent, they worked. In 1965, there was indeed a lot of coffee in Brazil, providing 44 per cent of the country's exports. Two decades later, manufactured goods accounted for 67 per cent. Most of Brazil's $13 billion trade surplus in 1986 was due to these investments. But the surplus was all going to repay the debt and the country was heading for a blind curve. The second oil shock in 1979 threw the juggernaut into a wild skid. Oil prices doubled, interest rates skyrocketed and commodity prices fell. Antonio Delfim Netto, finance minister during the Sixties surge – known for his autocratic, high-spending ways as the generals' economic tsar – was recalled from Paris, where the years as ambassador had put weight on him, but his myopia had not improved. He went about with a portfolio of pipedream projects borrowing as much as he could, to pay for oil imports and repay the mounting interest. It was credit craziness, doomed to default, and the banks accommodated him.

A year later, with inflation mounting, Delfim slammed on the brakes. Government spending dried up and recession hit. Inflation raced to 100 per cent by 1983 – the year that debt repayments from the Third World began to exceed aid and credit from the First World. Brazil asked for a $25 billion rescue package, but refused to accept International Monetary Fund conditions, claiming these were more severe than the ones imposed on Germany after World War II. In the deadlock, Brazil stopped repaying principal on its debt, though it continued to pay interest. A series of measures to stop inflation, freezing first wages, then prices, had little effect, except to change the name of the currency from the Cruzeiro to the Cruzado. Inflation reached 225 per cent in 1985 and estimations for the year in progress as the bankers and their recalcitrant clients sit at the table are much higher. The bankers in New York know that the Brazilian economy is in dire trouble.

In February of that year, President Sarney, the politician who inherited the mess from the outgoing military-controlled government, had announced that Brazil was also suspending interest payments.

'We will not pay for the debt with the hunger of our people.'

The interest had been costing Brazil all of its trade surplus – $13 billion in 1987 – the third largest in the world! *Imagine if that money had been spent in Brazil . . .* How many hospitals, how many factories, can you get for $13 billion? ask the Brazilians. Never mind that the debt was incurred by an unconstitutional regime. Never mind that there was no check on where the money went. For a developing country to transfer all its export earnings and 5 per cent of its Gross Domestic Product to the developed world is unjust! In the last five years alone, Brazil has paid over $55 billion – more than it borrowed in the first place!

These are not arguments to which the bankers are sensitive, but the Brazilian delegation is bullish as the session begins in New York. The consensus in Brazil is clear. The Workers' Party, backed by the unions, wants the repayments spread over twenty or thirty years at much lower interest. The majority Democratic Movement Party points out that Brazil spends seven times more servicing the debt than on social programmes, and wants to see interest rates reduced to the level they were at when the debt was incurred.

The American banks have threatened to cancel Brazil's current account credit line of $15 billion, but Black Monday has left them nervous of provoking more drama, and in need of this profitable short-term business.

Late on Sunday night, an agreement is reached.

Of the $4.5 billion in payments due since February, Brazil will pay a third and the bankers will cancel the rest. Brazil will resume payments on the debt and the banks agree to renegotiate, but only through the IMF. Until the final settlement, current interest rates will apply. The Brazilians had wanted to see the banks reduce their 'spread', the 1.125 per cent above the London interbank rate they are taking as profit for their shareholders and depositors in the First World. In Brazil, meanwhile, the new finance minister has announced an austerity programme. The IMF 'medicine', so bitter to Brazilian pride, is to be administered.

Eight months later, in June '88, a final agreement will be reached. The spread will be reduced to 0.8125 per cent – the same for intransigent Brazil as for Mexico, Chile and Argentina – and the $62 billion still owed will be rescheduled over twenty years, with eight years' grace. This means that Brazil will be paying $500 million less per year. A month later, the creditor governments grouped in the Paris Club, owed a further $15 billion, will agree to similar terms.

Qualifying these accords as reasonable for everybody, a banker says, 'We have reverted, in the Brazilian case, to a classic scenario.'

It had happened before. Defaults on Latin American loans floated in the 1820s were almost total. Three decades went by before Latin America was again the recipient of easy, boisterous credit.

In the early nineteenth century, the newly independent nations of Latin America were described as the retarded children of backward parents. These parents looted mountains of gold and silver to fuel a commercial boom in Europe, and forced their children into the economic inbreeding of mercantilism. Spain and Portugal also bequeathed a Renaissance love of splendour: lavish palaces built by a slave economy; Baroque cathedrals that were the centres of a society in which, having been ordained by God, privilege and position were eternal. The historian Gilberto Freyre describes post-colonial Brazilian society as medieval, ripe for the attentions of Protestant capital.

In the next spate of lending, from 1862, Brazil and Peru were the main beneficiaries. But by 1867, over a quarter of loans to Latin American governments were in default. The new Juarez regime in Mexico refused to recognise the debts incurred by the Emperor Maximilian and Venezuela had stopped paying interest. A charging bull market in London made up the losses, however, and lending continued. When the bull market ended in 1875, over half the loans to Latin America – worth £70 million – were in default.

In London, the cries of ruined investors led to a parliamentary enquiry, which concluded that 'the governments concerned were guilty of deceit and corruption. The loan contractors had extracted extortionate terms from and used infamous methods to deceive British bondholders, who in their turn seem to have behaved with avarice and stupidity.'

Rothschild's had enjoyed a special position as the issuing house for Imperial Brazil, and were relatively little-harmed. The rule of Dom Pedro II was benevolent – to bankers. Through thick but mostly thin – the poor coffee harvests and the terrible drought in the *Nordeste* of 1873–75 – the Brazilian treasury paid its debts. There were benefits: new railways, roads, docks, harbours and telegraph lines, even the beginnings of a public school system. Most Brazilian children, though, would never be able to read the document recording their birth, who owned them and how much they were worth. Rothschild's chief ally in Brazil was Ireneo Evangelista de Souza, Baron Maua. Trained in an English firm, he dreamed of an industrial revolution for Brazil, via the alliance of credit with technological progress. He built railways, ports and telegraph lines, established gasworks and textile factories in Rio, and owned huge estates. His steamships opened up commercial traffic in the Amazon. His bank was the major financial power of the empire, and was active in Montevideo and Buenos Aires to the south. For a quarter of a century, Baron Maua was the greatest entrepreneur on the South Atlantic coast. He survived the crisis of 1873–75, but not the next one, and ended up a vagrant wandering the docks he had built in Rio, sleeping on the benches in the nearby parks, one of which was later named after him.

Where did all the money go? I once asked a Brazilian friend, as we sat on the beach at Ipanema. He snorted, a mix of national humiliation and pity at my innocence. 'Look around you,' he said, indicating the luxury apartment blocks. 'A lot of it is right here.'

From Rio, there is one flight a day to Zurich, he explained, presumably full of Swiss holidaymakers. 'What would all those planeloads of Brazilians find to do every day in Switzerland, a cold, expensive country full of secretive banks?'

He guessed that about half of the money was stolen, say $40 billion, a figure that most Brazilians would go along with. We should not be surprised at the amount. Throughout the developing world, it's the same story: the diversion of public funds, the pillage of bank reserves, of gold, diamonds and precious metals, the inflated invoices for state contracts, the transfer into private accounts of the proceeds of corruption.

The Kleptocrats of Brazil remain at large, benefiting from institutional cover. Power in the federal republic is shared by an array of people at state and national levels, who came and went under the military regime, making corruption more widespread, difficult to trace to a single, plenipotent pillager. The presidents of the military years were the chief executives of concerted interests in a political charade of great sophistication. They were chosen by the votes of a few hundred senior officers in Rio's *Escola Superior da Guerra*, the country's elite intellectual academy. A liberal, General Geisel, was even elected in '74. He relaxed censorship, made a few reforms, but still left congressmen with little to do but rubberstamp decisions made elsewhere.

During the debt negotiations in 1987, Leonel Brizola, governor of Rio de Janeiro, accused foreign bankers of engaging in 'an orgy of irresponsible lending'. The secrecy of the military regime meant there was no control of the deals that went down between the generals, the industrialists and the lenders. When Pacific, Gas and Electric or Framatome came calling, who made the decisions and how? How much was pocketed in kickbacks, fees and commissions? Brizola wanted to set up a commission to look into how the debt was incurred. He proposed that the country would then repay the part of the debt that was legitimate, at low, fixed rates. It would have meant reopening wounds made by the military, financial wounds that, in the lives they cost, are as grave as any inflicted by torturers in the dark, early days of the regime. In '64, Brizola mounted the only challenge to the generals' coup, and twenty-five years later, his presidential bid will be headed off. *Imagine if all that money had been spent in Brazil . . .*

Hyperinflation – price rises of more than 50 per cent a month – has come to Brazil. People in the queues outside the banks on this October morning in 1988 look no more anxious. They are trying to work out how much cash they will need for the next few days, so as to leave as much as possible in the bank for the *overnight*. To work out how much things will cost tomorrow, they figure against the *black*, the unofficial dollar rate. Cars, real estate, medical bills and airline tickets are all priced in dollars. But the planes leave empty when the passengers don't show up. Because they are refundable, the tickets have become an inflation hedge.

Inflation is a rat-race towards a cliff that is always receding, a psychoeconomic fever. But the people in the lines at the supermarkets look no more agitated this morning. Next year in Argentina, at an annual rate of around 1700 per cent, looting will begin. The Brazilians, adepts of inflation, merely continue their calculations.

In his office, the owner of the supermarket tries to figure out how many kilos of mozzarella to order that day. He knows the supplier will bill him at next month's price, adding a margin to cover inflation. The owner could order two months' worth, gambling that the rate next month will be less than the rate the month after. In the meantime, he must change the prices on his stock, as he does every few days. He too will add a margin for inflation that will make inflation rise again when the shopping basket is tallied by the IBGE, the Brazilian Institute of Geography and Statistics.

Prices rise by the escalator and salaries by the stairs . . .

The IBGE will announce next month's figure, and the shelf-filler will get her monthly rise to compensate for inflation. But by then, prices will have risen again. To make ends meet, she must borrow or buy on credit, at a rate of 50 per cent per month or more, to cover inflation.

Because inflation rises faster than salaries, the supermarket owner finds he has made a small benefit from the payroll at the end of the year. This is when inflation is rising; sometimes it falls, but it always rises again.

With the profit, he juggles between the *overnight* and the *black* at first, then he buys an airline ticket and a couple of telephone lines. In São Paulo, the exchanges are old and overloaded and there is a growing demand for lines. Before long, the owner will be making as much from these activities as from the supermarket. He will have learned the lesson known by everyone in business in Brazil: *speculation is better than production.* The telephone lines prove a good investment. Three years later, demand is such that a secondary market has sprung up for the limited number of lines. Prices for lines in the different exchanges are quoted in a listing every Sunday on the back page of the *Folha de São Paulo.*

Eleven

The candidate steps out of a private jet, greeted by TV cameras and youths beating tribal drums. They wear fresh white T-shirts with the name *Collor*, the two *L*s coloured yellow and green, the national colours of Brazil. He dashes across the tarmac and into the terminal as the crowds swirl and jostle around him. A middle-aged man in a wheelchair is pushed into the fray, his face shining – a Latin-American photo-opportunity for Fernando Collor de Mello. The candidate beams, sweats, tries to keep his balance. People are expecting miracles.

Waiting to greet the candidate is the state deputy, Luís Irujo. A member of Collor's Party of National Reconstruction, he is co-ordinating the presidential campaign in Bahia. Like Collor, he looks young for a politician. He is heavyset and light-skinned. His father is the owner of a local TV station. He tells me the riotous welcome is 'spontaneous'. Several hundred young Collor supporters have come in buses laid on from all over Bahia, Brazil's third-largest state, to the airport in the state capital of Salvador. 'They don't mind leaving the beach today,' says Luís Irujo. 'They think Collor has a lot of charisma.' The Collor T-shirts have been given to them. At home, they have no sanitation; many are unable to read. But they have electricity and TV sets. On the channel that belongs to Irujo's family, they watch the *telenovelas* and the 8 p.m. news, currently displaced by campaign messages.

Collor's campaign message is simple. Two graphic bars coloured yellow and green smash through a series of obstacles: *Corruption! Poverty! Debt! Inflation!* These are words everyone understands. The bars turn into the two *L*s of Co*ll*or. The candidate is shown bathing in the cheers of a huge crowd, both arms raised in triumph. Little known just a year ago, Collor, aged forty, was too young to vote in the last direct presidential elections, three decades ago. Three weeks from now, he will be voted president of the world's fourth-largest democracy.

'You've come from Europe?' Collor's press agent had queried. She sounded surprised that I had made such an effort. 'Why do you want to meet him?'

I explained that, with its massive debt problems and its responsibility for the Amazon rain forest, the future of Brazil was of great interest. I added for good measure that Collor was a phenomenon, like Ronald Reagan, and the press agent agreed. I knew that Brazilians like to be confronted by their own enigma. In the press, Collor was being described as a populist with plenty of charisma but no policies. Despite or because of this, people said he was going to win. He had the backing of the two most powerful groups in Brazil, the TV and the military. His campaign was being fought with all the tools of modern marketing in a largely illiterate, though nevertheless democratic, society.

There was no point coming to the campaign HQ in Brasilia, Collor's press agent had told me. He would be too busy. He was on a hectic schedule of rallies, jetting around the country. His day began at 5 a.m. each morning and he flew back late at night. 'You should go to Bahia. Maybe you can see him there.'

In the airport lounge, chairs are arranged for a press conference, abruptly scrapped in the mayhem that greets his arrival. Collor sweeps through the crowds, replying to TV reporters on the run. It's a taste of his political agenda, seemingly composed on the spot, amidst mounting acclaim and confusion.

'Come with us,' shouts Ruy Pontes. He grabs my shoulder,

pulling me out of the crowd and onto the air-conditioned coach. 'It's always like this,' says Ruy proudly. 'Collor is like a football star.' He gives me his card. Ruy is in charge of 'political marketing' for Collor in Bahia.

The candidate sits at the front of the bus, conferring with state deputy Luís Irujo. His shirt is damp and he has lost his tie. He frowns at documents, falling quiet as he watches the sun set on the dry scrub. Irrigation is an important issue in Bahia, an agricultural region where the old colonial divisions of Brazil are still sharp. Business and administration remain in the hands of wealthy families like those of Irujo, of European stock, while the population is largely of African descent. In the Seventies, Bahia was the birthplace of the *Tropicalista* movement in Brazilian music, led by Gilberto Gil and Caetano Veloso, who coined the name after the title of a work by the artist Helio Oiticica. The week before I arrived, Paul Simon had been here recording with the drum choir Olodum, one of the *Blocos Africanos* who parade in the annual carnival.

We drive for an hour along a pot-holed highway to Feira de Santana, Bahia's second city, where the annual fête has been co-opted for a rally. The pop-corn and beer stands are plastered with Collor stickers. Through the open windows of the two-room houses, I can see the 7 p.m. *telenovela* unfolding on the TV sets, a daily mix of lust and intrigue depicting the idealised world of a Brazilian middle-class that Collor seeks to unify.

Collor's supporters have followed in municipal buses marshalled for the day, noisily drumming *batucadas* on the backs of the seats.

It is the day before Children's Day, a holiday weekend and, for Collor's supporters, a day out. From the buses, they give the candidate the Brazilian national gesture, a thumbs-up, before joining the thousands of local people thronging in the streets. The campaign committee has been busy here too. Girls in Collor T-shirts dance on the stage erected in the main square. Music booms from the speaker columns and green-and-yellow Collor balloons float in the clear night.

Descending from the bus, Collor has to force his way through more people struggling to touch him. He has learnt to move fast in public, smiling anxiously as he is tossed by a sea of shining faces, lit by the inevitable TV lights.

Reaching the front of the stage, he raises both arms to quell the roar of the crowd. 'You all know the crisis we are going through!' he shouts, his voice already hoarse. 'But if God has placed these obstacles before us, it's for me to overcome them and become president!'

His voice echoes through the PA, affirming that 'the people of the *Nordeste* deserve respect.' The government of Brasilia, he declares, 'will no longer be able to humiliate us.' Reaching the first station of his cross, he cries, 'I will bring water to the fields! Farmers need credit and not the theft that is the present interest rate.' He promises to end corruption in the farming administration. 'We need money for health, agriculture, housing. It has to be taken back from those who steal from the people – the *Marajás*!'

At this, a huge cheer goes up, drowned by Collor's campaign song, which also happens to be the national anthem.

It's what people have come to hear from the candidate likened to Indiana Jones by the popular press, the dashing *Marajá* hunter. Appointed by the military mayor of Maceio, capital of the small state of Alagoas to the north of Bahia, Collor won his first election to office as a federal congressman in 1982. With the backing of his family, he was elected governor of Alagoas in 1986. National fame came through his attacks on the *Marajás* – bureaucratic fat-cats – that coincided with cries for state 'deprivatisation', a sarcastic dig at public employees abusing their positions. In thirty years, the size of the administration has grown and so has the level of poverty, with half the population still earning less than the legal monthly minimum of $75. In his book *The Other Path*, Hernando de Soto highlighted the follies of a corrupt, runaway administration in Peru and, lately, newspapers in Brazil have been equating government with poverty, calling for less of both. The corrupt official has become the second favourite donkey on which to pin the country's woes, after the foreign debt.

Collor seeks to identify himself with the honest and hardworking people of the *Nordeste* in the struggle against the bureaucrats. He announced his candidature just a few months ago and has spurted into the lead like a Latin American striker going for the goal. His vote is assured in the semi-rural north, but that accounts for only 40 per cent of the electorate, and he must convince the urban populations in the south not just of his sincerity but of his ability to deal with chaos.

As Collor declaimed from the stage, I wondered what would make someone want the job of running a country like Brazil; a Quixotic task, requiring either cynical self-interest or selfless statesmanship, for the great presidents of Brazil would not make a very convincing football team in the eyes of their countrymen. *Corruption! Poverty! Debt! Inflation!* Armed with a foolhardy idealism, Collor is offering to slay dragons.

Critics accuse him of having youth and good looks but, so far, no policies. They add resignedly that this is fine for the people of Brazil. After the military handover in '85, an electoral college voted in a new civilian president. The first direct elections in two decades were set to be fought by long-standing heavyweights: Leonel Brizola, the sixty-seven-year-old former governor of Rio at the head of the Democratic Labour Party; and Ulysses Guimaraes, seventy-two, leader of acting President Sarney's Democratic Movement Party. When Collor entered the campaign, Brizola joked that he was a 'pebble in my shoe'. If a challenge came, it was expected from the Workers' Party led by José Luis da Silva, or 'Lula', the Brazilian Lech Walesa, an ex-steelworker with strong support in São Paulo – and not from Alagoas, the third poorest state in Brazil.

This arid corner of the *Nordeste* produces tobacco and the sugarcane alcohol that fuels nine out of ten new cars, leaving the air in the cities clean but the rivers full of toxic by-products of the refining process. It's from sugarcane that Collor's family derive their wealth. Here, the old colonial structures are still in place: whitewashed wooden *fazendas* and poor tenant farmers. Squeezed by high interest from the banks and low yield from the land, they migrate north to Amazonia, where the controversial development provides some work, or south to Rio and São Paulo, to scratch a living in teeming slums. Everybody blames the banks, or the burden of the foreign debt, while only priests and Communists talk of land reform, an issue stained with blood in Latin America.

After the rally, in a house on the square that serves as the local party HQ, Collor holds a press conference as the townspeople dance outside. The windows are open but the small room is humid with the heat from the TV lights. His knees jammed against a table with people crushed at all sides, Collor faces a Betacam. His lead in the polls is starting to slip, and he knows he must do something to hold the voters' attention. In a few days, he tells the newsmen, he will publish a policy document. He reveals part of the contents: a denunciation hot-line for the public to expose crooked officials. 'Corruption is linked to impunity. They parade in the streets of Brasilia with all the money they've made!'

As the fête continues in the square, Collor leaves for a motel on the outskirts of town to gladhand local campaign contributors. The motel is situated in the new Brazil that Collor espouses, near an industrial park with 120 small businesses. In this setting, he seems almost like a Kennedy figure; against the old, crooked alliances, symbolising youthful democratic hopes, backed by powerful interests. But Brazil is hardly enjoying the economic boom that North America was in the Sixties. And while Collor might be telegenic, he often looks distressed by the surging crowds around him, like a man riding a wave whose ferocity he didn't guess.

But, handsome and athletic – he has a black belt in karate – Collor has an appeal lacking in his seasoned opponents for an electorate whose average age is below thirty. He appears as a devout family man, avoiding political tags and calling himself a 'Christian reformer'. He articulates with pious gestures the simple creed of *Collorism*, a crusade against the injustices of corruption and poverty.

It's warm by the poolside but the candidate doesn't stay long.

By midnight, Collor is back in the Bahian capital, Salvador, in the studios of a TV station with his campaign manager, Luís Irujo. Irujo's father, who happens to be the owner of the station, is preparing to shoot a spot for Collor – against a backdrop of the station logo.

His associates leave him alone in the owner's office to prepare

109

his lines. The text was written for him by Sebastião Nery, a journalist and former Brizola supporter who swapped sides to work for Collor. In an article titled 'The Brizolin Cartel', Nery has recently attacked Brizola for his links with *Bicheiros* and drug barons from the *favelas* like Escadinha. Brizola promises to fight back with potentially wounding charges of corruption around Collor. But Collor is used to the media fray. His late father Arnon launched a newspaper in Alagoas, the *Gazeta do Povo*, expanding into radio and later TV. Collor's father was a friend of Dr Roberto Marinho, the powerful head of TV Globo, and the family's Alagoas station is affiliated, like the station in Salvador, to the Globo network. Collor's TV spots surpass those of other candidates for slick professionalism; staff from the nation's most popular channel have been on temporary leave working on his campaign.

I watch Collor rehearse his convictions in front of the camera, bathed in white light. He is tall, with the physical self-possession of the martial arts practitioner, though he stoops slightly. It's been a long day. The candidate still hasn't recovered his tie; his white shirt is looking tired, his expression haggard. Miracles are hard work.

The spot takes just a few minutes to record. Collor gets it right in two takes. Afterwards, Ruy Pontes ushers me in to the owner's office and introduces me to the *Governador*, who is sitting on a sofa, shuffling through papers. Everyone around him uses his official title as governor of Alagoas. Yet Collor appears a modest man. He wears a simple wedding ring and, like almost everyone else in Brazil, a plastic watch.

He invites me to sit down with him and, as he puts away his papers, I tell the candidate that the world is becoming alarmed at the destruction of the rain forest. 'Will you try to halt development?'

Collor answers firmly. He has rehearsed this. 'The problem of the rain forest is a problem for the whole world. But I think the solution will begin with us. I could not admit foreign participation. I think each country must find solutions for their own environmental problems. We have to sit at the same table and discuss this, each one facing their problem and seeing what contribution they could make for the others. Contribution and not interference.'

He is giving a polite rebuff to attempts to internationalise the

Amazon issue. The burning forest has now been seen by all from satellite pictures, but Collor defends Brazil's right to exploit its resources. Not everyone is interested in the Amazon for the same reasons. 'If foreign capital comes to this country we have to establish a good partnership, putting our resources at the service of our development.'

A large chunk of those resources presently services the foreign debt. To the alarm of its creditors, Brazil has, for the last six months, again suspended payments.

I ask Collor what he will say to the banks if he is elected. He chuckles, then pinches the bridge of his nose to concentrate on his English, learnt from Beatles records and at school in Rio.

'I don't want to fight against the IMF or other institutions. I want to fight *inside* them. There are many people who are very close to our position about the external debt. I think we are living at this moment in a very positive period because the bankers and these institutions know that it's impossible for the Third World to pay this debt at present.'

Collor's campaign involves millions of stickers and T-shirts and many TV spots, paid for by 'me and my friends – it's not a secret. We have to register with the election tribunal.'

'What is the cost?'

'I don't know – some kilograms!' he jokes.

'What is your relationship with Roberto Marinho?' I ask. 'A lot of people have told me you are the Globo candidate.'

'Not true,' he laughs, fingering a box of cigars given to him by the owner of the station. 'I'd like to be, but I'm not. My link is that I am in this profession. I'm a pressman too and my family has an organisation of communications. Our television transmits the programmes of Globo. My father was a friend of Dr Roberto.'

As election day drew close, Globo played a shrewd game of promoting Lula at the expense of the more moderate left-winger Leonel Brizola, knowing that the election of a far-left candidate would be anathema to the military, who, a few days before the vote, warned that such a result would be 'unfortunate'. It was their only statement during the campaign, but one heavy with meaning. With Brizola relegated to third place, Collor won easily.

111

Collor tells me that his vocation was not politics. 'I think my destiny took me into political life. I accept my destiny and try to do my best.'

I ask what he will give his children, aged eleven and thirteen, for Children's Day.

'The gift I make to them is the promise that when I am elected president, there will be no more children sleeping in the streets!'

When I phone Marly to tell her what Collor has promised his children, she is amazed. 'He said that?'

I tell her he sounded sincere.

'That's the problem.'

The next day, I meet Ruy Pontes for lunch. The restaurant overlooks the beach and the skyscrapers of downtown Salvador. Across the street is a modern conference centre, architecturally imposing with its vast postmodern canopy roof, next to empty, dusty lots and tin shacks. Brazil has been described as one computer-literate Mediterranean country and twenty dirt-poor Caribbean ones. It is often reminiscent of the Spain of the Seventies, with construction work going on everywhere, but never fast enough to catch up.

Ruy is pleased to be putting to use his degree in communications to 'market' Collor. Usually, he markets the less glamorous fare of local companies. He won the Collor assignment after working on Luís Irujo's campaign for state deputy. Their primary medium, he says unsurprisingly, is TV. 'The visual aspect is important, our people like to see and listen.' During the military years, TV was used to homogenise a far-flung and disparate people; two countries, who didn't know each other. 'Our continental area is large, so if you control communications, you have power,' he says.

In his early forties, Ruy, who has three children and a pleasant home, has realised the Brazilian dream. He is part of the urban middle-class glimpsed nightly in the *telenovelas*. But he fears for his country's stability. They live with hyperinflation, which boiled over into rioting in Argentina last year. Their salaries suddenly eroded, the middle-class there found themselves sharing the deprivations of the slum-dwellers, while the slum-dwellers took to looting. It's a prospect that nobody wants to contemplate. 'Brazil is a different case,' insists Ruy. Collor represents the hopes of Brazil to move up to the First World, the world of the *telenovelas* whose room sets are juggled by Globo to generate four hours of dream-Brazil a day.

Ruy asks me what I think of Collor. It's a question everyone asks me, but not for conversation or a political debate. I feel as though, unsure themselves, they want only to be able to believe in him, and are hoping my objective view might confirm their stronger, subjective one. I tell Ruy that Collor is an idealist for an idealistic people. Cementing a stable middle-class, if he can do it, would be safer than a leftist transformation, which might just lead to a military clamp-down, the cycle of revolution and repression that characterises Latin American history. But the middle-class in Brazil is fragile, a television fiction.

I had asked Collor if he was afraid of what happened in Argentina. 'No,' he replied evenly. 'The new president has taken good measures with determination and now Argentina is in a good way.' Nor would he want to see Brazil go the way of Bolivia, a laboratory for the theories of Harvard economist Jeffrey Sachs, who strangled inflation with tighter money than even the IMF would have dared to impose. 'It's different because in Bolivia there was a very long period of recession. I think in Brazil we will not have this recession. It will be hard for the most part of our people but not, I think, as hard as what happened in Bolivia. I think we have a target to reach: to be placed in the group of the seven richest countries on the planet. We have the resources and potential and population and climate. What we have to do is administrate these resources without complexes.'

Critics like Gilberto Gil, now a local councillor in Bahia and Secretary of State for Culture, argue that Brazil has Third World problems that need to be solved first. He would prefer to see the country at the head of the Third World than at the feet of the First.

Brazilians as a whole are more likely to make an affective choice. Collor is playing to the tele-literate society. Schooled in communications, Collor sells himself simply but skilfully to this electorate. Hoping for miracles, they settle for promises.

Ruy tells me that Collor the crusader has made one more promise: a strong state education system.

He falls silent for a moment. 'Our problem in this election is that half of the voters are illiterate. And these are the people who will elect our next president . . . '

———

Within a month of Collor taking office in the Spring of 1990, rows of black limousines are to be seen parked along the streets outside the presidential palace in Brasilia, next to a sign that says: 'See the end of privilege in our country. These cars are for auction!' At a televised cabinet meeting the following month, the new president hands out memos to his ministers detailing how many civil servants they have to sack: 360,000 out of a total of 1.6 million state employees.

He cuts the number of ministries from twenty-three to twelve and only the remaining twelve ministers have the right to an official car. Federal police chief Romeu Tuma – who now devotes his energies to chasing people evading the freeze on 80 per cent of savings in personal bank accounts – has to take the bus too. And even this is no longer free in what was once the civil servant's paradise. Ministerial mansions are up for sale, while billions of dollars have been earmarked for public housing. Collor's economic adviser Antonio Kandir proposes an $18 billion sell-off of state companies and a social spending programme of $94 billion financed by raising taxes by more than half. But tackling the rampant cronyism in Brazil's public sector will not be easy and the new measures are complicated, with fresh amendments coming each day. By May, however, the monthly inflation rate is down to 3 per cent – compared with 85 per cent before Collor took office. He had promised it would be down to zero.

With the middle-class unable to salt their savings away in US dollars and workers faced with massive unemployment – half of São Paulo's 700,000 engineering workers were sacked or laid off and thousands more fired from coal and steelworks – Brazilians resign themselves to further chaos, the only way left to fight chaos. Order – the military solution – brought them to this point in the first place. Some have been striking, demanding consultation but accepting cuts. Riot police dispersed protesting school teachers in

Brasilia, where the distribution of school milk is halted because of suspected frauds. By June, though, Collor's plan still has the support of 54 per cent of the population.

Wearing combat boots and fatigues, the president flew north in May to the Amazon, followed by TV cameras. He met leaders of the Yanomami tribe to hear their complaints of the violence and disease brought by the 40,000 *garimpeiros*, gold prospectors who have invaded their lands. As the cameras rolled, Collor told Police Chief Romeu Tuma to dynamite the prospectors' airstrips. To the satisfaction of the international ecological movement, Collor appoints José Lutzenberger, a fierce critic of Amazon development, as his environmental secretary. More importantly, Collor has taken control of the region out of the hands of the military and given it to a new civil agency, headed by Lutzenberger. The governor of the affected region says, however, that 'we can't just sit back and look at a mountain of gold.'

The president resumed payments on the foreign debt that had been suspended for six months, but at a rate lower than the banks might have wanted. They 'welcome' the move, however, combined as it is with a drastic austerity programme. The left accuse Antonio Kandir's team of tight-money zealots of going too far. He says it's just the beginning. 'If we have to,' he promises, 'we'll go as far as a recession.'

Meanwhile, at the weekends, Collor has been busy demonstrating the attributes of a leaner, fitter Brazil, roaring on a Jet Ski, jogging in an 'Eco '92' T-shirt, flying a Brazilian-made fighter jet. Perhaps he is trying to escape from the contradictions of ultra-right monetary policies and spending on housing and education, a contradiction at the heart of old-fashioned Latin-American populism. Some people say Collor has the makings of another Peron. While Collor lacks the military background and is no protectionist, his attempts to embody the vigour of the nation combined with a self-righteous streak might lead to personal delusion. When he talks of his political 'destiny', it's the language of pious humility appropriate to a Catholic nation. When he promises to bring water to the fields, I only hope he doesn't have to eat his words.

Reading of Collor's actions, I think of Ruy Pontes, with 80

per cent of his savings frozen. While prices have stabilised for the moment, business must be thin for Ruy, as wages are cut and unemployment grows.

Brazilians won't be in much of a mood to be marketed anything at present, let alone promises.

Twelve

In May of 1991, Zelia Cardoso de Mello, Collor's finance minister, resigned, taking with her the justice minister – with whom she had been passing love notes under the cabinet table – the president of the central bank, several Secretaries of State and 100-odd civil servants.

They were the Campinas Boys, though their leader was a woman; ultraliberal young disciples of Chicago economic guru Milton Friedman, flush with doctorates from the University of Campinas in São Paulo, and they were going to strangle the inflation culture with tight money: Zelia Cardoso de Mello (no relation to Collor de Mello) at the ministry of finance; Eduardo Texeira at the head of the superministry of mines, energy, telecommunications and transport, controlling 112 enterprises with a total turnover in 1989 of $55 billion – 15 per cent of GDP – a state giant ripe for auction. Other figures reveal the paradox of Brazilian industry. Half a century after the doctrine of planned development – substituting national products for imports – the profit margins of Brazilian firms are among the highest in the world. The wage costs of Brazilian industrialists are less than those of employers in India. With the profits, they join the wealthy old agricultural elite in the exclusive clubs, ones with swimming pools and ones with electronic databoards. Like the *fazendeiros*, they find they can make more money when production slows from betting short on the markets.

As the Campinas Boys set about cutting the tariff barriers that allowed domestic industry to thrive, industrialists fear the worse. Brazil satisfies 94 per cent of its needs, importing only oil and high technology, but the captive market is to be thrown open to the foreign capital hated by nationalist dictators like Brazil's Getulio Vargas and Argentina's Peron – inventor of the doctrine of import substitution – and by socialist ones like Cuba's Castro.

The Campinas Boys, a late-arriving Latin version of Wall Street's Yuppie heros of the Eighties, created the Collor plan, freezing $100 billion of savings – every bank account with a balance of over $100 —so as to dry out excessive liquidity, and with it, inflation. But this has merely choked industry by cutting consumption. Recession has hit, with a fall in GDP of nearly 5 per cent and a brutal industrial slowdown of nearly a quarter. Even with prices for raw materials frozen and wages held in check, inflation continues to rise and the *descamisados*, the people without shirts, are in danger of losing their shorts as well. The Collor plan to stabilise the economy has added 2 million more people to the unemployment list. These are just the ones eligible to register for social security. 'We are supporting the insupportable,' says Edson Nunes, the director of the national statistical institute. 'We are in a process of Africanisation.'

Collor promised inflation of 3 per cent per month. At the end of his first two years in power, inflation averages 18 per cent a month. He promised growth of 10 per cent a year. He delivered 1.2 per cent in his first year, and recession in the second year. He promised to sell off unprofitable state enterprises. There is nobody in Brazil to buy them. He promised to build each year 1,250 CIACS, the cheap pre-fabricated school buildings that can be put up in a day. Only three have been built. He promised to root out and prosecute those who enrich themselves from public office. Halfway through the third year of his five-year term, proceedings will begin to impeach him for corruption.

Addressing a conference in New York on the eve of Eco '92 – the first ecological world summit, José Lutzenberger, nominated

Secretary of State for the environment by President Collor, tells the delegates, 'Don't bother sending your money to save the Amazon, it'll only get stolen.' The following day, he learns on the phone that he has been sacked.

Lutzenberger was referring to the diversion or misuse of funds in government agencies, for which – despite bureaucratic muddle and a lazy judiciary – there is plenty of evidence. He was fired because *Brazil is not a serious country* but you don't go around saying it. Especially not when the president's brother-in-law is suspected of attempting to assassinate the mayor of a town in Alagoas, the president's home state, who furnished details to the press of the misuse of funds from a charity presided over by the president's wife, Rosane Collor de Mello, to buy votes for the president's political cronies.

While his brother-in-law awaits bail in a private cell, with a TV and open visiting hours, Collor's wife is sobbing at a mass held on the forty-ninth anniversary of the Brazilian Assistance League, a venerable charity with a $1 billion budget and 10,000 employees, occupying three floors in the ministry of social action. Rosane – like her husband, from a wealthy estate-owning family in Alagoas – was sobbing because her efforts as head of the charity, showing the League's good works to Barbara Bush and Danielle Mitterrand, who both have *their* charities, and distributing food-hampers wherever the president passes, had displeased her husband. His efforts to distance himself from the scandal could have been dictated by the scenarist of a *telenovela*. He is photographed without his wedding band, and publicly refuses to kiss Rosane on their anniversary.

If President Collor knew of the diversion of the charity funds, no one in Brazil would be surprised. In 1988, a state commission found that, to get federal aid, mayors in Brazil were calling on one of the sixty-three lobbying agencies in Brasilia, who took 20 per cent for their trouble in finding a 'sympathetic' ear. Of the 30 billion Cruzados distributed in 1987, nearly a quarter went to Maranhao, home of only 3 per cent of the Brazilian population, but the state where acting President Sarney was born and built his political career. Another quarter of the aid went to Minas Gerais, where the minister in charge of distributing the aid had made *his* career.

While Rosane was sobbing and the president huffing, his brother

Leopoldo Collor de Mello and some friends of the minister of finance were answering questions over dealings in coffee futures in New York, dealings that occurred immediately before Brazil decided to suspend coffee exports. One of the inside traders, who had never bought commodity futures before, made $168,000 in six days. Who said Brazil is not a serious country? In fact, it was General de Gaulle, on a state visit in the early Sixties, a passing judgement Brazil has never been able to live down.

As the congressional committee continued to investigate the misuse of Rosane's charity funds, Antonio Magri, the labour minister, was found to have diverted some $30,000 into a nice ranch for his summer vacations. A former electrical worker, he became a union leader and was given the labour post by Collor. He soon learned the complex truths of government administration in Brazil. Brazilians took the evidence of Magri's misdeeds with a shrug. They sighed a little heavier, knowing that the syndicalist and former working man had acted from the self-interest that he once fought so bitterly. 'I had to do it,' said Magri, 'the job wasn't going to last forever.'

We may assume that he wasn't acting in a unique flash of genius; that he was, as many Brazilians suspect, merely the *boi do Piranha*, the weak cow sent across the river to be devoured by carnivorous fish while the others cross in safety. If so, we may also admire the cattle-driver's sense of tragedy; the cynical or political point he was making by throwing Magri to the reputation-eating journalistic fish. The onus on those who claim higher moral principles – socialists like Magri or crusaders against corruption like Collor – is to live by them.

The movement to impeach Collor is another carnival campaign, like the one for direct elections. His convocation before a tribunal in 1992 is an excuse for Sambas in the streets. There is embarrassment, mitigated by pride that once-illusory institutions have become real enough to deal with a corrupt president. It's the first time in Latin American history that a constitutional process has triumphed over guns or money. But no one really cares if Collor built himself Babylonian gardens with a campaign slush fund. He is sacrificed not for his hypocrisy but his failure.

The Campinas Boys brought Brazil that much nearer the abyss. In 1985 the Brazilian economy grew by 8.3 per cent, faster than any other in the world. Five years later, it was in recession. Brazilians look back at the Eighties in sorrow and confusion, calling it the lost decade. The economic surge that began in the Sixties and brought them to the door of the First World had ended with Brazil once again relegated to the Third.

The Sixties had been the era of giant projects, a decade that began with the inauguration of the new federal capital of Brasilia, a city built from scratch 1000 miles from the coast where most Brazilians still prefer to live, a city far from the follies of Brazil that is still its biggest folly, that cost $12 billion – more than all the money in the country when building began – and remains astonishing today for its strange, sinuous architectural forms; a brazen, hallucinatory challenge to the empty interior.

From Brasilia in the Sixties came the directive to build the *Transamazônica*, a highway traversing the rain forest, linking Caracas on the Caribbean with Buenos Aires to the south, but still a red dotted line on the map in many places, unpaved dirt roads with virtually no traffic. Built by army engineers in cahoots with the powerful construction lobby, the roads were part of a military strategy to link the Amazon – which was even then coveted by 'international agencies' and might one day have to be defended. The military also gave the go-ahead to Brazil's $2.5 billion nuclear power programme. The reactor was built with German technology 100 miles south of Rio, in a region known to be geologically unstable by the Indians, who call it Itaorna, which means rotten stone in Tupi-Guarani. It now lies virtually idle, serving little purpose in a country with ample hydro-electric capacity, other than as a potential cover for developing nuclear arms.

Brazil is the world's fifth-biggest arms producer, an industry that earns the country $3 billion a year in exports. Engesa, a private firm launched in the Seventies, has sold more than 5000 light tanks named after a poisonous snake. The steel plate is Brazilian, the engines and parts either Brazilian or bought from foreign motor manufacturers. Being cheap, uncomplicated and sturdy, Brazilian arms are popular with countries like Iraq, a big client during her devastating war on revolutionary Iran.

The moral prejudice to the peace-loving Brazilians, who only crushed the Paraguayans to stretch their stiff old imperial elbows, and that more than a hundred years ago, is extreme. To prevent their own people dying, world commerce leaves them no other route than to contribute to the slaughter of others, equally or more wretched. The First World, meanwhile, continues to receive interest on the money it lent to build the armaments factories.

But the choice was also Brazil's, a decision with the horizons of a general. Armaments was a business they knew. The military placed patriotic orders for the products of fledgling companies like Embraer, founded in 1971 by Ozires Silva in the city of São José dos Campos along the Rio–São Paulo highway, where an institute of aviation technology has existed since the Forties. Now the world's sixth-biggest aircraft manufacturer, the company began by catering to the demand in rural Brazil for a light plane. The Tucano, their jet fighter designed on Brazilian computers, is versatile and popular. When Britain's Royal Air Force placed an order for 130 Tucanos, Her Majesty's Government, while hypocritically upholding the lantern of free trade, imposed the same kind of conditions on Brazil that protectionist, economically backward Brazil imposes on governments selling to her. The jets had to be manufactured under licence by Short brothers in Belfast.

To pay for her stalled miracle, Brazil has substituted arms for coffee. To service the loans and build an industrial base, Brazil tries to make finished goods for export instead of agricultural products and raw materials. With a kind of lumbering arrogance – confidence undermined by lack of confidence – she fights against history repeating itself.

In the past it was raw materials that were exported, and finished goods that were imported, an arrangement that usually left the colonies owing money to the people who invested to extract the raw materials. When Potosi was exhausted – the biggest silver mine the world has ever seen, a whole mountain that ate Indian slaves who weren't allowed to leave its tunnels until they were dead – Bolivia found it still owed money to London for all the fine linen and fancy churches.

Brazil has managed to clamber on to the first rung of the industrial ladder, smelting its own ore into iron and steel. But the cosmopolitan style that comes with imported goods still leaves Brazilians feeling that their cars are not as good as American or European ones, though Brazilian Fords and Volkswagens share the same parts – parts which are produced in Brazil.

As for Japanese cars, well, President Collor, on a visit to Japan, says Brazilian cars are like *chariots* alongside these fine new Hondas.

When Brazil started manufacturing cars, everyone laughed. It couldn't be done. Now they build, from Brazilian parts, 25 million a year. But the Gol, the Brazilian version of the Volkswagen Golf, had to have 243 modifications before it was good enough to be exportable.

Newspapers took up Collor's cry of 'poor Brazil,' comparing everything to its foreign rival. Everything was a *chariot*. Two months later, Collor acted. The list of 1200 articles that it had been illegal to import disappeared. Tariff barriers on everything else were to be reduced to a maximum of 20 per cent. The negotiations to do this proceeded sector by sector. When the cementation industry proved intractable, the government threatened to drop the barriers entirely. The industry responded by reducing its ample profit margins by half.

But behind the dash for growth lay more than just the rhetoric of Latin American populism, more than the anti-imperialism of the Communists even, more than just the pride of the struggling giant.

Announcing the first debt moratorium in 1987, President Sarney said, 'It's a miracle the torch illuminating Latin America at the moment is that of liberty and democracy – not convulsion.'

One of the keys to this is growth: the great dream, the only hope. For without growth things would stay as they are. And they are intolerable. Poverty – not something that anyone in Brazil feels is inevitable even if they have become used to it – instead of being the temporary symptom of a society going so fast that some lag behind, would become the permanent condition of a society standing still.

If Brazil's growth rate were to fall too close to its rate of population increase – around 2 per cent – then poverty might turn to revolt.

'We have opted for growth without recession,' said Sarney. 'We won't submit to conditions that force us to relinquish development.'

Development is a race against a population bomb, against the spectre of political upheaval, against a tide of hunger and disease that swells behind, already swallowing too many of the weaker.

Thirteen

The old factory district in the north of São Paulo is a vista of razed terrain, empty lots, a flat spread of nothing waiting for a planning decision, for fresh investment, with only the contours of the freeways for geophysical relief; a past too recent, a future too far off, the flat, barren crossroads outside American towns where boom meets bust.

Lining the road are the Over-nite motel, the Roman-Ville motel, the Broadway restaurant, the kind of places that spring up wherever six-lane highways come together to give access. Plasterboard villas with red-tiled roofs, they are new, but already grey with dust. The signs have dulled and rubbish blown by the wind accumulates at the feet of security walls. Between the walls and the road there is no sidewalk.

Jori worked the windscreens at the roundabout, holding the buckets of water for the other kids, then jumping out as the lights changed to clean them herself as soon as she could reach across the hoods. From the traffic island, she watched the motels being built. It was an encouraging sign. It meant her world was improving.

Being all she knows, she cannot think like me that it looks impermanent, like much of America, that it didn't quite come off, forming an independent nexus, before the money ran out halfway, before someone stole it or saw a better prospect.

Between the district headquarters of Alcoa and Unibanco, there along the road that leads in and out of the city centre, living on a traffic island beneath a flyover, Jori grew up; like millions of others, modern Brazil buzzing past their ears in a nerve-racking haze while they make love in a shack, on a torn mattress, on a cardboard floor.

The thing that shocks me the most is how unsanitary it is. I stifle my revulsion, for this reaction in me upsets me as much, measures the distance between us. The *favelas* of Rio, with their semi-official status, sewage and lighting, and their superb views, had not prepared me for the squalor of those of Brazil's largest metropolis, at the engulfing edge of the tide.

Waste living off waste, refuse off refuse. There are several tons of garbage behind the shacks where Jori was born, the garbage of garbage. I look carefully to see what it consists of, since it doesn't resemble the garbage I'm used to seeing. It's uniform, every piece the same size and texture, without colour; millions of small pieces of nothing. The garbage of garbage.

There are no empty cans; these have all been recycled. There are no bottles either, for the same reason. No bits of broken glass; these have all been collected. There is nothing that might have been thrown out of an ordinary home, for this garbage has been salvaged, sorted, broken down, picked clean by children looking for food or amusement. All that's left is shards of wood, the broken scrap of scrap, pieces of pieces, small scraps of paper or cloth. It is the size of each piece that gives this garbage its homogeneity. Each piece is small because anything big enough to be used has been saved. What has no value for people for whom a broken piece of plywood is the wall of their home?

These homes are being bulldozed, after six years, and the dusty street beside the flyover is full of squashed rats, flattened by the advance of the bulldozers as they fled from their nests in panic. The rats are about a foot long. I try to avoid stepping on them. In Jori's nightmares, the rats nibbled at her ears. Waking up, she found it was true.

One family has salvaged from the bulldozers, from their home made of salvage, the corrugated tin, the broken pieces of plywood, the old fenceposts, the door, the tattered chairs, the electric juicemaker, the occasional table and the lamp. Everything is broken, frayed, bent or rusted and it's all piled high on the back of a white flat-bed truck with the town logo on the side and beneath it, the slogan of the new mayoress: 'São Paulo – A City for All'.

Six years was not so long. Jori will miss the place. She will miss the makeshift school where Old Man Nando showed her letters and numbers. They had found some paint left over from the construction of a motel and painted the words *Escola Infantil* on the side of his shack. She would miss the little shop belonging to G.G. The shacks had padlocks and chains on the doors, to keep out the dogs, and the thieves. People with nothing stealing from people with nothing.

On top of their possessions, cheering and waving as the truck drives away, sits the family. There are eight of them. They lived in two shacks, which meant they got $4000 indemnity from the city, $2000 for each shack. They have paid their debts and opened a bank account with what's left. And they are going to be rehoused in a new bungalow.

Watching them go are some boys. There is a skinny boy, aged about twelve, thin and sweating, clutching at his scrawny elbows and shuddering, a feverish fear in his eyes as he watches the bulldozer flatten his home with a rev of mechanical fury. Now he has nowhere to sleep, nowhere even to lie down, and his jaw shivers with cold and fright. He is suffering from secondary malnutrition, its effects reversible in time. Recurring dysentery has left his knees protruding like tennis balls from thin legs. He must find somewhere to sleep. The other boy is in better health. He is a few years younger. He scratches a distended belly with his jaw open, watching the bulldozer. A smaller boy digs with a spoon at the rice left in the corner of a saucepan. He returns to sit with three other children on an old sofa. The youngest is about two, and sucks her pacifier, staring without the energy or understanding to be afraid, as the bulldozer passes before them, churning dust and debris, to

127

raze another shack.

The trucks take away the broken planks, the old furniture and the plates, the primus stoves and the nailed-up curtains, and the people in the back with them, piled up on top, garbage on garbage, going off to their *casa popular*. Funded by the Banco Nacional de Habitacao, the *casas populars* are far from the city. That's the problem, but it's a real house at least. Living under the freeway interchange had its inconveniences, but it was central.

Jori is going to miss the wastelands they played on here in the Barra Funda, where no one stopped them and no one cared about them. They had that wild, fervid look in their soft brown eyes that made people flinch, as though at dogs. She knew a boy who had been shot, like a dog. An older boy. He was crazy, dangerous. He spat and stole. They found his body a few hundred yards away.

Under the flyover now only a few houses remain. There are thin, mangy chickens picking at the dust, and sick, exhausted dogs snapping weakly at the flies that circle them. Across the railway tracks is the church of *Deus é Amor*, the cathedral of the poor, a converted factory building. Old Man Nando had taught Jori to read the big neon letters of the sign on the front of the church: 'God Is Love.'

———

Fleeing the tide of poverty and hunger, they hang on outside the doors of the trains, or crouch like surfers on the rooftops of the carriages. It's 7 a.m., and the trains arriving at Pirituba station are already full. Pirituba is one of the outlying suburbs of São Paulo. The trains are coming in from the satellite towns that comprise Greater São Paulo – population 20 million – crammed with construction workers, cleaners, maids, clerks and shopgirls.

Across the road beside the railway tracks is Pirituba's municipal yard. Diggers and dust-carts are parked there in neat rows, idle; the workers are on strike today. But they have come to the yard nevertheless to hear the mayoress, Luiza Erudina, a member of the Workers' Party, who is coming to Pirituba this morning to put the city's case.

Pirituba is another featureless suburb that flew up in the Sixties, until growth flew past or stalled, leaving everything half-finished: unfaced two-storey concrete houses along unpaved streets; empty, muddy lots in which the shacks crowd; a bus terminal, a square and a church, the vestige of the old village. To the north, there is some relief in the patchy, interminable suburban landscape: the tallest peak in the precincts of the city, the Pico do Jaraguá.

It's in suburbs like this that the majority of people who voted Luiza into power in January '89 live, people who were glad to hear that she was going to transfer resources out of the wealthy city centre, where the garbage was collected fourteen times a day, to the suburbs, where it was deposited.

Luiza is small and compact as a goat, tough and tenacious like one too. She wears a white blouse, blue skirt and a red scarf. She has the pale skin of an office worker, despite her *Nordeste* origins. She came to São Paulo more than thirty years ago and worked as a cleaner before becoming a social worker and later an activist in the Workers' Party, who won the mayoral race with a vow to 'make the rich pay'.

She climbs on to a wooden platform left over from her campaign and takes the microphone, her voice booming in the open yard. Now, instead of stirring discontent, she must quell it. She talks about priorities, 'what we have achieved, what we can't do anything about, like land reform and *inflacão*'. Her tone is strident, emotional, almost impatient with the municipal workers' demands for higher pay. They earn $120 a month, and grumble about inflation. She promises fair salaries, a future for their children, a hospital bed, and warns of 'criminality, marginality'. But there is no more money . . .

Only 5 per cent of municipal levies stay in the city. The rest goes to the federal government, in part to pay the foreign debt. Brasilia takes 70 per cent of all taxes. The municipalities then get money from the federal and state governments. 'This is the way they control the municipalities,' explains Guimercindo Milliomensen, a Workers' Party state deputy who has come with Luiza. The Workers' Party controls only twenty of the 5000 municipalities in the state of São Paulo, but among these are the largest ones: São Paulo, Port Alegre and the port of Santos. If the city workers are on strike today, it's thanks to Guimercindo and Luiza. 'Ten years ago, no government workers had rights to association.'

At that time, Guimercindo was a teacher. Federal spending on education had shrunk from 12 per cent to 5 per cent of the budget. 'And the conditions!' He shakes his head. 'Without democracy, nobody was in control . . .'

When union rights were granted in the new constitution, he became the head of a teachers' association that sought to monitor spending, but found only waste and wreckage. 'The schools were destroyed when Luiza was elected. Our priorities were buildings and equipment, then paying professional teachers.'

The city now spends 25 per cent of its budget on education, but this still isn't enough. In the city of São Paulo, 100,000 children between seven and fourteen still have no school places. In Greater São Paulo, the situation is far worse.

Across the street, the trains slither past. When they stop, there is a worsening crush to get on. At least on the roof, or hanging on to the door rails, there is a breeze. They are not joy-riders, or fare-dodgers. They have tickets, but no places.

To make the rich pay, Luiza has raised taxes on large properties to 15 per cent. Under previous right-wing administrations, they had shrunk to 1 per cent. The move has made her unpopular with wealthy liberals, who accept the need for improvement, but didn't want to have to pay for it themselves. The state prosecutor has taken the city to court, claiming the new tax is unconstitutional. 'The tribunal has judged that it was OK in other cities,' says Luiza, 'so we will win – but when? We have urgent needs. They can wait till next year.'

With the proceeds, she has proposed to make public transport free. Luiza used to change her car every two years, but now she can't because, as mayoress, she is not earning as much as before, and the rent on her apartment has just gone up.

Luiza works eighteen hours a day to stay ahead of municipal business, managing 100,000 staff and a budget of $3 billion. But Paulistas still wonder who the strongman is at city hall. As a woman and a *Nordestino* – 'my greatest handicaps' – Luiza faces the scepticism of macho Brazil and the contempt of middle-class Paulistas for the poor brown people who clean their apartments – a race apart, slow and laggardly, many of whom had never seen a vacuum cleaner before.

There are many women in the crowd – office managers, secretaries and social workers – who listen intently to Luiza as she tells a homely story about her father.

She was born in the state of Paraiba, in a poor town. Her father was a *Cabeça chata*, a 'flathead', a nickname for *Nordestinos*. Many of the municipal workers and most of the people of Pirituba share his origins.

It's a hot day. 'We should have flat *hats*,' she jokes, fanning herself.

In the eyes of many European-descended Brazilians, the *Nordestinos* are doomed by a curse of hereditary feeblemindedness, a tarnish that apparently only years of scrubbing floors can erase. They are short, either because of Indian blood or malnutrition. When a news magazine published a photo of a midget, claiming he was a member of a new race, named *Grabitos* after the rats who live off garbage in the impoverished cities of the *Nordeste*, nobody doubted the hoax.

A young journalist named Wilson Rossato who is covering Luiza's beat for a popular daily explains to me what *Nordestinos* are.

'They are animals,' he spits.

He is referring to the one million lately arrived *favelados* in São Paulo, who have yet to find a dirty floor to occupy them, other than the one, made of dirt, that they sleep on.

Instead, 'They live from recuperating paper and bottles,' he explains.

What do they think of Luiza, I wonder?

'They don't understand her job, her function. They don't even know *they* exist.'

A private education has confirmed to him that he exists, and travel has broadened his horizons. He wants to leave Brazil and move to Miami, where he recently spent three months. There are 200,000 Brazilians living in Miami, the home of the Latin Yankee. Miami is the most popular international destination from São Paulo

131

airport.

'It's paradise,' he says, beaming.

He assures me that the newsmagazine story about the *Grabitos* was true.

The mayoress has an explanation for the half-made world that is Brazil – and the whole of America.

'We are preoccupied with our image of ourselves as settlers, developers, builders. We are always ready to launch a new project without caring for what has already been built.'

She has tried to preserve what had already been built in São Paulo. There wasn't any choice. The previous administration under Janio Quadros left $6 million of debts to municipal suppliers alone. The city had run out of credit locally and firms refused even to bid for city contracts. 'We had to pay for everything cash-on-delivery. So we had to be thrifty.' A system of 'popular control' – union-based watch on corrupt practices – helped reduce costs by a third. Worker participation in administrative decisions brought more efficiency, and Luiza is proud of the fact that she has less personal power now than when her mandate began. 'We're in a position to build now.' Her monuments will be socially useful, she promises. 'Health centres and schools.'

To persuade her critics, she goes from the municipal yard to a lunch with local businessmen at a country club in the nearby hills. More than a hundred local businessmen are there, the people who will be paying Luiza's new property tax. They are curious about Luiza, but hungry. They begin eating their steaks as she talks about compromise. Four years of city government has taught her about the need for this. She is counting on the support of business. 'We have to be free and open with each other. We have to work together to build; lots of children, lots of *empresários*!' she laughs.

'My party had many prejudices against you businessmen,' she continues. 'We are radicals, left-wingers. But now we're learning from businessmen, about how to get things done.' The businessmen pause, chewing their steaks, to wash down this flattery with some beer.

'I had a lot to learn. First of all, I'm a woman. Second, I'm a socialist. Third, I'm a Brazilian. All I knew was that many of you were against women, against workers, the poor, the Blacks. Improving their lot is good for society – and good for business. The municipal improvements that we've brought about have helped this.'

A downpour outside sucks the tension out of the air. The businessmen and Luiza are comfortable with each other now. The men have something in their bellies. Luiza's food waits in front of her. But she doesn't stop.

'São Paulo is a major city, with ten million people. But three hundred thousand children don't have places in the public schools. They are the future of our society. Without kids, without education, we don't have a future.'

She stands on her toes, throwing herself forward to make her points in a gruff, practised voice.

'The international minimum for hospital beds is four per thousand people. São Paulo has only 1.8 per thousand . . . You can't measure the progress of a society just by counting the number of supermarkets,' she cries, to a room full of supermarket owners. 'Capital isn't just for businessmen and investors, it's for constructing the schools and hospitals that we need for the whole of society!'

She turns to the debt problem . . . and thunder breaks. She calls the debt problem 'a profound crisis of conscience'.

Then Luiza sits down to eat. She eats heartily, and leaves nothing on her plate.

Fourteen

———

Her brown hair falls on soft brown shoulders. I have to sit down when I see Marly again, there beside her on the bench seat in a Japanese restaurant, after she wiggles her hips to make space for me.

She offers me sake from a square cup. Several years have passed since we first met. She has finished school, and works with a construction firm. 'You should see her in a hard-hat!' says one of her friends.

I'm asked, with genuine curiosity, why I have come, because not many people come to Brazil outside of the carnival season, and few come to São Paulo.

I reply that I'm writing a book.

'What kind of book?'

'A book about Brazil . . . '

The people at the dinner table look perplexed. What can you say about Brazil? Where do you start? That I am interested in it merely deepens the mystery.

'About cities and jungles,' I offer. 'Mostly about cities.'

The sake hit. 'About the tension between the jungle and the city, primal dreams and contemporary reality. We have a nostalgia for a mythical, early space that we see on the packaging of

cosmetics and food. We fear that we've lost touch with something in ourselves and we're destroying it in our environment.
But all across the world, people who still live in those places, in
Africa, India, Asia, they want to leave to come to cities like this
one . . . São Paulo is the future of the Third World. I wanted to see
what it is that's made ten million people come here over the last
two decades.'

We talk about São Paulo. 'You'll like it,' says someone. 'It's
big.' And the Paulistas at the table agree.

Here, too, I knew my encounters would be ruled by libidinous
magic; I would find a world like the one I knew but which, barely
able to believe in itself, was a fable to me. It is with a sweet,
helpless sense of alarm that I sit down.

Marly drinks her sake and tells me it always goes straight to
her head. Then she drinks some more, and the sake spills from the
corners of the square cup, splashing over her legs. She wipes it off
with innocent grace, childlike unconcern. I try to picture her in a
hard-hat.

'We're going to the beach this weekend,' she says. 'It's nice,'
she promises.

I am careering towards industrial apocalypse: switching lanes with
weekending Paulistas returning home on a Sunday night. I've been
to the beach with Marly and her friends, who complained about
the Jet-Skiers polluting the shores with noise and fumes, but whose
families all seem to have one of these new distractions in the garages
of their beach homes.

The freeway from the coast cuts into the Valley of Death without
warning. No signs tell you to don oxygen masks as you pass the
outskirts of Cubatão, but your sinuses remind you that you are
leaving behind the sea breezes for the humid fumes of the city.
And in the distance, there are the lights of the first refinery . . .

There is no man-made structure more beautiful than a refinery,
no bridge poised in sublime equilibrium, no soaring skyscraper, no
jumbo jet. I've always felt a thrill at the sight of these places, at
the smoke from smelting ore and fumes of boiling petrochemicals.
In the region known as the Valley of Death, between São Paulo and

the coast, smoke, flame and sparks spew from the devil's foundries, surrounded by excavations that seem to go deep into the guts of the earth; under tall chimneys belching so much smoke, copious and dense, of such deep grey. The clanking engines of a century of miraculous growth, you feel that if they stopped, if the fires went out, then everything else would sputter and die, and you're right.

These installations rapidly lose their gleam; from shiny technological symphonies of tubes and silos with their neat perimeter fencing, bathed in the orange glow of sodium lamps, they rust and turn black with their own soot. In the tropics, where they are regularly washed by the rain, the gleam turns to a kind of sweaty patina, as though they are beset by fever.

The lights grow brighter as we approach, the road curving gently upwards to provide a better view. They fan out below and multiply: some turn out to be small, intense flames, others are whole suburbs or plants. People once travelled to find the world as it was, or a world utterly different from their own. Increasingly one finds the same world, with superficial differences, surprising in its familiarity but staggering in its multiplication. Cubatão, the biggest industrial park in Brazil, as big as those on the Rhine or the shores of Lake Michigan, has a special character. It offers the sublime juxtaposition of heaven in the still-virgin forest, nursing in her green valley bosom hellish metallic tumours, the plants spitting fire and funnelling black smoke into the heavy sky, smoke that causes babies in the nearby shacks to be born without brains.

It was almost night by the time we reached the dark, churning heart of the Valley of Death, half an hour after we first saw it. There was no sign to indicate that it was known as such, just the last gleaming of twilight that seemed to mark the end of an idyllic day and the beginning of a dark industrial night, bringing with it pollution, mutation, overheating, the cancer of uncontrolled growth, the migraine of television, shanties multiplying like abcesses, infrastructural infarctus, the burning jungle, the shoals of dead fish floating in mutant algae, sensations of blotched and prickly skin, melanomas, lymphomas and leukaemias.

People have tried to halt the industrial juggernaut ever since it was set in ineluctable motion. Those, like myself, who have never been near a furnace that can melt rocks into iron, boil sand into glass, or transform oil into plastic, indulge our nostalgia with a periodic revival of the romantic, the spiritual, the handmade, the natural, the biological and, now, the ecological. We would not want to return to a level of pre-industrial comfort of course, to candle and horsepower, except as a kind of theme holiday, and so we ride the juggernaut, while others run alongside, leaping desperately to get on, leaving a trail of mangled limbs and bloody, dusty rags.

In the Valley of Death, these forces are thrown into relief. Lightning streaks down, a silver bolt of nature's contempt, containing, in a second or two, more energy than all the factories in the valley can consume in a week. Steel funnels streak up the green mountainsides to unleash billowing black toxins into the clouds. In the *favela* alongside the highway, a child flies a kite in the glowering sky. Rain falls in the valley like a curse.

As the freeway rises upwards to cross the coastal ridge we pass plant after plant nestling in the verdant hillsides. Ultrafertil is the name of one, a producer of stockfeed and fertiliser. The plant looks old, though it's not, a deadly rusting grey, and the paint on the sign has faded. The name is a grinning mockery of the petrochemical poison it produces. The contrast between the tree-covered slopes and the defiling industry of the valley floor dramatises the battle between conservation and development.

The dense sub-tropical vegetation of the valley is already thinning, as die-back affects the trees, weakening roots and causing landslides of red dirt. These avalanches have undermined the viaducts carrying the highway and threaten to bury the *favelas* below. To seed the hillsides, a group of Brazilian ecologists came in hanggliders, a dangerous stunt in the turbulent winds. The federal authorities had already spent $100 million on filters for the chimneys – after the babies started being born without brains. In the Seventies, pollution was identified as the cause of cases of encephalitis in children born in Cubatão, the dormitory town for the 50,000 who toil in the Valley of Death.

The freeway rises higher – till we are almost under the low clouds, heavy and pregnant with effluent, spilling a soiling, stinging rain. Looking back, we can see the port of Cubatão, with its old

137

colonial-era church, perched on some high ground in the Valley of Death, a fading, insufficient spiritual balm for the iron soul of the Valley. Old blue and white buses queue at the factory gates, pulling out in convoys to take the workers home from the Sunday afternoon shift.

On the train to the suburbs, crowded with people going places on a Sunday, I kiss her again, something I had wanted to do – uncontrollably and delicately – for six days and nights, ever since we got back from the beach.

'Brazilian men are very macho,' Marly had told me over the phone, on the second day. 'They want to be in control.' She was having problems with her boyfriend. 'I can't see you.'

On the third day, she told me about a friend whose ex-husband doesn't want to pay maintenance for their seven-year-old daughter. 'He says this to her: you're a liberated woman. You have a job. You can pay. That's Brazilian men!'

'That's men,' I offered.

'No,' she said, 'they're insecure.'

She explains that he doesn't pay for his daughter's upkeep – though as the owner of a business, he could – but he dotes on the girl, wants to know where she is all the time, and takes her away every weekend.

'That's Brazilian men. They make great fathers but not good husbands.'

On the fourth day, she told me about her best friend. 'She's married, but she has a crush on this guy, who's very nice, but he doesn't want her. It's driving her crazy. Why shouldn't two people be together if they want to?'

On the fifth day, she told me about Brazil. 'Brazil is hard on relationships. Nothing works here . . . I'll call you.'

On the sixth day, she called and asked me what I wanted to do. I told her, a little reluctantly, that I wanted to see some of São Paulo, the old parts of the city. I'd expected that it wasn't what she had in mind, but she said she'd take me.

We could see it best from the train, she said. We have to stop several times to ask for directions to the station in São Paulo's inner city, located to the north, across the Tietê River. 'The Portuguese language is not very concrete,' complains Marly. 'They don't know left from right.' But we find the railway station and park the car between a group of drunks and a tired, ugly prostitute, who is standing in a street empty of cars apart from a large new American model parked near her.

The street is lined with old warehouses with broken windows. From inside come the screams of children and the wailing of babies. Tin pipes protrude from holes in the walls carrying the stodgy odours of simmering rice and beans. The poor, squatting this abandoned factory, are enjoying their Sunday *fejoada*.

It's hot in the railway carriage, full of people with sweaty, weary faces. The crowding is oppressive; even on Sunday, the train is crowded. The press of bodies, during the week in jeans and shirts but today in shorts and T-shirts, brings us closer. In the crush, as the train rocks, with the windows open for ventilation, my nervousness, which I have felt in her presence, has gone, and we are dancing in the breeze from the windows. She throws her head back to catch the air, which is not cool but in motion at least. The train begins to slow down . . .

She has brought me to see the station, built by the British – who also built the railway – at the turn of the century. It reminds me of any number of European stations, with a glass roof supported by wrought-iron vaults on red-brick pillars. For Marly, its grandeur and age lend it a rare dignity. She leads me through the marble booking hall. The marble is Italian, and, apart from posters warning about cholera, we might be in an Italian railway station. The station is in Mooca, pronounced 'mocha' – the area where Italian immigrants settled in the early part of the century, perhaps pleased to find an Indian word that resembled an Italian word.

The Italians opened stores and built factories. Matarazzu was the head of the community, a *fascisti* who made a fortune from machine shops, buying land to build more factories that, within less than a decade, was worth more than the factories had earned. The Italians kindled the Brazilian industrial revolution, here in the north of São Paulo, displacing the old Portuguese coffee aristocracy of the *fazendeiros.* Marly's maternal grandparents came from Italy, from a village in the Po Valley. Mechanisation on Italian farms had put her grandfather out of work. There were no more jobs in the factories of Turin, so they sailed for São Paulo, to do the work the slaves used to do. It was New York or São Paulo. They dreamed of owning a farm, but her grandfather went to work in a factory in Mooca and ended up owning that instead.

Marly says she always liked the station, because of its pretensions, which remind her of Europe.

'It's seven p.m.,' she says, turning the dial on the car radio and hearing only news programmes, 'the hour when Brazil talks.'

All the stations broadcast the hour of stolid news from the government agency in Brasilia, a hangover from the military years.

The cars crawl along, their drivers resigned and courteous to each other. Part of the Brazilian enigma is their relative lack of Latin characteristics, like impatience in traffic. In a Mediterranean country, they would be jostling furiously, if going nowhere. If you can read the nature of a society in its road habits, Brazil is an ordered country that, when not held up, goes very fast. And when it is held up, it waits.

The fastest Brazilian on four wheels – which is saying something – is Ayrton Senna da Silva, the Formula One driver from São Paulo. Before a race, he used to walk the first bend, just staring at the track. His intensity was mistaken for arrogance, until he started winning in '85. A shy youth, he practised on a kart in São Paulo's Parque Anhembi every weekend for five years. His father, who had built him his first kart when Ayrton was four, bought him a new kart, a couple of spare engines and a van with a workshop inside, to bring him out of his shell.

Marly sighs at the traffic, and makes a U-turn in her Volkswagen Gol next to a sign that says 'No U-turns'.

'Illegal,' I remark.

'*Completamente!*' she says, rolling the word around her tongue, savouring the fact as she glances in the mirror to check for traffic police.

Fifteen

———

In São Paulo's Museum of Modern Art is a small study by Francisco Rebolo Gonsales, entitled 'The Suburbs of São Paulo'. It depicts a scene of pastoral quiet, an unassuming impression of a small rural corner of the Brazilian Eden, a simple stucco house with a wooden fence, an outhouse for the pigs and chickens, near a bend in the road down to the river. Now there is a twenty-storey block on that corner, nowhere to park on the road and the river is buried somewhere, full of sewage.

Gonsales had put up his easel there in 1938.

He worked in watercolour, flooding the sky with a soiled grey, the characteristic hue of the sky over São Paulo; intensely luminous at times, dull and dark when it's about to burst with rain. Gonsales' sky is grey not out of verisimilitude, however, but for reasons of cultural politics.

Brazilian landscape artists of the nineteenth century would have derided his choice of subject, and regarded his style as amateurish. So cowed were they by the cultural omnipotence of Europe that they copied their French contemporaries to the last brushstroke. So scornful were they of the attributes of their country that they engaged in a bizarre quest to find their subjects. They looked for a European classical landscape in the *Mata Virgem*. In the groves

141

of ipê and *jacarandá*, they searched for eucalyptus and olive trees. They weren't alone in this forlorn pursuit. Others built the palace of Versailles, the châteaux of the Loire and the cathedral of Chartres in precious hardwood. They copied the manners of Europe as others copied the dogmas, writing glowing constitutions that ignored the reality before them.

The artistic results, collected in the National Museum of Rio, are betrayed not by any failure of technique but by the blandness and unreality of the transformed landscapes, based on ones that many of the artists had never seen, and which they painted only by reference to other paintings.

Gonsales was free to paint what he saw. He owed this freedom to artistic emancipationists like Tarsila do Amaral. Influenced by the Surrealists, she drew on the Brazilian unconscious, on its folk art. In a marvellous painting, 'The Iron Road of Brazil', she depicts factories, railway signals, churches and small houses. They are arranged in a dream-like cadence, floating across the large canvas. The colours – which would be bright in a merely naïve rendition – are muted, as though by a tropical haze.

Tarsila belonged to a group formed in the wake of Modern Art Week, which took place in São Paulo in 1922, and included Emiliano di Cavalcanti, the Cariocan artist who painted cubist portraits of mulatto families: black or *caboclo* fathers, blonde mothers and their children. His heresy was stylistic but also political. He was contradicting the old view of Brazil as a white nation, a Portuguese Dixie or Cape, in which blacks, since they had no legal status except as property, had no civic existence; neither did their lives have any reality, at least not one worth recording, despite their vastly greater numbers. The heresy of di Cavalcanti, apart from the pleasure he takes in a naive style, was a prophetic one on the symbolic level of images, the view that Brazil was a black nation that was becoming white.

In the previous century, not even the iconoclastic Machado de Assis had strayed far in his novels from the habitual concerns of the French drawing-room, even if his salon looked out onto the streets of Rio. What was unnatural, and now remarkable, about his naturalistic novels wasn't the social setting, but his stylistic devices – disorienting the reader with his own disorientation. 'The whole is suggested by the fragments, the structure by ellipsis, the emotion by irony,' wrote one critic. Brazil's greatest novelist was the curly-haired son of a mulatto father and a Portuguese mother, who had his portrait painted in a velvet jacket and silk shirt. He becomes bored with his characters, perhaps realising that they, like Brazil, are only half-made, and treats them with quintessential Brazilian irony. They are like orchids that hide a jaguar's smile. He is impatient with their intrigues and jealousies too, perhaps realising that in faithless Brazil, infidelity is too limp a peg on which to hang a moral drama. And as our world too comes unmade, losing its moral and rational bearings, so Joaquim Machado de Assis becomes the subject of literary investigation in American universities, where he is hailed as the avatar of Magical Realism by Alfred MacAdam, who says Machado disbelieved in 'the reality of Brazilian, and perhaps all, history'.

The Modern Art Week in São Paulo was, like everything of cultural value, imported from Paris, though paradoxically, it was a cry of unfettering from Europe. Native writers, poets and painters attended to see what the fuss was about cubism, lettrism, futurism and other isms. In the exhibitions and cafés they found the European traditions they had been fettered to smashed by Europeans, who distorted perspective in search of truth, stole from the instinctual force of African and Asian art, and recorded the modern world of radio towers and radiant factories, which was just then being hammered and riveted into place around them in São Paulo. *I love this town*, wrote the French poet Blaise Cendrars, one of the visiting cultural ambassadors . . .

Saint Paul is my kind of town
Here no tradition
No prejudgement
Neither ancient nor modern
All that counts is this furious appetite this absolute confi-
    dence this optimism this audacity this work this labour this
    speculation that gets ten houses built in an hour of all styles

ridiculous grotesque handsome big small north-facing south-facing egyptian yankee cubist

With no other motive than to follow statistics predict the future the comfort the usefulness the profit and attract a huge immigration

All the countries

All the peoples

I like that . . .

The two or three old Portuguese houses that remain have blue tiles

Cendrars noticed the eclectic energy – and the Portuguese *telhas*. He came from Paris for Modern Art Week but fell in love with Tarsila – whom he brought back to Paris for a show in 1926 – and stayed to investigate the enigma, fascinated by the diabolical, *Macunaíman* side of Brazil.

The shock of the new was total, and it gave Brazilian artists a new self-possession. They even rejoiced in their former shackles, declaring themselves Anthropophagists, eaters of culture, devourers of all, open to any influence. They digested with a loud burp all that Europe had fed them and promised to eat whatever else came along, beginning with Brazil.

In literature, this movement produced *Macunaíma*, the epic poem by Mario de Andrade, published in 1928, that borrows the story of the Tupi Indian hero, Macunaíma. But de Andrade's hero is black. He doesn't speak till the age of six, but busies himself fondling female relatives, beheading ants and bothering his brothers, with whom he bathes in a magical lake. Macunaíma emerges blonde with blue eyes, while one brother, bathing afterwards, becomes bronze, and the third, bathing last in the dirty water, remains black.

In São Paulo, the brothers confront a giant 'eater of men', so they go to Rio to get help from Exú, the avenging demon of the slums. Drawing on Indian, African and Portuguese myths in a narrative full of low dialects, de Andrade constructs a fantastic farce whose wit and resonance weren't lost on the Brazilian public. 'Do you know,' writes Macunaíma to his wife about the 'sophisticated' Paulistas, 'the richness of their intellectual expression is so great that they speak one language and write another?' One critic proclaimed that the hero is no lesser a figure than 'young Brazil, the astute but unlettered heir to all the cultures, all the instincts, all the customs and music of the most ancient races'.

The Museum of Modern Art, where Gonsales' painting hangs, occupies a small, low building in São Paulo's Ibirapuera Park, amid the tall *pinheiros* – pines – and the smooth ebony trunks of the tropical oaks. Next to it is the larger Museum of the University of São Paulo, a vast rectangular slab of glass and concrete.

In it, a collection of contemporary Brazilian art occupies a corner of one floor. The pieces – big colourful canvases filled with broad gestures and figuration derived, inevitably, from Indian and African art – readily embrace the profusion of Brazil, but the size of the museum building, which is otherwise empty, leaves them floundering. The pieces make a brave stand against this emptiness. The artists battle with brash brushstrokes to make sense of their heritage, in the face of a disinterested world. These artists labour in a double isolation, that of Brazil; and the dilemma of contemporary art: no shared programme, no shared ideals, no shared language, no way to touch more than a few specialists. It's here that the São Paulo *Bienal* is held, when the museum fills up with foreign works and the specialists of São Paulo come together to measure the distances between them.

But the museum building is what impresses me; so big that the generations of artists who have passed have barely filled it, a Corbusien space on the scale of the continent, virgin and empty, waiting to be conquered and filled. Not far away, at the entrance to the park, is one of the nerve centres of this assault, the Legislative Assembly, built like the University Museum by Oscar Niemeyer in the Fifties. It's another oblong block that floats, according to the wishes of Le Corbusier – the Godfather of Brazilian monumental architecture – above the ground. Le Corbusier wanted to preserve the flow of nature around his buildings, a balancing act of delicate proportions ignored by the post-war town planners of Europe who used his model on an industrial scale. Niemeyer built even bigger in Brazil, challenged by nature's dynamic, one of astounding volume and grace. He built waveform apartment blocks to lap the toes of Rio's mountains – with, instead of nature, a highway flowing under them; and the Assembly building, a vast, squat forum; a hovering block of concrete and glass, cathedral-like in its minutiae – thousands of small inset windows – and in its repetition – rectangles within rectangles within rectangles. This mystical aspect surprises me, and must have filled with awe the democratic government of the time, as they gave him afterwards the whole city of Brasilia to build.

Before we abandon or flee them for good, I would like to hear an elegy for cities, something with the excitement that Cendrars felt, unclouded by the dismay we feel at what, little more than half a century later, cities like São Paulo have become. Brasilia is the world's most improbable city. The ugliest city in the world that I have seen is Medan in Sumatra, the safest, Tokyo, the most beautiful, Rio, the most efficient, Singapore, the most pleasant, Perth in Western Australia. I get nervous in towns, which seem like villages to me. I find the countryside – repetitive fields and vaulted forests – claustrophobic. There is nothing more exciting to me than arriving in a new city, greeted like an old friend by the same chain of international hypermarkets, the same auto distributors, the golden arches pioneering the greenfield sites, on freeways that stream and entangle. São Paulo is no disappointment in this respect. Eventually – and the longer it takes, the more comfortable I feel – one reaches a crowded old centre, the nostalgic heart paved over and populated with shoppers. Here there are cafés where the same cultural debates rage, linked by satellite with cafés in other cities. I feel that those city dwellers who yearn for the countryside, who rush away at weekends, are blasé. The whole world is moving to the cities, imagining themselves on a high-rise balcony – the best place to view the city – and cities the world over are coming to resemble each other, with the same signs, the same activities. The anthropology of cities even unearths the same histories.

This is a source of dismay to some, though most people, when they travel, look for exactly this familiarity, an instinct that has allowed international hotel and restaurant chains to thrive. The differences now lie in mere details, vestiges of habits and beliefs, customs and rites, decorative traditions and food cultures, languages and myths.

People who live in São Paulo had said you should see it. When I asked why, they thought for a second and – as though they didn't want to spoil the surprise – said, it's different. I think they were hoping I could make sense of it for them. Their confusion is understandable. It looks the same from every angle. From everywhere, there is the same view of rolling hills and skyscrapers. It happened so fast, they wonder how. From the first factory to the megalopolis – the third biggest in the world after Tokyo and Mexico City – in less than a century. Nobody planned it. Nobody would have dared to conceive of such a terrible, exhilarating future.

Le Corbusier dreamed of skyscrapers knitted by highways and walkways, and if he had woken in latter-day São Paulo, he wouldn't have been disappointed – until he tried to walk in the heat and congestion, or drive in the traffic jams, or find his way out, only to find that he was still dreaming, that his dream had no end. He sketched a project for central São Paulo in the Thirties, of the Piratininga River Valley criss-crossed by highways. In his sketch, there are just four skyscrapers.

Standing where he made the sketch – just down the hill from the São Bento monastery, where the settlement of São Paulo de Piratininga was founded 400 years ago – looking across the central bridge, I see *hundreds* of skyscrapers now, and behind them, in the suburbs and satellite towns, *hundreds* more crowd the horizon in every direction. His Radiant City has become a dazzling enigma. The river he drew has become an eight-lane freeway.

The bridge was built by a Scottish firm at the turn of the century to carry a new tramway from the centre to the elegant villas that lined Paulista Avenue. Behind the villas were empty fields. Now the avenue – Brazil's Park Avenue, the most expensive real-estate in Latin America – is lined with skyscrapers housing bank and corporate headquarters.

As Modern Art Week was laying the plans of cultural independence in São Paulo, a bustling new commerce was piling concrete in the sky in tribute to itself. The Sampaio Moreira building was the first *arranha-céu* in São Paulo, next to the old bridge. Finished in 1924, it was twelve storeys high. Work was already under way on the nearby Martinelli building, twenty-two storeys high. By 1930, there were ten more buildings of more than twelve storeys. The modern era was well under way. The old terraced cottages that lined the slopes, incongruous and stuffy like those of Sydney, built by a British company to a design appropriate to Britain, with sash windows made of red Paraná, had been torn down. The old five-storey *blocos* were already shabby from the fumes. Now these tenements have sunk to a level of dangerous squalor, and the real housing scandal of São Paulo is not the *favelas* but the *blocos*, where three million people live in overcrowded rooms.

The new skyscraper blocks were gleaming white in the Thirties. By 1950, there were hundreds of them, ten to twenty storeys high. The accelerated cycles of cities like São Paulo suggests that these too will soon be grimy and decayed, becoming twenty-storey tenements. Already, there are cracked walls and burst pipes in buildings only ten years old, the hurry to build the future bringing entropy forward.

In just two decades, hundreds. Up went the billboards and electric signs. Up went the Neo-Fascist mansions on the Avenida Brasil, with their Italian marble floors and tall windows, attempting to impose order on a vegetation that rapidly sent its aerial roots shooting around them, entwining them like snakes. And in came the popular dictator Vargas to impose order on Brazilians. But once the agitators in the factories and the anarchist columns marauding about the countryside had been imprisoned or shot, in came – paradoxically – voting rights for women and a legal minimum wage.

Often called the Chicago of the South, São Paulo had a late start. Chicago's boom came with the railroads that brought iron ore and men. By 1900, the population of Chicago had swelled to half a million. The world's first steel-frame skyscraper, the Home Insurance building, had gone up in Chicago in 1885, followed by twenty-one more. At this time, São Paulo was still enjoying its afternoon coffee, a quiet and prosperous town at the centre of a region of palm-lined *fazendas* and old mission settlements; a landscape of gently rolling hills laced by waterways that were ideal, in the words of Francisco Varnhagen, for transporting 'large, heavy objects such as cannons and church bells', instruments with which to make the music of Latin America.

The rivers linked the *fazendas* and led out to the port at Santos, the nation's biggest port and once the largest coffee shipping port in the world. On the rivers could still be seen Indian *pirogas*, light navigable canoes woven from bark. There is a *piroga* in Ibirapuera Park now made of granite, a detail of the monument to the *bandeirantes*, the Brazilian pioneers, who a hundred years before Davy Crockett led the wagon trains, opened up the interior of São Paulo state, stealing cattle and land from the Spanish. Looking north as always for a reflection of itself, the *bandeirantes* have been raised as Brazilian frontier heroes. These brave *caboclo* scouts hired by the captains and the landowners hunted, caught and sold their half-brothers to make the land safe for investment, decimating the missions of the Jesuits where the books were written in Guarani and property didn't exist.

The new constitution guarantees Indian land rights, but makes no provision for a memorial to the *misiones*, the greatest tragedy of all the Indian nations – for in this story one can find all the greed and bloodlust, all the contemptuous, unfeeling horror of the destruction – by sword, musket and, with God's permission, the teeth of dogs – of the Aztecs, the Incas and the Sioux, but also glimpse the compassion that might have saved them. Worse, in the communes and farms so coveted by the kings of Portugal and Spain is an image of a world that might have been, an experimental marriage of Old and New Worlds – primitive and modern technologies, beliefs and forms – that was never again attempted after the expulsion of the sons of Loyola, and, on such a scale, can never be again.

In contrast to the hedonism of Rio – a decadent beach resort in the view of the Paulistas – the work ethic rules under the cooler climes of São Paulo. 'That's why God made São Paulo so ugly,' joke the Paulistas, 'because it was the only way to get the Brazilians to work.'

He removed them from the proximity of a beach in São Paulo, so the women would not walk through the streets in their bathing suits. He kept them away from any high mountains that might remind them how small were their endeavours; and He gave them a subway, clean and bright, to ease their three-hour journeys to work. He gave them a river, the Tietê, to carry away their waste, until it was brimming with it. He gave them rolling countryside in which to put up as many skyscrapers as they pleased and – a safe distance away – a wild coast, Brazilian *lebensraum*, to line with condominiums for the weekend in reward for their efforts.

The city was built by Italians for the most part, who were followed by Portuguese, Spanish and German immigrants. São Paulo today has a level of German investment higher than that of most cities in Germany. Volkswagen is based here and the whole country was, until the last decade, full of scuttling, noisy Beetles in every possible colour. The Germans settled here and in cities like Joinville or Blumenau to the south, in the state of Santa Catarina, which counts 300,000 German descendants. German dialects can still be heard in Pomerode, a delightful Bavarian town with the highest suicide rate in Brazil. During the Second World War, Hitler planned simultaneous fascist uprisings in São Paulo and Buenos Aires, looking to swallow Uruguay and Paraguay in the new German America. The Rio de Plata, rich farmland, was to be the base for the Nazi drive northwards, marching across the *sertão* and through the Amazon, which the Führer also had plans for, into Central and North America.

Another city with a Germanic backbone is Curitiba, the capital of the state of Paraná. Set 250 miles southwest of São Paulo on the inland plains above the Serra do Mar, Curitiba is a Brazilian contradiction, a South American city that works. Its 1.5 million residents enjoy fast, efficient public transport, selective waste collection, and four times the ratio of green space recommended by the World Health Organisation.

The architect Jaime Lerner led a team of young urbanists who developed a plan for the city in 1965. He became mayor six years later, and since then, his opponents can only gripe that 'even the sunsets are prettier since he's been in power'. The city recycles everything: the old wooden electricity poles became bus shelters, footbridges and municipal offices, bottles became lamps in the florid parks, old buses became mobile kindergardens and schools for the *favelados*, who have grown with the recession to number 8 per cent of the population. But in Curitiba, they have access to twenty-four-hour medical centres, while the rest of the population has a twenty-four-hour shopping street. Such innovations cost them only an average local tax and the public debt is no greater than in other Brazilian cities. 'Our initiatives, if they have any originality, are simple and cheap. They have more to do with compromise than with miracles,' says Lerner, who receives delegations from New York to see how it's done, and is thinking of bidding for the mayor's office in Rio to see if he can do it again.

As well as Germans, large numbers of Jews, Syrians and Lebanese came to São Paulo in the early decades of the new century, and, a little later, 100,000 Japanese immigrants. They brought the financial, human and technological capital to set in motion an industrial revolution, a brutal, rapacious machine that swallowed people and spewed out goods. In 1986, there were 700,000 industrial accidents in São Paulo, three times the rate in the First World, affecting a quarter of all workers.

Bustling, violent and bursting with commercial and cultural ambitions, São Paulo is hampered by a sense of isolation and inadequacy. In the art galleries and rock clubs of São Paulo, an optimistic society but one crucially lacking in self-confidence searches for expression.

They suffer, especially the cosmopolitan Paulistas, from what Australians call the cultural cringe. In this, at least, they aren't alone. Even New Yorkers, for all their pride in living in what they fondly imagine to be the city at the edge of modern civilisation – poised on a precipice over the AIDS-crack inferno – are still not immune to the charms of a British accent, which continues to be a mark of unattainable refinement in the old colony. North Americans, of course, are not obliged to take Britain seriously and do it out of fondness for their crusty forebears.

A hundred years before they threw their tea party in Boston, the Brazilians were treating their Portuguese rulers to ridicule. The seventeenth-century poet Gregorio de Matos described a Portuguese second son:

> Barefoot, naked, save for his rags
> Ah, there upon the wharf he springs
> And a few lice and filthy bags
> Are all the capital he brings

When, in 1649, the Protestant Dutch were driven out of Guararapes by Catholic Brazil, the *mazombos* – Brazilian-born – ceased to cringe at the *reinóis* arriving from Lisbon. The flight to Rio of the Portuguese crown and 20,000 members of the court – saved from the onslaught of Napoleon by the British fleet – put paid to any remaining colonial abasement. But the deference, the sense of distance, isolation and unimportance remain. Rather than Europe, however, the Brazilians measure woefully their distance in this century from North America.

Unsurprisingly, considering the resemblances, the United States views its large southern cousin as a kind of underdeveloped alter-ego, though, in Freudian terms, Brazil is the id, the child and the woman.

New York took the cultural spoils of the Second World War, when the best of Barcelona, Montparnasse and the Bauhaus fled there. Brazil had laid its claim to a modern, independent artistic identity in the flurry of activity following Modern Art Week in 1922, but there was no coterie of exiled Cubists to give it lift, and not much in the way of patronage. If the Italian-born di Cavalcanti had gone to New York instead, more people would surely have heard of him.

Sixteen

São Paulo is big, too big. The city makes Nilson tired. He has grown used to its size, its scale and repetition – apartment blocks all the same marching up and down the hills, balconies saluting balconies. He knows his way around, and doesn't get lost the way he used to at first, finding himself staring up at the wrong skyscraper, which looked just like the one he was supposed to go to, for his job as a cleaner. And he has grown used to the bustle of the people, the way they are too busy to notice him. He feared at first that he had become invisible, that he had ceased to exist, died and come to São Paulo. Then he thought it was because he was shorter than them. Then he realised it was because he was less important.

They have bigger things on their minds, bigger problems to deal with. That's why they are always so busy. They dress well and talk about important matters; they have cars and apartments, they come home with big shopping bags, they are always coming back from the sports club or going out to dinner. He often wondered how they managed. They drink and smoke, and talk loudly. Since he has been in the city, Nilson has tried to copy them.

'Inflation.' He shakes his head. 'Now you have me . . . ' says Nilson, lighting a Parliament cigarette.

'Everything rises.' He exhales . . . 'Prices are always higher.'

When Nilson was a boy, he didn't know about inflation. It's only since he's been spending money that he's learnt about inflation.

As for President Collor, since he's been there it's worse. First he froze the money . . . Nilson's mother had money in the bank and couldn't get it. She was mad. Then when he unfroze the money, Nilson couldn't buy anything with it because of inflation.

Nilson would like to buy a house. There is one for sale in a small *favela*, just a few houses in a nice area with brick walls and window frames but no windows. He has $500 saved at the bank, but the house costs $1000, and his savings always seem to be going down. He gets interest, inflation plus a half per cent a month. But it's his mother's account. And prices always seem to be going up. His mother's grocery bills are higher all the time.

Prices go up but Nilson's salary doesn't. For the last year, he's been making $100 a month working for Tony, more than the minimum. The girl he met on the bus on the way down, Marly, has given him a part-time job. He cleans her apartment three times a week. He makes a little extra with that. But it's never enough.

His boss Tony must make a lot of money. Nilson saw a cheque once and it was for a large sum. Tony once told him about how he arrived in São Paulo from Maranhão, the same state as Nilson, fifteen years ago. Tony slept on the sidewalk when he arrived. 'Look at me now,' he said to Nilson encouragingly. 'I'm thirty-eight. I have a business!'

Tony remembered Nilson's father's shop in Ribamar. He was glad to help Nilson get started. Nilson was working for Tony six days a week, twelve hours a day. On top of that he spent two hours a day getting to work, which was OK when he could get a lift in Tony's van. Then he cleaned Marly's apartment some days, which was OK because she wasn't like the women who stood and watched while he vacuumed or pointed to the corners of the windows he had forgotten to wipe. She didn't mind if he was late, and told him to help himself to snacks from the refrigerator, an offer he was always too shy to accept, though he was hungry, and it would be another two hours before he got home to the room he shared with two other guys in a lodging house.

'When I was a fisherman I was much bigger,' Nilson complained to Marly once. He shrugged his scrawny shoulders and shook his head. 'I was eating better. Now I get sick. I have to work a lot harder, and I get sick. I was never sick before. I have no lunch break . . . ' She made him a sandwich and told him not to bother to clean that day.

Nilson sometimes thinks about going back to Maranhão. If he had some money, he would. He thinks about the girlfriend he had there but then he feels better when he remembers the two he has here in the city. Preta and Vania are their names. He's been going with Vania for five months. He likes her a lot. Preta, his old girlfriend, is jealous, and he has been seeing less of her lately. Vania's father has a clothes store and sometimes Nilson stays at their house at weekends. They go to the Chic show together to dance. With Vania, Nilson doesn't feel so invisible. People look at them, admiring the girl on his arm. He can forget about inflation, forget about his worries.

Now he has a new worry. His sister Meris is coming down to São Paulo too. Meris is sixteen years old, and she has just had a baby. The guys there in Maranhão don't want to look after babies, they just want to make them.

The hotel where Nilson has been living in a room with two other guys is not somewhere he could bring his sister. A prostitute stands in the street outside – a *Nordestina* who laughs like a little girl, but her teeth and nose are broken and there are stains on her underwear, which she likes to flash for the guys at the bar on the corner. Late at night, he would hear them drinking and fighting while she laughed.

When he first moved there, Nilson had considered paying her for sex. He was lonely, but fatigue soon made him oblivious to his solitude. It became bearable with time. He played cards with his room-mates and went to church with one of them for a while, though he thought it was stupid to give your money away like that. And there was something about the girl that scared him, a look of confusion, craziness and hatred in her stare. He told himself he couldn't afford it.

Seventeen

Nilson will be working in the *jardins*, the wealthy hillsides where the streets are lined with *jacarandás* that give a soft, diffused shade from their fine, lacy leaves, the lightest of green, like a delicate fern at the end of branches large and strong enough to reach across the street. The force of tropical nature in the midst of this polluted, concrete environment is a constant wonder, a constant reminder. The pavements swell and crack from the force of roots pushing up from the giant tropical chestnuts, as though the earth beneath São Paulo were truly a living thing, a Gaian entity that will one day wake and shrug off this giant city.

It's in these suburbs that the fabled violence of cities like Rio and São Paulo is most tangible, or at least the fear of it. Here, and in the downtown district, near the overcrowded tenements, where the pimps and thieves mingle with the office workers by day and control the lobbies of seedy hotels by night. Elsewhere, in the modest residential districts, in the poor, dusty suburbs and in the *favelas*, there is relatively little of the random violence of North American cities. Nilson's job will be to hold off the desperation of people like himself, the unskilled poor. And to hold open the gates for imported cars.

These are the leafy suburbs of the *telenovelas*, where the mistress of the house complains – like a Victorian lady or Southern dame – of the impossibility of finding good servants nowadays, and has to make do with five where before she had twelve; where swimming pools nest in a profusion of emerald fronds. It's here that the violence is done. Muggers in the streets outside; and respectable, corporate muggers in the living rooms inside, with their walls covered with Indian art, drinking imported whisky from cut crystal.

At a party beside a pool in the *Jardins*, I am introduced to Victor Civita, the grandson of Victor Civita Snr, founder of Abril, the publishing company that owns most of the magazines on Brazilian newsstands, including *Veja*, the Brazilian *Time*, which sells almost a million copies a week. The group is now headed by Victor's father, Roberto, and has branched out into television. They have licensed MTV in Brazil, broadcast on UHF in most urban areas.

The warm evenings compensate for the humid tropical days; the temperature descends enough to liberate the scents from the walls of verdant fronds. The people at the party work in the media, in advertising, publishing, fashion and television. They are mostly in their late twenties, the sons and daughters of people in control of the media. I'm asked the inevitable question. 'What do you write about?' And when I hesitate, someone adds helpfully, 'Arts, politics or ecology?'

In Brazil, as much as anywhere else, ecology has become a buzzword, a growth sector, a career. I was almost sorry I wasn't an ecologist. As a foreigner, I would have satisfied an image they had of themselves, of a nation with environmental issues to resolve that matter for the whole world. Ecology, for cosmopolitan Brazilians suffering from the cultural cringe, has given them new status.

Instead, I say I'm interested in television in the developing world. Brazil is the tele-literate society, a model for the next century. TV in Brazil, as everywhere else, has become more real than life: the collective memory, the collective unconscious. Television shares and validates experience. In Brazil, it has brought about the political enfranchisement of the sub-literate, a revolution more instantly far-reaching than the printing press. Television has opened a transamazonian highway in the depths of the jungle. In the centre of the new settlements is a post with a television, which a local functionary comes to switch on every evening. The whole village gathers around to catch up on Western civilisation. Indians, like the military and the industrialists, have sensed the power of this new flickering totem. Some tribes have their own cameraman, providing material for government agencies, universities, BBC and HBO documentaries.

Bringing MTV to the Brazilian public, I tell Victor, is worse than opening Pandora's Box. He was contributing to the destruction of history. Once, as a magazine editor, I had been accused of this myself, and with reason. If I can never think of an answer to the question of what I write about, it's because of accelerated data flow, multi-channel bombardment, electronic reincarnation, image proliferation, poor concentration, vision-bites, fuzzy logic, parallel architecture, infotainment, expert programmes, colorised movie classics and the rest. 'I'm just trying to compete with television,' I tell him.

'You should meet my dad,' says Victor. 'He hates television. It's against everything he stands for. It's anti-culture!' Victor's dad publishes educational material at a loss, 'because he feels he has to.'

I feel a little sorry for Roberto Civita, who still believes in content, and doesn't realise that form, or surface, over which the modern attention skates, is all that remains. But his ideals didn't stop him buying a franchise on Music Television, and CNN, and ESPN, and TNT classics, and two other channels.

'He had no choice. It's the future. I made him do it,' says Victor.

He grows dejected. 'It doesn't fill your mind. What do pop videos make you think about? More pop videos!' The station also runs public service announcements about drunk-driving, AIDS and, of course, ecology that Victor enjoys making.

'I like the language at the same time. I'm a Gemini. It's a new language trend. "No language" is a language, but sometimes I wonder what I'm doing . . . '

Victor studied politics and media at Columbia University. He wanted to be a musician, but accepted this alternative for the sake of the family. Troubles with the military censors had led to a spell

158

in exile in London in the Seventies after one of their magazines, *Realidade*, was forced to close. At college in New York, he read Neil Postman's influential study of TV, *Amusing Ourselves to Death*. 'I hated TV. I thought it was the end. Now here I am.'

He predicts, 'We'll all go back to storyboards. Instead of rapid editing, it'll be one long take. It's been overused already. The limit is the imagination.'

History will fall back into place? Content will be revealed? Maybe not. 'Non-verbal literacy' is the term for what MTV is teaching America. The following day, on the top floor of the Abril tower, in the executive restaurant overlooking São Paulo, Victor introduces me to the advertising executive who helped to set up MTV in Brazil. He too is interested in television in the developing world. He has a large file of clippings on the subject of non-verbal literacy. He says the problem is that it leaves people with no facility to verbalise an argument . . . I would go further, and say it leaves them without an argument to verbalise.

Victor's grandfather started out by publishing Donald Duck comics. The company still does, and Brazil is the only country in the world where they are writing new adventures for the feisty fowl. Brazil, which, before television, was two nations, rich and poor, urban and rural, that didn't know each other, is becoming, like the rest of the tele-literate world, one big all-seeing but unremembering child.

Downstairs, Denise is visiting the new pop music TV station, to meet the VeeJays. She is fifteen years old, and wants to be a secretary when she leaves school. Her visit to MTV was the prize for answering a survey about her attitudes.

She is interested in conservation. She knows the crocodile is in danger but puzzles that they've been found again recently in São Paulo's Tietê River. She thinks pollution is the most serious environmental problem in Brazil, followed by deforestation and litter. Some of her friends have taken part in local clean-up campaigns. She is careful not to litter the beaches and the streets. She tries to save energy, conserve water and re-use plastic bags. It's something all her friends do.

Denise is conservative about sex, and wants to remain a virgin. 'Men want to marry virgins. Girls want to wait for the right man.' She twists her mouth and shrugs. The contradiction is hard to support. She has been *ficar*, going out, with someone. 'We petted a lot – hands all over the place, but . . . '

Smoking, she says, is *brega* – tacky. She knows a lot of girls who smoke, however.

Her favourite VeeJay is Astrid, a corkscrew blonde with brown skin and plenty of bounce who has become the first Brazilian MTV star. She is also the first Brazilian TV showgirl I see who is not out of the Barbie mould.

'Oh, she *is* white,' insists Victor. 'Brazil is a white country,' he ironises. 'But she has one foot in the kitchen, as we say.'

As for the rest of the MTV fare, Denise – who is 'white' too – likes Paula Abdul and Madonna but says, timidly, that she prefers Brazilian music, artists that she mentions to a nod of agreement from Victor: Caetano Veloso and Gilberto Gil.

'The truth is you have to go Samba eventually,' says Victor. The government imposed a protectionist 50/50 rule at first – but there was nothing to protect. 'There weren't any Brazilian pop videos. Now it's getting better.' *Musica Popular Brasileira* is where the market is, he explains. '*Sertanejo* artists, Brazilian Country and Western, *Caipira* duos like Xitãozinho and Xororó, who sold six hundred thousand copies of their last album. Guns'n'Roses sold only forty thousand copies, to the kids of AB consumers.'

Denise's little brother likes Guns'n'Roses, and would probably buy their albums if he could afford to. His favourite VeeJay is Thunderbird, a good-natured geek who connects with the surf and rock crowd. Victor takes Denise off to get his autograph.

That night, Victor invites me to join the MTV party at a rock concert in an old movie theatre transformed into a nightclub. There is a group on the bill he thinks I'll like, Moleques de Rua, which means street kids, a Samba-rock group from the *favela* of Vila Santa Catarina.

'We're children of the recession,' says Duda, the thirty-one-year-old guitarist with the group. 'We started in '83 but we relaunched in the Collor era. The idea was to do music to let go, to turn aggression into art.' Duda is an ex-communist and a fan of groups like The Clash and The Sex Pistols. He has the long, bushy beard of a Marxist intellectual but says Moleques de Rua were inspired by London's punk rock movement of the late Seventies. 'With the difference that we didn't just want to destroy things. It's up to people to find solutions, like the way we've organised the band.'

The Street Kids slap colour-coded plastic pipes with sandals. The instruments are made from materials recuperated, like the *favelas*, from construction sites. Duda created tuned percussion instruments to give the drum fetish of the local kids some musical expression. He painted the instruments different colours so they could learn the names of the notes. Their rhythms have the energy of *batucada*, but their music is made with rock guitars for this rock city.

Like all good rock groups, they are self-conscious rebels. One of their songs, 'Public Enemy', equates the police with bandits. Because they are black, they are often compared to the *Blocos Africanos* of Salvador. 'But we don't go along with the spiritualism of the *Blocos* of Bahia. Even if Samba is the base, our music comes from the industrial and concrete art tradition of São Paulo.'

Their names are Felipe, Garge, Caio, Gelo, Pelé, Naldão, Bombinho, Ivan and Osvaldinho.

The youngest of the Moleques is only twelve years old and brings a crate to stand on to reach his drum. The singer, Bombinho, dresses like Axl Rose, surf-bum-cum-gang-warrior. Victor enjoys my surprise at finding this LA style flourishing in São Paulo, largely because of MTV. To explain his surly stance, the singer of Guns'n'Roses has described a traumatic, wrecked childhood. Axl comes from a dysfunctional family, and America, north and south, is one big dysfunctional family.

The Street Kids are appearing as the support act to the rock group Titas – a kind of group art project with four singers, all of them poets who have studied the words of Baudelaire and understudied the epileptic dervish of the singer Ian Curtis. One of them, in a white shirt and black trousers, screams 'I'm not Brazilian, I'm not foreign!' It's the Brazilian equivalent of stubbing a cigarette out on your forearm; a fine mix of alienation and self-contempt to judge from the chord it strikes with their young middle-class fans.

Many of these are girls. One girl explains to me that this is due to the fact that there are four singers, so every girl can find her type. More surprisingly, they are Brazilian girls who can't dance. The Brazilian fashion and glamour photographer Bob Wolfenson is annoyed when I recount this. 'That's just another stereotype. All Brazilian women are sensual. Of course they are, but they can't all dance.'

He is a Paulista, of course. São Paulo, said Vinicius de Moraes, is the tomb of *Carnaval*. In São Paulo, people watch the carnival on TV. A popular Rio comic was asked: what's the strangest place you've ever made love?

'São Paulo,' he replied.

Eighteen

Among Marly's friends is Winston, a TV journalist who, between assignments, enjoys dwelling on the contradictions of his homeland, and offers to show me around. Winston was educated at the French *lycée* in São Paulo. There, the Jesuit teachers impressed on him a fact known to all French schoolchildren, that of the superiority of French culture. To be able to follow the lessons – in French – he endured the scorn of his Brazilian friends. Now, at the age of twenty-eight, having travelled in North America, Europe, Russia and China and lived for a year in Japan, he has a wider perspective.

'If you had to sum up Brazil in one word,' says Winston, 'it would be *corruption*.'

He isn't talking about government corruption. He is bemoaning the degradation of forms under tropical skies. 'That's why everyone loves the Japanese food in São Paulo. It's one of the few things that hasn't been corrupted.'

Once, he was ashamed of this. 'Now, I don't think this kind of corruption is bad. It's mostly for the better. It's a way of undermining foreign values and institutions. It clears the ground for fusion and the creation of something new.'

Winston takes me on an informal gastronomic tour of São Paulo.

'The degradation of Italian food in the São Paulo region is instructive,' he says. Where Italian immigrants have managed to preserve their cuisine in other parts of Europe and America, even in the hotter climes of Australia and North Africa, the Brazilian experience has been an exception. There is no wine in Brazil to console them; no possibility of cultivating anything but some modest whites in the southernmost states. Economic protectionism puts high taxes on imported bottles, and without wine any meal begins to lose its savour. But the pastas are made with the wrong grade of wheat and the restaurants – even the large, family-run ones – do not always have an espresso machine; a shocking lapse, like not being able to get a G-and-T in the British Raj. The pizzas are large, Chicago-style, for we *are* in the Chicago of the South, but often bland and overloaded with mass-produced Brazilian mozzarella. Winston thinks that Brazilian pizza is the best in the world, 'better than anywhere in Italy, except Naples, and only equalled by Japanese pizza'. He takes me to the largest pizza restaurant in the world, seating seven thousand people, in a converted factory.

Portuguese cuisine has likewise gone through a process of decline. Brazilian cuisine is an American version of Portuguese cuisine – American not in its ingredients but in its quantities – which even in its highest form, in the restaurants of old Lisbon, is not one of the great culinary arts, consisting mainly of grills accompanied by rice, potatoes or *farofa*, cassava-root meal browned in oil or butter. The vegetables are generally over-cooked and the desserts over-sweet.

In Brazil, this style has been preserved at the expense of any contribution from native cuisine, like the tasty *macacos* or *jacaré*. Even the native tomato is used less than in French or Italian cooking. The cornucopia of tropical fruits provides exotic milkshakes known as *vitaminas*, popular on Rio street corners. But that's all. No sour chocolate sauces as in Mexico. It's indicative of the false idea of Brazilian integration that the food cultures of the people who comprise the nation have not met and mated. Rather, the cuisine of the dominant Portuguese culture has been little improved by Americanisation. This in itself is appealingly unpretentious. In the *lanchonetes* that resemble North American diners you can eat a hamburger or a steak sandwich, a grilled sliver of tender skirt, plus the same amount of cheese, spilling out of a roll. The local beverages are Guarana, a dark, perky soda made from the Amazonian root, and coffee. There's a lot of coffee in Brazil, much of it badly made, however. The seven best grades are all exported.

The sugar is refined to a delicate, powdery lightness. In this state, it resembles other South American stimulants, a reminder of its potency. Watching the Brazilians spoon it abundantly into their coffee cups, Winston wonders if they know the sparkling crystal was once so rare as to be included in the dowries of European princesses, and whether they care to recall that the addiction of Europeans to this cheap energy source – it powers both workers and their cars in Brazil – was the chief reason for the birth of the colony.

The above-average Brazilian has a diet rich in protein, dairy products, starch and sugar. The below-average, less of the same. It's unsophisticated and heavy. The *churrasco* – charcoal-grilled chicken livers and sirloin served with *farofa* – is the height of good bourgeois eating. The *feijoada*, an African-influenced pig-foot and bean stew served with *farofa*, sliced oranges and hot-pepper sauce, the reward of a working week.

The *lanchonetes* – homely emporia in the mid-century modern vernacular of chrome and formica, lit by fizzling neon, with rows of tinned produce on the shelves – now face competition from fast-food chains. In a month when inflation topped 20 per cent, McDonald's *reduced* its prices. Bob's, the national chain, tried to compete with two burgers for one. In recent years, golden arches have appeared on the fringes and in the centres of Brazilian cities, and the *lanchonetes* find their custom dwindling.

There is an argument that protectionism reinforces cultural isolation, reinforcing in turn the cultural cringe as imported goods are made even more expensive, rare and desirable. When President Collor, after cringing at the quality of Japanese cars, decided to scrap the list of nearly 1200 restricted import items – everything from tractors to computers, vacuum cleaners to golden arches – he was applauded by European and American economists. Always so ugly in others and right and natural in ourselves, protectionist rhetoric – pro and anti – hides obvious economic interests. Winston

165

is delighted, however, because it means he can get pasta made with hard wheat.

He is dismayed at the proliferation of golden arches, but pleased to be able to get a Japanese fax. And he suffers from this contradiction. The self-proclaimed anthropophagist worries about being swallowed by other cultures. He wants to be part of the world, but fears that the world will eat him.

Winston is an estranged son of Europe, with a grudge against it. He has a grudge too against North America, a tendency to side with the underdogs against the Yankees, though he regards communists, who traditionally capitalised on such sentiments, as 'impossible, a joke'. He dislikes the greed and arrogance of North Americans but it's the snobbery of the Europeans that really galls him.

He confesses that he used to be helpless before the haughty self-possession of European women, swooning over them and sending long letters from the depths of his cultural and emotional abjection. But he has grown out of this. Now he prefers Brazilian women. He ardently wants to be Brazilian, but doesn't know what that is.

Brazilian logic, says Winston, is 'fluid and circular, spiralling to reach the place it started from'. He repeats this often and I find it hard to divine what he means. 'We don't follow rational, linear thinking. We're influenced by the mysticism of Blacks and Indians.'

Is he talking about the superstitious nature of Brazil, the world of dreams and coincidences in which all Brazilians seem to live? 'Lapsed Catholics, we are still fervent in our belief in something, anything.' When a landslide kills thirty-four people in the state of Mato Grosso, occupying the headlines for three days, the following people appear on the TV news to comment on the catastrophe: an attractive spokeswoman from the governor's office calling for federal aid; the mayor calling on the governor for more resources; the housing worker blaming the mayor for squandering resources that might have prevented the red mud from swallowing fifty-odd shacks; an astrologer, who pointed to the ominous conjunction of Uranus and Saturn.

Is he talking about the Dionysian nature of Brazil? 'Its proximity

166

to Eden was undoubted by the early colonists.' For latterday tourists, it still represents the libido at play. The God of Brazil is no moral authoritarian but a priest in drag licked by a lascivious people, a people whose sturdy designs are mocked by the bounteous, ripe nature that surrounds them, a constant invitation to a languorous idyll. Plans for hydro-electric plants, for chemical factories and communications empires, for sending children to school and becoming the eighth member of the G7, plans undertaken with such epic intent, are ridiculed by circumstances and by nature. For every paradise spoiled there are still a hundred more, supine, waiting, ripe, embracing . . .

In the absence of a solid religious foundation in Brazil, Winston is thinking of launching a religion himself. He tells me, only half joking, that he has dwelt long and hard on the religious mysteries.

At the age of eleven, he began to think he was Jesus Christ.

By the age of fourteen, he became convinced. His friends took him to a whore, who laughed. They had turns with her in the car until it was his turn, and he couldn't. They all laughed. She was ugly, was his excuse.

He began to wonder if he might be a homosexual, but discounted this, as the only man he dwelled on was Jesus Christ.

He idolised Christ but also Che Guevara, who looked a bit like the Son of God in that poster, though the thing about Che was how much it infuriated his father. His mother was concerned about his obsession with Jesus, but hoped he would grow out of it.

It was more difficult with his younger brothers, who at first admired his fixation as a sign of maturity, then saw it as a mark of idiocy, and savagely mocked his insistence on saying grace, in Latin, before meals.

At the age of eighteen, long after everyone he knew, he finally lost his virginity, with an older woman. He confided to her that it was the first time he had made love and she told all her friends, who told all his friends.

Soon after, she left him. He was heartbroken. He thought he could never love another woman, but at least he thought less about Jesus

Christ, about His body racked and dying on the cross. He began to think instead about women's bodies.

The religion he wants to start will be a cult of Diana, which will seek out and worship beautiful, intelligent women!

Nineteen

The cathedral of the poor is an old factory. Bare iron uprights and crossbeams support a low zigzag roof made of corrugated tin. A downpour clatters on the roof like a never-ending train, and the sun heats it like baking foil. The roof hangs hot and heavy over the heads of the congregation. They hang their heads, listening to a loud, distorted voice from the speakers.

Maybe you haven't got a job, maybe you're looking for work . . .

The long, wide building – occupying a whole block of the inner-city wasteland left over from São Paulo's first industrial surge – has been painted bright blue and white vertical stripes. Above the entrance are neon letters five feet high, set against a rainbow backdrop, advertising the *Igreja Pentecostal Deus é Amor*. The paint on the building is fresh, a thick coat that is regularly renewed. The surrounding factories and walls are streaked with grime from the pollution and the rain but the church is clean and bright. The paint is important; devotional paint, offered, along with the buckets and the hands, by the congregation. And the colours – a factory-line version of the colours of the old Baroque churches – are significant too, the colours of the Holy Ghost, of the skies in the kingdom of the poor.

Maybe you haven't got any money . . .

Outside the cathedral of the poor are stalls selling popcorn, candy-apples, sweets, hamburgers and fruits. It's Sunday, and people have been coming and going all day from the non-stop services. Down a side street buses are lined up. They enter through the factory doors, under the eyes of attendants wearing white shirts and ties. Inside, there are banks of seats, stretching forward to a platform with a bare wooden table.

I say don't worry about a job! Don't worry about the money you don't have!

The table is so far away I can barely see it for the rows of arms waving in the air, arms raised with banknotes, or holding books stamped with their attendance records. Many of the arms are sagging. They've been working all week, carrying and scrubbing, and they are heavy. They are held up at the elbow by the other arm, framing a lolling head, eyes screwed shut and brows sweating under the hot roof.

Because you may not have money now, but if you give your money now to Jesus . . .

The preacher gives a signal, and attendants move forward holding straw baskets.

Give all that you can to Jesus . . .

The congregation sways and shouts. *Jesus!!* They flap the notes in their hands to get Jesus' attention.

Then Jesus will take care of you. Jesus will help you!

The money flutters into the baskets, piling high like damp leaves.

He will help you find that job! He will help you get the money you need!

The donors sit down, exhaustion and satisfaction on their faces. They lean forward to press their foreheads to the backs of the bench in front and pray. Next to them, others are asleep. In their faces there is pain and relief; tired, weary brown faces, sagging in supplication, gazing up at the roof of the cathedral of the poor, above which the leaden sun beats down. I realise that I've seen these faces before, in the sculptures and paintings of Aleijadinho, the 'Little Cripple', the greatest of all Baroque artists, who painted on the effigies of saints the faces of those who slaved in the mines, digging out the gold that paid for the splendid eighteenth-century churches of Ouro Preto. Aleijadinho was a mulatto like them. When disease took away his legs and the Little Cripple could no longer climb the ladder to reach the ceilings, he had himself strapped to a winch and hoisted up to paint the little white clouds in the blue skies. When the pain burning in his hands became too much to bear, he gave his assistants the scissors and told them to cut off his leprous fingers, then he tied his brushes to the stumps and carried on painting his devotional masterpieces. In the cathedral of the poor are the faces he painted, 250 years later, still gazing up in anguish and hope.

The congregation is split between women and children on the left and men to the right. The young women wear knee-length skirts, no make-up, and have their hair loose. Most of the women are middle-aged or older. 'Jesus is really here,' one of them whispers to me, though over the din from the speakers I can barely hear her. She is aged around fifty, and wears a neat, bright blouse. When she came the first time, she explains, she couldn't even walk and the hospitals didn't know what was wrong with her. She used to attend a church where 'the blood and body of Christ came only once a year. Then I came here – and I got up and walked! Praise the Lord!'

The woman is a *crente*, a believer. In the world's largest Catholic nation, they have abandoned the Church of Rome for new Pentecostal and Protestant churches like this. To the side of the platform at the front, by the altar that looks like a committee bench, are a group of handicapped *crentes*, arranged in a pitiful tableau, waiting for the Holy Spirit to lift them out of their wheelchairs.

The most ardent of the *crentes*, all middle-aged men, have left their seats to press at the front of the platform, their heads bowed in prayer and arms raised with their offerings. From behind a bare wooden table on the platform, the preachers take turns at the microphone. Each sermon lasts twenty minutes, a hectoring crescendo that ends in a shower of bills. Like the attendants, the preachers wear white shirts and ties. They look like businessmen, and come and go from side doors carrying briefcases stuffed with church literature and cash.

Don't give your money to prostitutes! Don't give your money to drug dealers! Give it to Jesus!

171

The Pentecostal Church of God Is Love offers solace to the new urban poor, and they in return donate a portion of their income to Jesus. It's impossible to guess how much money Jesus receives this Sunday, from a congregation of several thousand. The church is one of the oldest of the 'sects', as the spiritual father of Brazil, the Pope, has called them. It was launched in 1962 by David Miranda, a plump, strait-laced, self-styled 'missionary' who offers a strict interpretation of biblical doctrine. No smoking, drinking or gambling, no contraception and no trousers for women. You can only be baptised if you are free of demons. Epileptics must have a medical certificate, as the trance techniques used by the preachers to expel 'demons' have caused deaths in the past. The 'offence' of homosexuality can only be expunged by five years' work for the church, sex with animals by three years' work, masturbation by two years and extra-marital sex by one year. The disco and the beach are forbidden. A first visit to the beach entails six months' suspension, a second visit, one year, a third visit, expulsion. You can only listen to recordings of Miranda or his preachers, on sale at the church. If you buy a video, you are suspended from the church until you sell or discard it. You are forbidden to have a TV set but radios are permitted . . . There are no icons in this church, and the only illuminations are the signs on each side of the altar advertising the church radio station, whose studios are in an outbuilding next door, near the church cafeteria, where old women sit in their best clothes, hunched and grateful, eating a cheap lunch from a paper plate.

This part of the cathedral that I'm in is grubby and unpainted, lit by white neon tubes. Next door is another, even larger section, part of the same building but with walls painted white and white cloth over the plastic seats. There, music plays, and it's in this section that the best, the most extolling, exhorting preachers can be heard. To gain admittance, church members must show their attendance cards; then they can be 'baptised'. Not surprisingly, with such severe rules of entry, the kingdom of David Miranda is full of old women, who have washed floors all week to give Jesus his tribute.

A few blocks away in a converted cinema is another Protestant church, the Universal Church of the Kingdom of God, which throngs with *crentes* every weekday afternoon. There, in the company of the faithful, singing and crying under a roof freshly painted white but seeping with rain, I witnessed a miracle.

The minister called on us to pray, to pray hard, because Jesus was listening, and in five minutes' time, his divine powers would become manifest. We bowed our heads. Assistant preachers in white shirts and ties moved among us; one placed his hand on my head and pressed hard, muttering a prayer to drive out my demons. Next to me a woman fell to the floor, trembling and crying. On the old cinema stage, an assistant handed the minister a portable phone. On the line was a woman who had been listening to the service on the church radio. A miracle had occurred, there in her kitchen. She had received Jesus. We began to sing; a jolly tune that told Satan to shoo away.

Across the street, in the Catholic cathedral that once filled with factory workers on Sundays, just three people sat in the pews.

To found a new church in Brazil is not complicated. You just go to city hall with a copy of the lease to the property, a plan of the property, a copy of the articles of the new church and the ID of its leader. No problem. You can now open for spiritual business, free of tax.

This is what Edir Macedo Bezerra did in the late Seventies. An ex-employee of Loterj, the state lottery, he opened a storefront church, the Universal Church of the Kingdom of God, in Rio de Janeiro. His church was not very different from others: white paint, rows of seats and bright lights; a clean interior belonging to the congregation, not one they cleaned. From it, 'Bishop' Macedo launched a crusade, a 'holy war' against the 'satanic machinations' of the *Macumba*, against the cults that came from Africa to Bahia and down to Rio. To fight the African devils, he used their weapons: trance techniques, chants and exorcisms; but away from the beaches where women in white dresses – and men dressed as women – strewed flowers on the sea to placate Iemanjá, away from the suburbs where the Mothers and Fathers of the Saints slit the necks of chickens and danced in the blood; in nice, clean, modern premises. His 'pastors' weren't drag queens in head-dresses, they wore the white shirts and ties of TV presenters. They offered civilised miracles to a credulous, newly urbanised flock; miracles they were soon hearing of via the church's twenty-two radio stations.

A little more than a decade later, with the proceeds of the weekly donations, Macedo bought the Record TV network, based in São Paulo, for $45 million. The Universal Church had more than 800 branches in Brazil and more in Argentina, Spain and the United States. On behalf of Jesus Christ, the forty-six-year-old 'Bishop' was estimated to be collecting a dollar a month from some six million *crentes*.

'Money is a profoundly spiritual thing,' says Pastor Paulo de Veloso of the Universal Church. 'God only asks for ten per cent! When you give this, it's a way of saying, Thank you, Lord. For it's through the grace of God that you have all you have. And he lets you keep ninety per cent!'

The pastors have a Cariocan showbiz style and the unctuous manners of salesmen. They compete to exhort God's 10 per cent. The Bishop keeps a league table, showing how much each pastor has pulled in from exorcising the 'devils', the headaches and the woes, of their congregations. The church literature explains that 'poverty and misery are the work of the devil, and riches a gift of God'.

Macedo thinks money is important in the earthly life – a preoccupation he probably shares with his *crentes*. 'Jesus wasn't poor. He said, "I am the lord of lords, king of kings,"' says Macedo. 'A king is never poor.' He knows the devil exists, but, unlike his followers, doesn't believe in him. He is plump and taciturn, notably since his acquisition of the powerful TV network, which aroused the attention of the government. He agrees that television can be an 'arm of sin' and doesn't appear in person on his channel. His favourite book is the Bible, and his favourite film, *The Ten Commandments*. Being a Lutheran, he says he has no respect for the Pope, nor for any Brazilian mystic, such as the seventeenth-century Bahian Jesuit father Vieira. He gives a zero to Brazilian politics, and puts his faith in God, with whom he has 'made a pact through Jesus'. God, he affirms, is not Brazilian. The quality he admires most in a woman is intelligence, and in men too. He has never been psychoanalysed. Revealingly, the Bishop's favourite dish is rice, beans, cabbage and meat. He hates anything cooked in palm oil and the African-influenced cuisine of Bahia.

In five minutes, the holy spirit will descend! In five minutes, the holy spirit will descend . . .

The huge electronic signboard in the Maracana stadium announces the imminent miracle as though it were the next fixture. On the stands of the giant soccer arena, 200,000 *crentes* are gathered for the start of the Easter weekend; crowded, sweating and mumbling with their eyes shut tight and their hands pressed on the top of their heads. There aren't enough pastors to move through the crowds like pickpockets, placing their hands on the heads of the faithful to exorcise the demons, and so the faithful, moved by the reverberating voice of the Bishop, in white shirt and tie in the centre of the field, perform their own auto-exorcisms. When they open their eyes, they will be filled with divine light.

'If you trust in Jesus, you'll be able to see. You won't need your glasses,' promises the Bishop. 'Throw away your glasses, for He is coming!'

And thousands of pairs of spectacles shower onto the soccer field.

Bishop Edir Macedo, who has 'made a pact with Jesus', does not throw away his glasses, however.

While he preaches his sermon this Good Friday in the Maracana, a woman is writhing in religious ecstasy, one of the thousands possessed by devils who can't bear to hear the pure white words of the ex-lottery employee. The woman, middle-aged and dressed for the day in her best clothes, is gyrating, breathing hard and deep as a pastor presses her skull with both hands, muttering imprecations to the devil to leave this suffering soul. She starts to tremble, racked by violent shudders that leave her gasping for breath. The pastor releases his hands and raises his arms to heaven, his work done, crying out thanks to God. The woman collapses on the floor, still shuddering, breathing irregularly now.

This has been going on all morning, throughout the stadium filled with devils this Holy weekend. There are so many devils, the pastors must work hard to drive them out. The woman is still shuddering, her eyes are still closed. She is gasping now, choking for breath. The people around her want to help her up, but the pastor says no. They are dealing with the devil, with powerful forces that only men in white shirts and ties can master. They know the devil's work.

The woman stops shuddering, her eyes opening wide. Her pupils are fused a cloudy white. She has seen the light of lights . . .

Afterwards, Bishop Macedo expresses his regret at the ways of God. The woman's death, he says, was 'doubtless due to a lack of faith'.

Iemanjá is the Yoruba goddess of the sea, a vain, capricious spirit, who expects and gets a tribute of boats laden with flowers and beauty products at the beginning of February. If the boat drifts back to the shore, it means she has refused it. She is sore at something. Iemanjá has been receiving these flowers since men first set out on boats from the shores of Guinea and Angola. When they came to Brazil, lying chained in rows, their noses pressed to the next rack of human bodies, smelling their own fear and faeces, they prayed to her.

When the Catholic priests of Bahia banned such rituals, the crafty orixás hid inside the statues of saints. Iemanjá ducked under the skirts of her pious little sister, the Virgin Mary. The mortal hand-to-hand combat of African villages became the ritual dance of the capoeira, often described as a kind of Brazilian martial art; in reality the ceremonial vestige of an ancient political process. Eventually, seeing with what fervour the black folk of Salvador washed the church of Nosso Senhor de Bonfim, Our Lord of the Good End in the Bay of All Saints, a noisy ritual that announced each January a cycle of Candomblé ceremonies – its practitioners drunk on prayer, drums, trance, dance and sugar-cane alcohol – the ban on the Candomblé was relaxed.

The rise of an urban class of free blacks and mulattos with the status and pretensions of whites in the last century led to the development of the more intellectual Umbanda, which borrowed from the spiritism of the French poet Alan Kardec and formalised the syncretic cosmology of the Catholic-African *orixás*. To outsiders, the rites and sorceries of both sects are known as *Macumba*.

Now, when Iemanjá comes to receive her flowers, she finds her followers dwindling in numbers. And she hears a strange chant over the drums, the sound of passages from the Bible being screamed at her by members of the Charismatic Renewal, Catholic proselytisers who, with the blessing of the Pope and the eminent Cardinal Ratzinger, are doing battle against so-called New Protestants like Edir Macedo for the souls of the poor.

John Paul II has come to Brazil, the world's largest Catholic nation, with the express intention of kindling a Catholic revival in the face of increasing desertion from the one true faith. In his last encyclical, he has warned against the menace of the 'sects'. In the world's largest Catholic nation, there are more than a hundred more 'sects' like that of Edir Macedo's, with an estimated 12 million members, and their numbers are growing.

In Natal, on the *Nordeste* coast, the head of the Catholic Church is greeted with a red carpet and cannon-fire for his first public mass in 1991. But the crowds are not large enough to fill the main square of this provincial city, dressed in flowers and roped in red cord for the occasion, with portable toilets, a rock concert PA system and numerous 'points of communion' emblazoned with the name of their sponsor, the Bank of Brazil. In front of 200 bishops, the Pope goes on the offensive: 'The Christian vocation of millions of souls is being menaced by sects, by violence of all kinds, especially that linked to drug trafficking, by consumerism, by anti-birth campaigns. It's urgent to return to the moral values of the Christian tradition.'

But the sellers of merchandise bearing the image of the Pope – everything from T-shirts to credit cards – are disappointed. They hope things will improve when the papal tour hits the larger cities.

The day before, as the Pope arrived to attend a congress of Brazilian bishops, 'Bishop' Edir Macedo held another spectacular prayer meeting in front of 200,000 *crentes* in Rio's Maracanã – the sixth in two years. It was a deliberate show of strength to His Holiness. While it was going on, the Pope was telling his bishops

177

that the expansion of the New Protestants in Brazil ought to provoke them to take up position. They should be out there occupying the terrain with the sects, 'provoking in people the joy and rapture of belonging to the One True Church of Christ'. And he added that, with the collapse of Marxism in eastern Europe, 'the theology of liberation, based on ideological concepts, has been deprived of meaning.'

'Protestantism is very individualistic, a "me" religion. It's dogma and TV,' says Hamilton Caldozo, a black journalist who has followed the development of the sects. 'It's for the cities where everyone is your enemy. And things are getting worse for you every day.'

He concludes that Luiza Erudina, the mayoress of São Paulo, and Edir Macedo – who has found ample new flocks in Brazil's biggest city – have the same constituency. 'She was elected out of frustration. Collor was elected out of frustration.'

In the last days of his campaign, Collor appeared on TV with a chorus of black Protestant women behind him, moaning, swaying and singing gently, '*Col . . . lor. Col . . . lor.*'

Marxism has failed the people of the badlands, declared dead before it has even reached them.

The badlands, the *sertão*, a parched scrub of black legend, plagued by periodic droughts. The cursed 'green drought' is the worst. The grass soaks up what little water falls on the surface, quickly irrigating useless scrub and giving an impression that all is well, but leaving the rivers dry and the fields gasping.

The *Nordeste* has a population of 40 million and the highest birth-rate in the country. Most are born into feudal poverty, virtual slaves of the *fazendeiros*, ruled by debts and guns. The tenant farmers find they owe more than they grow, when they can grow. A monoculture of sugar has returned to fuel the cars. When the droughts strike, they drift to the coastal cities, where the convulsive quick-slow pace of industrialisation leaves them crowding in ubiquitous shacks.

Land reform, which even His Holiness admits is necessary, has failed them too, evaporating like the rain. Among the programmes of the transitional government headed by José Sarney, who was born in the *Nordeste*, was an attempt to redistribute idle land to 1,400,000 peasant families. Federal funds would be used to buy and redistribute small, unused plots from *fazendeiros* – at the values declared in their tax returns. It was land that the landowners found more profitable to use as collateral for playing the markets. Laws governing land occupation that were proposed for the new constitution should have given another 5 million families the chance to subsist independently on their own farms, instead of coming in despair to overburdened cities – a desperate measure to stem the rural exodus and halt the growth of the *favelas*.

The new constitution, established in 1988, recognised the right to strike, limited the working week to forty-four hours, abolished censorship, made torture, terrorism, racism and drug trafficking crimes without remit and established a right of 'popular initiative', allowing laws to be proposed by a petition of 1 per cent of the electorate. But the powerful lobby of the *fazendeiros* obtained all they wanted, an improvement even of their rights under the statutes of 1964. All they have to do to retain their ample properties intact is demonstrate a productive activity. To achieve this is easy. The Brazilian agricultural landscape is now the province of a few cows roaming over vast empty acres.

The forced expulsions of peasants occupying empty land, the battles between *posseiros*, squatters, and *pistoleires*, hired killers, have been too numerous, too far from justice, or from an interested media, to record. The cows need only give milk now and then to enjoy a lifestyle denied to people who have given their blood.

Movements like *Sem Terra* fought for squatters' rights under the military dictatorship but, with a forcedly political complexion, their margin for action was limited to self-defence, backed by a few legal struggles. The only people in a position to take up the cause of the peasants were the clergy. The peasants are miles from justice, miles from the media, miles from schools and stores – stores owned by the *fazendeiros* to whom they end up owing their lives – but never so far from a church. The Pastoral Land Commission, created under the auspices of the National Episcopal Conference, which groups the Catholic bishops of Brazil, reported in 1990 that

179

of the 1560 cases of assassination that had *resulted in judicial dossiers* – and not simply gone into police drawers or unmarked graves – over the previous fifteen years, just eighteen had come to court. Of these, guilty verdicts were returned in eight cases. Two of these were for killing Indians, two for killing priests and three for homicide against lawyers. Just one peasant had received posthumous justice. Until the Chico Mendes case – the shooting of the Amazon rubber-tapper who tried to organise resistance to the landowners – no enquiry was ever made into who ordered the killings. The *fazendeiros* roamed their lands with impunity. Behind white palisades, under tall palms, with their powerful friends, they sat and contemplated the changeless skies. A year later, the Pastoral Commission reported again. This time, they had evidence of 4501 cases of slavery, of labour at gunpoint.

There was other evidence – unproven – of extreme-left, revolutionary elements infiltrating the Pastoral Commission, using funds from a West German charity for the purchase of arms. It was part of the continuing attacks on a church that was the only recourse for many during the military dictatorship. At least thirty Brazilian priests received death threats in 1989. They had chosen 'the priority of the poor', first proposed at a conference of Latin-American bishops in Medellin, Columbia, in 1968 and adopted at another conference in Mexico in 1979. It was this choice that the Pope intended to call into question when he arrived in Natal for the twelfth Episcopal Congress.

The Church in Brazil had readily taken up the theology of liberation, one of the leaders of which was the Brazilian Franciscan Leonardo Boff. The priests – especially younger ones – left the musty Baroque confines of a Church constrained by authoritarian rigour inherited from the colonial era, and looked for their vocation in the community, helped by lay assistants who had no legal rights to pursue what would otherwise have been a political struggle. Father Boff was condemned by the Vatican to 'obsequious silence' in 1985, and forbidden from teaching or making public statements after the publication of his book, judged sacrilegious, *The Church, Charisma and Power*. The same year, Dom Helder Camara, the popular archbishop of Recife, a native of the *Nordeste*, was replaced by an obscure canon from Rome who took residence in the palace deserted by his predecessor, reopened the seminary that Dom Helder had closed, re-established internal regulatory councils, and took away the authority of rural pastors whom he accused of indiscipline and financial irregularities. In contrast to his predecessor, the new bishop has also never said a word about sackings, inflation or the death squads.

If the progressives were still in the majority when the Pope arrived for the twelfth Episcopal Congress, the signal from Rome was clear. Cardinal Paulo Arns, the archbishop of São Paulo, saw his diocese dissected in 1989, reducing his influence. The papal delegate to the conference was Cardinal Eugenio Sales, archbishop of Rio and a firm adversary of liberation theology. Some conservative bishops at the conference felt that 'the priority of the poor', which may have been right in Brazil when the poor had no other representation, was no longer so urgent in the new democracy. As a result of this, and of the changes imposed by Rome, many of the lay preachers – experienced in community organisation – had moved into the unions and the new political parties. The interdiction of the Jesuits from the dominions of Spain and Portugal had once before satisfied the interests of rulers and their wealthy clients, leaving the weak to a wretched fate, but the threat to the validity of the Church in Brazil was now coming not from dereliction of its moral duties, but from its new and growing Protestant rivals.

To win back the flocks, instead of political bread, the Catholic Church will be offering cathode circuses, part of an aggressive tele-evangelical drive sanctified by the Pope that includes plans to launch a Vatican satellite, Lumen 2000. Against the Protestants in Brazil, the Catholics employ the weapons of the enemy, attacking, like the Protestants, the *Candomblé*. Thus the new archbishop of Salvador, Cardinal Lucas Moreira Neves – who feels that the established church in Brazil has been more mindful of social needs than religious ones in the last decade – has forbidden the ceremonial washing of the Church of *Nosso Senhor do Bonfim*. He wants to channel back into his aisles what he describes as the 'effervescent religiosity' of the Brazilian masses.

Twenty

There are 365 churches in Salvador da Bahia, overlooking the Bay
of All Saints, a saint for every day of the year. Levi-Strauss was
photographing them in the Thirties, and the urchins scampered
around, begging not for coins but to have their picture taken.
The French anthropologist turned to oblige them with his new
Leica. Further down the road, he was detained by two plain-clothes
policemen who had been following him. They cautioned him against
taking photos of the brown children. It might lead people to think
that Brazil wasn't a white country.

The urchin following me is still brown, however. He presents a
photocard identifying him as a language student and official guide.
For a gratuity, he will show me the Baroque treasures of Bahia.

The old quarter of the city of Salvador in Bahia des Todos
Santos has been designated a conservation area by UNESCO, the
grandest and most important collection of colonial-era buildings in
the world. But this four-hundred-year-old outdoor museum is not
overrun by tourists or inhabited by a discreet bourgeoisie, it's not
a Boston or a Florence, though it's bigger than any historical part
of New England and flourished soon after the Italian Renaissance.
No inch of historical patrimony in North America or Europe has
run to such ruin, though the far older temples of southeast Asia

seem to merit even less concern. And despite the attentions of UNESCO, old Bahia appears never to have been restored. Instead, it has slumbered through centuries of heat and rain – and recent decades of pollution – to reach a state of magnificent dilapidation.

Apart from the churches, it seems not to have been painted in four centuries. The colours have become a memory in the stone-and-plaster walls of the one-storey terraced houses, faded and grimy beyond belief. Their decaying, tumbledown aspect belongs more to Portugal of the Middle Ages than early colonial America, though the streaks of black that cover them, running down from broken red tiles and bent gutters, are a mark of our century. The shiny black cobbles have been rubbed slippery-smooth from the feet of processions winding their way up to the gorgeous churches with their gilded frescoes, and by the everyday activities of the inhabitants of this living relic.

From the churches built of amazing riches and competitive fervour, as though the captains and barons who endowed them needed to signal God's attention so far from home, or else had much to atone for, my young guide leads me down the hill, to show me the house where Jorge Amado lived – now a small museum dedicated to Brazil's greatest contemporary author – and the square where they sold the slaves, millions of them. For nearly three centuries, ships arrived in the bay below carrying their bitter cargoes, and left full of sugar.

The carefully nurtured myth of a white Brazil was indispensable to the colonists, who were vastly outnumbered by the Africans. But, inferior beings, they weren't counted except in the ledgers of the traders and the plantations. Thus, Bahia was white.

From here, almost as soon as the first ones came ashore in the sixteenth century, the slaves ran away. They founded the nation of Palmares. The first independent colony in the New World happened to be black.

> *Folga nego/ Branco não vem ca . . .*
> Rest, black man/ The white man doesn't come here.
> If he comes/ the devil will take him.

Runaways tasted freedom in the sweetwater they drank, hiding in rivers as the dogs snapped at their ears. On nights without a moon, they crawled, stumbled and ran as far from the fields and the canepress as they could, to the groves of Palmares in the Serra da Barriga, inland from the Alagoas coast. Here the Caeté Indians lived too, until the Pope declared open season on them for eating the first bishop of Brazil. Here the *quilombos* were established, the hidden villages, protected by sharpened stakes and jaguar traps, where the runaways lived free during the seventeenth century, profiting from the diversion of the thirty-year Dutch invasion that began in 1624, and later employing the subterfuge of the bush to thwart the raids of the Portuguese. In Palmares, the palm trees brought from Africa flourished, providing oil for cooking and lighting, fibre for weaving, fronds to cover the huts and the beds, a continuation of Angolan traditions. The different tribes spoke a common language, Portuguese, using Guarani names for places and things and African names for spirits and feelings.

One of the things they felt was that *the remedy for man is man*.

Father Antonio Vieira chided the gentlefolk of seventeenth-century Bahia – 'not all that gentle', according to the poet Gregorio de Matos – reminding them who carried their litters and parasols. 'It could be justly said that Brazil has its body in America and its soul in Africa.' Brazil was dependent on Angola as Portugal was dependent on Brazil; Angola, 'with whose unhappy blood and black but happy souls Brazil is nourished, animated, sustained, served and preserved.' The Jesuit priest, an enemy of the Inquisition – which had its hands full rooting out the devil's work in the colony – angered the barons with his sermons.

São Salvador da Bahia was the capital of Brazil, seat of the viceroy and the archbishop, the biggest Portuguese city after Lisbon. It rivalled Lisbon in sumptuous wealth, in gilded churches and glorious ladies. Through the main square, the slaves were paraded for sale, a natural selection of the best of the Bantu, because only they have survived.

Father Vieira said the ancient prophets were right to read destiny in the guts of the animals they sacrificed, not in the brains, because a prophet who can love is better than one who can reason. From the pulpit of the Ayuda church, the oldest in Brazil, he asked: 'Does it make me a lord that I was born farther away from the sun, and others, slaves, that they were born closer?' He was born in Bahia, and knew of its shame. 'Although we are the sinners, my God, today it is you who must repent!'

The not so gentlefolk of Bahia enjoyed the Jesuit's defiance of the Inquisitors, and tolerated his compassion for the slaves, whose beds, after all, they were not averse to sharing. But enough was enough.

The Guarani-speaking 'captain' Domingos Jorge Velho had come north from the state of São Paulo, where his troop of mongrels and thieves in the pay of landgrabbers had been settling disputes over the titles to what once belonged to nobody. The Indian hunters were usually Indians themselves, or *mamelucos* like the captain, half Indian, the other half Portuguese. They turned or were turned against a part of themselves, like animals tearing at their own wounds.

Domingos had come to quell the rebellious Janduim tribe. It took six years to do this, and afterwards, a new commission awaited. He was offered lands, slaves, pardons and decorations to lay low Palmares. Domingo paraded with his band of cut-throats in the streets of Recife, a telescope slung across his bare chest, drumming up recruits. The runaways were an affront to God's order. The scandal of the *quilombos* had persisted for a century and endured more than forty expeditions.

Nine thousand men were mobilised, mostly hungry peons – for droughts were taking their periodic toll – the biggest army Brazil had ever seen, bigger than the one that repelled the Dutch. Cannons wrecked the fortifications of Macacos, capital of Palmares, and flames burned the huts. Chief Zumbi escaped, to be betrayed by a comrade. His head was brought back to Recife to rot on a pole. So ended, in 1695, the first independent colony in the New World.

Brazil is a white nation. In 1648, the Portuguese declared that any man who fought the Dutch would be a freeman. Henrique Dias, from Luanda, rose to the rank of captain of a black legion

185

consisting of Minas, Ardas, Angolans and Creoles. By 1796, money had already become the great leveller in the New World. Mulattos could purchase a document that declared their slave grandparent a free person, allowing them to wear a sword and be escorted by slaves carrying silk parasols. In 1870, among the group of abolitionists at São Paulo University was Luis Gama, who had been sold by his father in Bahia. At that time – just twenty years before abolition was declared by Princess Isabel – the average *fazenda* had more than a hundred slaves and in the cities, carriages were advertised for sale with their drivers. But Brazil is still a white nation.

Thunder breaks over Salvador da Bahia, the thunder of drums ... In the old quarter of Pelourinho, near the post where runaway slaves were tied and flogged, a doorway leads onto a yard the size of a basketball court. In the yard, one of the *Blocos Africanos* are rehearsing for *Carnaval*.

The *Blocos* are the new musical sensation of Bahia, a neighbourhood drum choir. Forty drummers are lined in rows, with the deepest drums, the size of oil cans, slung around the necks of those at the back. They take small steps back and forth in rhythmic formation to the beat of the drums, so loud and low that the ground seems to rock. The pop musicologist Paul Simon came here to record their martial syncopations for one of his albums, and later took them to perform with him in New York's Central Park. He says he was going back to the source, looking for inspiration in the West African roots of rock and roll music.

The drummers are mostly in their teens, and around them, sitting on the stairs, on the tops of the walls and in the branches of the trees, are dozens more local teenagers. Some of them take turns at the microphone, holding scraps of paper with the words they've written. They sing a couplet and – *boom!* – the drums kick in. The rhythms are slow; more disciplined and warrior-like than the carefree, rollicking *batucadas* of Samba, they are closer to the music of the canefields.

If Jorge Rodriguez doesn't like the song, he raises his baton and the drums cease as suddenly as they started. The singer dejectedly passes the microphone to someone else.

Jorge is the leader of Olodum, the best-known of the *Blocos*. Twice a week, Olodum gather to rehearse here in the evenings. Since 1987, they've sold hundreds of thousands of records in Brazil, but Jorge says the purpose of the group is not commercial. 'We have a role here in the African community of Bahia,' explains the genial Brazilian Rasta. 'Kids come to us because we're an alternative to the violence of the streets. We're fighting against the racism of Brazil, trying to take pride in an African identity.'

They are fighting against the racism that exists even between Africans. More than four hundred years after the first ships arrived, a hundred years after they achieved a nominal equality, the Yorubas still think they are superior to the Bantus.

Bahia was the birthplace of the *Tropicalismo* movement in the Sixties, led by the singers Gilberto Gil and Caetano Veloso. Their music succeeded Bossa Nova as the cosmopolitan Brazilian sound, employing electric instrumentation and mixing in the musics of the Caribbean, not much farther away from Bahia than Rio. Reggae from Jamaica, Calypso from Trinidad, Merengue and Cumbia from the Hispanic islands served to change the temperature of their Sambas, and a lyrical slyness in the face of censorship gave them resonance.

By 1989, Gilberto Gil was preparing his thirtieth album, and had been elected to the town council of Salvador. 'I'm defending in politics the same things I was defending on stage: African culture, the preservation of the environment . . . ' He had been put in charge of cultural activities in Salvador. From an office overlooking the bay, wearing a shirt and tie that had an air of carnival pastiche on him, he surveyed the city that was then enjoying the sudden attention of musical luminaries from the US like David Byrne, who had been making a film there about the *Candomblé* and collecting recordings of *sertão* singers for a series of compilations of Brazilian music.

Carnival came to Rio from Bahia, and to Bahia from Europe. What had been in the Mediterranean countries a period of festivities celebrating death and renewal, a ceremonial mimicry of the earth waking and rejoicing in spring, uprooted and replanted between tropical latitudes has taken a different cast. With the change of season less marked, *Carnaval* comes not as the augur of summer but in late summer, a brief, exuberant hiatus in the eternal torpor. Behind the grimaces, the satire of a world turned upside down, is a kind of melancholy, a fatigue, the weary satiation of those doomed to endless pleasure.

Among the sources of *Carnaval* is the Sybilline festival of Attis, a herdsman loved by the Mother of the Gods, who castrated himself under a pine tree, causing spring violets to bud from drops of his blood. The eunuch priests of Attis, banging drums and tambourines and carrying an image of the Goddess, celebrated a three-day spring festival that culminated in the Day of Blood, when the priests whirled and gashed at their bodies with knives, splattering the altar with blood in offering to the Goddess.

At similar festivals in Syria, swords were arrayed in public so that holiday visitors, mesmerised by the crimson orgy, 'veins throbbing with music', in the words of Sir John Frazer, could join in and castrate themselves on the spot. The zealot then ran through the streets and threw his bloody manhood into a house, whose occupants, so honoured, had to provide women's clothes, which he wore for the rest of his life.

The cult of Attis spread to Rome when the Phrygian religion was adopted in 204 B.C. The sanctuary of the Mother of the Gods – a small black stone brought from Pessinus in Phrygia – was situated on what is now Vatican Hill. Inscriptions relating to the stone were found under St Peter's when the church was extended in the sixteenth century, a dramatic archaeological instance of the Church's assimilation of similar festivals of renewal throughout Europe in Lent and Easter. In the New World, in New Orleans, Jamaica, Trinidad and elsewhere in the Caribbean, these festivals were assimilated by the displaced slave population, who hid their own rites in them. But with no new season to celebrate in the permanent tropical fecundity, the rites became an expression of lugubrious weariness, the abandonment lost its purpose, becoming delirium, like sex with a sated lover.

The newly dismembered devotee of Attis could take comfort in the violets blooming under the pines. The day after, the 25th of

March, reckoned to be the vernal equinox, became in Rome, *Hilaria*, the Festival of Joy. 'A universal licence prevailed,' says Frazer. 'Every man might say and do as he pleased. People went about the streets in disguise. No dignity was too high or too low for the humblest citizen to assume with impunity . . . Even the eunuch priests forgot their wounds.'

As in *Carnaval*, so drums and cymbals were important in the rites of Attis. In rhythm was liberty, imprecation, delirium . . .

The Sybilline priests lived as women, like the transvestite priests of the *Candomblé*, the African religion of Brazil. In homage, sacrifice, or in order to invoke the Goddess – loved and feared, kind and cruel – they became a caricature of women. To allow real women the task would be to give them too much power.

The Africans knew this. The American anthropologist Ruth Landes, who visited Bahia in 1939, noted that the black priestesses of the *Candomblé* take lovers, but refuse husbands. They weren't interested in the prestige of marriage. 'They moved like Queens of Creation, condemning their men to the incomparable torment of jealousy of the Gods.'

The truculent, warm raconteur of Bahian life is Jorge Amado. He was born on a cocoa plantation, but the son of a *fazendeiro* chose, in the Thirties, to side with the Communists.

It was the era of Luis Carlos Prestes, the most infamous Latin American revolutionary before Castro, an ex-officer who led 1000 men on a long march through Brazil. For two years, over 15,000 miles, they were never beaten; the federal army was content to dynamite the fires in the towns and villages where Prestes had passed, preaching agrarian reform, free schooling, universal suffrage and an end to exploitation and corruption.

Amado joined Prestes in prison in 1935, and was imprisoned eleven times more over the next decade, the period of the *Estado Novo* of dictator Getulio Vargas. In 1945, his reputation as a novelist already established by his first book, *Bahia of All Saints*, Amado was elected to congress as a Communist deputy but in 1948, after Vargas changed his mind about democracy, he left for exile in Europe, where he lived for five years with his wife, the writer Zelia Gattai. For eight years, Amado's novels were banned in Brazil, but, in 1955, he left the Party to concentrate on writing. At this point, he admits, the poor ceased to be the only virtuous characters in his books. Bahia has been the inspiration and the setting for many of his novels – which have been translated into 100 languages and turned into mini-series and films in Brazil – a panoramic oeuvre, broad as Brazil, full of desperate adventurers, golden-hearted whores, ruthless landowners, thieves, poets, strong women, arrogant priests, corrupt politicians, bandits and pioneers. They are rich in political and romantic intrigue, the smell of spicy dishes, the fury of hooves, the flash of gunfire, the flames of illicit love and the mysteries of belief.

As a deputy in the constituent assembly, Amado proposed a law in 1946 guaranteeing religious liberty in Brazil. He was a friend of Procopio, the great Father of the Saints, who was regularly beaten by police during the attempted repression of the *Candomblé*. At that time, as again now, the reactionary cardinal of Salvador had forbidden the washing of the church of *Nossa Senhor do Bonfim*, the beginning of a week-long ceremony ending in the eight-mile procession of the Waters of Ochala to the beach and another church, Our Lady of Beach, brought stone by stone from Portugal but secretly dedicated to Iemanjá.

The ceremony begins with a mass given by a Catholic priest. From the start, the *Candomblé* has dissimilated and assimilated. The slaves who came from Nigeria, the Congo, Dahomey and Angola brought different, though similar, animistic beliefs with them. In the slave markets, buyers avoided choosing slaves from the same tribes, who spoke the same language, to avoid them fomenting revolt. Their new owners baptised the slaves first with a hot iron, then with holy water. Content to see an eager clientele, the Catholic priests turned a blind eye to the fetishes, the statues of Catholic saints covered in shells and stones, that the slaves brought with them.

Amado was born with hair, a mark of destiny in the *Candomblé*. He is himself an *obá*, which means master or ancient in Yoruba, the highest civic honour the religion bestows. Shango, lord of war, had twelve *obás* and the tradition of nominating these wise-men is still widespread in Bahia, where there are today 10,000 *Candomblés*, registered as businesses, though much poorer than they once were. In Amado's youth they owned large properties where whole communities lived. There was the house of the saints and the house where the initiation was performed, a series of ceremonies lasting several months, in which the head and body are shaved to allow the *orixás* to slip more easily through the skin. Now, the properties of the *Candomblé* priests are much smaller – and the city has grown much bigger.

Twenty-One

In the big cities, the void is growing, the lonely crowds, the empty stares . . .

Shango, Ogum and the others came to Rio and took rooms, offering advice, healing and orientation first to the people who cleaned apartments, and then to the people who owned them – or, more exactly, their wives. Unable to believe in official reality, they believe in a magical one.

The 'effervescent religiosity' of the Brazilians – nearly all of whom are baptised but less than half of whom can name the Pope – remains, even in the cities, the apartments . . . Many younger, liberal, middle-class Brazilians, especially those in Rio, have had some experience of *Macumba*; a teenage darkside flirtation which leaves them admiring the tenacity of this African folklore and, somewhere, mindful of their personal *orixá*. Everyone has their own *orixá* – their guiding spirit – as well as subsidiary ones who, once revealed, can never quite be detached from one's self-image, like the astrological figures that cause even sceptics to read with helpless foreboding their daily horoscopes.

If these guiding spirits have survived for hundreds of years, only to be shooed away by white-shirted materialist Protestants – ministers of the monotheism of money – the lapsed Catholics who comprise the modern Brazilian middle-class, like the middle-classes elsewhere, are also searching for a spiritual compass. They are disenchanted with political doctrines, they wonder why they can't buy happiness, the price of which is always rising, though they can and do buy organic products, in Brazil as elsewhere. Lately in Brazil they've been buying the books of Paulo Coelho, the most widely read Brazilian author of the last five years. Coelho's books aren't novels – though critics persist in classifying them as fiction – but autobiographical accounts of his experiences of magic.

His first popular success, *Diary of a Magus*, which has sold almost two million copies, relates his discovery of the powers of magic. *The Alchemist*, published in 1988, recounts his pilgrimage along a wilderness road in Spain, the Santiago de Compostella trail. The latest, *Brida*, tells of his encounters with an Irish witch. Sales of these books in Brazil have been second only to those of Gabriel García Márquez. Many take this to be a mark of the effervescent *credulity* of the Brazilians. But Coelho is serious about his work.

'Can I ask you a question . . . ' he says. 'Do you believe in magic?'

We have been talking for an hour and a half in his garden, a small tropical oasis surrounded by the back windows of apartments, on the ground floor of an apartment block in one of the most densely populated metropolitan districts in the world, central Copacabana.

He lives here, he explains, because he benefits from the energy of the urban environment, but on the ground floor because 'to practise magic, you must be near the earth'. It's an eerie, unnatural place, a nest of green foliage at the bottom of a concrete canyon with, all around, but somewhere outside, the never-ending argument of the traffic. Coelho is in his forties, and looks less the magus than the ponytailed playboy in a white T-shirt and white shorts, though he becomes so engrossed in our conversation that dusk turns to night before he realises we are sitting in the dark and turns on the lights.

I tell him, reluctantly, that I don't believe in magic. I clarify this by saying I don't think it's a question of belief, and I quote from Frazer, who said that 'magic is the history of failed experiments'.

Coelho looks disappointed at this piece of rationalism, however enlightened.

'Magic is a tool,' he says. 'It's not a religion. It's not about personal transformation, although . . . ' He leans forward over the garden table and attempts to give a precise definition.

'Art, science and the spiritual search – religion, magic, et cetera – have been important to the world, and when they touch, it can make sparks.'

He leans back again. 'When you start to follow the magical path, you start to fear, so you try to explain, and the magic disappears . . . Magic, like love, is *unexplainable*.'

In his books, he describes a personal odyssey that begins with the chance meeting in an Amsterdam café with an ordinary-looking middle-aged man. Coelho feels drawn to him, and when – there is no coincidence in Coelho's world – he meets him again in another city, he pesters the man to reveal the significance of the encounter, and learns that the man is a magician. After first proving himself a worthy pupil, he prevails on the mage to reveal his secrets.

Coelho's latest book carries a warning to readers about attempting without supervision the hyperventilation exercises he learned from a magus in Spain. Coelho's books recall those of Castaneda, who wrote of his initiation into the peyote-induced mystic rituals of the Central American Indians. But even during his out-of-body experiences Castaneda kept somewhere about him an objectivity that Coelho, with a characteristic Brazilian mistrust of rationalism, feels no need for. He wholeheartedly undergoes the magical experiences he describes, and the question of their literal truth, if it vexes the critics, is not one that troubles him. 'The critics don't like me,' he says slyly, 'but their wives do.'

The son of an engineer, Coelho was educated in a Jesuit school, though his family, he says, were lay Catholics. His mother was involved in the Liberation Theology movement for a time. 'Now she doesn't believe in anything. She asked me to read the *I-Ching* and I said no, you don't believe in it.'

Earlier, I had also quoted Aleister Crowley – *Do what thou wilt shall be the whole of the law* – provoking a jumpy anxiety in him, as though a wasp had come into the garden.

194

'*Aaiee!* Don't say that!'

He had what he calls a hangover in '74 – 'a very bad one' – as a result of dabbling in the oeuvre of the notorious black wizard. Coelho was a lyricist at the time for the singer Raul Seixas. 'My work had a close ideological link with Aleister Crowley.' Like the transsexual flirtations of Gilberto Gil and Caetano Veloso, this was a means of dissimulating protest under the dictatorship. The censors were perplexed by the men in make-up or black goatees, but couldn't find any Marxist maxims on which to wield their scissors. Camp and satanism, popular in Anglo-American rock of the time, became political weapons in Brazil. 'People couldn't talk about politics, so this was a kind of alternative. But I didn't believe in magic.' The bad waking dreams that he blamed on Crowley left him shaken, however. Earlier in the Seventies, when the regime was less strict, he had been involved in the free press, publishing the work of Burroughs. He read Sartre, Bukowski, Ginsberg, Alan Watts and Aldous Huxley and had a rucksack plastered with stickers from the Hippie trail. He had meditated by the pyramids; on Mount Sinai; with the Yogi Sri Ramaja; in the Patagonian desert; in the holy city of Teotihuacan, Mexico; on the slopes of Machu Picchu in the Andes; in the Milky Way coffee bar in Amsterdam . . . He came to London in 1977, feeling mature enough to write what he felt would be 'the book of my life'. The result, a book about vampirism published in the mid-Eighties, he now disowns. 'It was quite a frustration.'

It was only after his initiation that he acquired the confidence and style that has clicked with the public. 'My books come from an established tradition,' he says, 'and my only merit is to put it in a simple way.' He readily agrees that his books also satisfy a spiritual need in the Brazilian middle-class. 'People can't continue to neglect their dreams,' he says. 'They are unhappy because they can't hear them.'

He agrees, too, that the Americas, with their traditions of religious liberty, their hotch-potch of peoples and beliefs, are fertile ground for cults, from the cargo-cults of the old slave coasts to the 162 registered religions of California. Of every ten letters he receives, three are from Pentecostalists accusing him of being the devil's agent, three are from people saying his books changed their lives, and four are from people asking him to be their guru. 'I could earn a lot, more than I earn from the books, but I had this experience in '74 and I don't defy these powers. I have four disciples because I have to, because I'm in a tradition.' The tradition into which he was initiated is *Regnum Aginus Mundi*, founded by Catholic Templars in the *annis mirabilis* of 1492. 'It's an oral tradition. It's easier to maintain intact that way than if they write it down.'

Among their precepts are: we cannot delegate any power; we must take risks; we must pay . . . but he is uncomfortable explaining this to me. 'This . . . *language*,' he says, 'doesn't speak to your conscious mind, it speaks to your unconscious mind.'

Twenty-Two

The *Beijoquero*, the Serial Kisser, is a Brazilian saint who blesses with a kiss.

He has kissed Pelé and Xuxa, the most important people in Brazil. He has kissed the rock stars Peter Gabriel and Sting. Gabriel looked on in helpless bewilderment as the security men bundled the *Beijoquero* back into the crowd. Sting was equally surprised, but kept on singing. The *Beijoquero* comes to their concerts and waits by the stage. He waits by the exits, and then he rushes up and kisses them, in front of TV cameras and photographers. Who is the Serial Kisser? A former Rio taxi driver, he arrived penniless from Portugal as a youth. His address was an open sewer until he received his divine mission – to kiss people. No one is safe from his kiss: passers-by on the streets of Rio, presidents in their palaces.

When Frank Sinatra came to Brazil, the *Beijoquero* read in the papers that he feared the bullets of an assassin. He resolved to give Sinatra a kiss, to show the singer, and the world, they had nothing to fear from Brazilians. In front of the TV cameras, he clambered up on stage and gave Sinatra a kiss. Sinatra pushed him away in disgust.

Afterwards, the *Beijoquero* received a thorough beating, first from the security guards and then the police. Through the kiss, he found his worthless life redeemed, though his wife left him. He became, inevitably, a celebrity; he bares his scars on TV shows as though they were stigmata, marks of the physical suffering he has endured to impart his kisses, the blessings of a fifty-year-old lunatic. A psychiatrist tried to cure him with a mix of antidepressants and rationalism. For a while, there were no more kisses.

When the Pope came to Brazil, the *Beijoquero* announced he was going to kiss him too. The psychiatric cure had made him feel worse than he felt before, so he decided to go back to being the *Beijoquero*. Figuring security around the Pope would be tight in Rio, he went to Brasilia for His Holiness's appearance there. But the police found him loitering on the route of the popemobile and gave him a good, dissuasive beating before putting him on a bus back to Rio. Perhaps the Holy Father still knew nothing of his eventual love assassin. Surely, had he known, he would have suffered the Serial Kisser to come unto him.

Back in Rio, broke, but still determined to kiss the Pope, the *Beijoquero* announced he would make a public subscription to raise the money for the bus fare north, to catch the Pope at another of his shows. He stood on the street with a placard. The money poured in. Brazilians have a touching faith in beautiful fools. The money didn't stop flowing in. The Serial Kisser appeared on TV, and someone, an ex-journalist, showed up with an offer to manage him. Newspapers that ran the story were deluged with mail. Everyone wanted the Serial Kisser to achieve his goal of kissing the Pope. It was a kiss from all of Brazil. From the beautiful fool in everyone.

The police were tense. They had tightened the security cordon around John Paul II. They were taking seriously the threat to kiss the Pope. The Holy Father had almost reached the end of his tour in Manaus, in the middle of the Amazon jungle. He was far from the media centres, and so perhaps he thought he could relax his vigilance. He sat in his episcopal throne in the middle of the local football field, listening to the choir, the band, the drummers from the Samba School, waiting for the last rays of the sun and the lights to go on around the field, which would be his cue to get up and walk across to the podium, where his lectern was ready to be picked out by the lasers . . . It was as he walked across the field that the *Beijoquero* struck. He ran on to the soccer field, chased by security guards. The chief representative of Christ on earth didn't see him until it was too late: he turned, startled and unsure . . .

Overcome, the Serial Kisser fell to his knees and kissed the hem of the Pope's robe. He was after all a beautiful Catholic fool. He was dragged off by police and given a tremendous beating. But he rode the bus back to Rio a few days later, a king!

It was his greatest exploit. Much easier than kissing Collor – a deal fixed later on between his new manager and the presidential office – though there was no police beating to endure that time. He was hauled away and let out the back door.

Now he has a new wife, a professional nurse who looks after his wounds. When George Bush came to Rio for the Earth Summit in 1992, to explain that he couldn't allow US businessmen to lose their competitive edge by having to pay for an environmental clean-up, the *Beijoquero* tried to kiss him too. But security this time was too tight. There were warships in the bay with their guns trained on the *favelas*.

The Serial Kisser is a modern Brazilian saint. His message is one of universal human brotherhood. He is a minor TV star, as any modern saint would have to be. In North America, his bullets would be made of steel, but in Brazil, they are harmless projectiles, custard-pie kisses.

Twenty-Three

São Luis is the capital of the state of Maranhão – a small city, hot and poor, languishing under the equator on the tropical rump of Brazil. Not as big as Belem to the west, that colonial gold tooth set in the immense mouth of the Amazon, nor as important, historically, or as at ease culturally, as Fortaleza or Recife to the southeast.

The population is mainly, but not quite, black. They are *mestiços*, *mulattos*, *mamelucos* or *caboclos*: old words tinged with different shades of opprobrium. First it was European, largely Portuguese men who mixed with the Indian women. This mixing was accomplished with the sword, usually, with brutality – but sometimes also with tenderness. Indian daughters were sold for trinkets or bottles of liquor, or gave themselves to the men from the East with their metal chests, tall and powerful men who conspired with strange beasts, the horses. These men found the women raw, beautiful and irresistibly compliant. The men of the women had hidden or been shot or torn apart by the teeth of dogs. And the women were quite naked, apart from some threaded beads at the crotch; an unconscious nakedness, wild and tantalising to the men who stepped ashore after half a year at sea, in a New World. The apparent amorality of the women delivered Catholic sinners of guilt, the shiploads of thieves and wharf rats, orphans and whores, second sons and arch-seducers.

It absolved such moral trifles as rape, adultery, bigamy, incest and murder in a humid sexual fever. Sometimes the Indian men took revenge, which often ended in their massacre. But the revenge of Indian women was more subtle. It was visited on the descendants of the European settlers, who became less than European – but also less than Indian.

In the south, in the state of São Paulo, they were known as *mamelucos*. Women of the Tapuia and the Tupi-Guarani, whose men were dead or gone, gave birth to the children of Portuguese settlers. This bastard race was quite distinct, and thought to resemble the Mamelukes, a military class that sprang originally from a group of Caucasian slaves to rule Egypt from 1254 for six centuries, whose women were noted for their beauty. There is an engraving of a *mameluco* woman in a book by the German artist Von Meier that provides a glossary of racial features in Brazil in the nineteenth century. The woman is carrying a pot on her head and wears rudimentary clothing that distinguishes her from her Indian mother. But she has inherited the Amerindian features – a flattened nose and broad cheekbones – and a soft, innocent gaze. There are few faces quite like that in Brazil now. But it's a face that's everywhere, that has become generalised, glimpsed in millions of faces. And the distinctive name for that face has been lost in a generality. They are the *caboclos*, who serve at tables and man the petrol pumps, wearing the same soft expression, the trusting smile that readily breaks out, accompanied by the Brazilian national gesture, a thumbs-up. Is it the smile of the liberated European spirit, I wondered, every time I took my change, or the resigned and suppliant Indian one?

Nilson was a *caboclo*, a *Nordestino*. The one indignity was heaped upon the other, like dung on dung, refuse on refuse. And Nilson accepted it, compliant like his forebear, the Indian woman who had submitted or given herself to a European bluebeard. As a result, Nilson was condemned to come to the city, to work like a pack horse, to cough black dust from his lungs and grow thin and weak; to ride on the rooftops of trains, to make love in ditches and make his home under a freeway interchange. All this because he had the good fortune to be born in our century.

This is not something that Nilson was conscious of, this compliancy that he had inherited, nor did he ever think about how it had come to him. It never occurred to him that he was the son of an Indian mother and a white father, that the jungle was his mother and the sea was his father. It was never the other way around. Once, Nilson had an Indian grandfather, but that was two or three centuries ago.

And so he complied. It was a question of time. The Indian woman knew what the Portuguese bluebeard had yet to realise; that time had stopped as he passed out of the busy Christian world, with its directive to multiply, to create the world in the image of the European God. And the conquering settler only dimly realised at the end, as he surveyed the wooden world he had constructed and where he would die, that he had passed into and back to where there was no time, no hurry, no importance, where the world was created anew every morning, and; thinking he had penetrated – the woman, the jungle – he had been enveloped and consumed.

In Nilson's veins ran the blood of the European bluebeard and the Indian girl, the blood of Dutchmen who overran the coast for a time, and whose expulsion helped unite the captaincies of Brazil. The blood of Frenchmen too, freelance adventurers of all sorts, swords for hire, men who had left their mistakes behind in Europe, looking for wealth or solace. The lugubrious daughters of the forest, whether bought, bartered or won with a simple gift of beads, became their mates, and often enough they gave their children back to the forest, happy to forget European practice, enticed by the promiscuous nature around them into a parody of baronial prerogative.

In Nilson's veins ran sugar too. A few precious grains of the white crystal, the privilege of a prince's tongue until the enterprising, scientific Dutch drained the swampy delta of the Demarara River, planted cane and harvested death. But the Indians of the *Mata Atlantica* were disinclined to labour on the great plantations. Having lost the war, having seen their fellows slaughterd, their settlements burnt, their women and children herded away, what point in staying to witness the settler's ultimate purpose?

202

What purpose the hissing, boiling sugar refinery, spewing sweet black clouds and scorching the tropical air, to produce the white powdery crystals that melted on the tongue and burned in the heart? They fled inland, where the fish still jumped from the rivers to greet them and fruit still fell into their hands when they were thirsty. They took with them their customs and rites (thought to have nothing to impart), their blood (thought not to exist), and their seed. There is no lower status in the New World than to be born the son of an Indian man. This has become a privilege reserved for Indians.

The Indian or *caboclo* children born in captivity – who sensed somehow that their Indian fathers had been cowed or that their Portuguese fathers would spurn them – were docile but unproductive. Caught between the whip and the dogs they worked without will. The effort that built the plantations that began where the sun rose and ended where it set, the houses that rose tall as oaks in the sky, seemed to them futile, insignificant. In impressively large numbers, they preferred death.

But the West Africans who came in stinking ships and even greater numbers to replace them, chained to their dead, chained to the post in the market square, chained to the house, chained together under the blazing sun, were more sturdy. They worked harder. Perhaps it was simply that they had fear, unlike the Indian men. Not quite naked like Indian men, they wore loin-cloths, a concession to public modesty. Fear had somehow been instilled in them. They feared the sting of the sword. But whether they were born afraid or it had been branded into them like the marks on their skin – the slashes on their cheeks that they made themselves or the weals made by the branding iron – they were afraid. And as such – and like everything that was imported – they cost more. So the master was more careful with them. The foreman would have their injuries deducted from his wages. This was the only esteem they enjoyed, the only weapon. Other than to be born the son of an Indian man, there was no lower status in the New World than to be born the son of a black man.

If you were lucky, you became the playmate of the master's children and a common nickname for you would be Punchbag.

203

Later you went to the master's bed, then to his fields, to cut the yellow cane that grew high as a house in muddy canals thick with mosquitos and dark as an eclipse. For sustenance, you sucked the juice out of the yellow cane, sweeter than any fruit, till your teeth were black. Then you sucked with your gums. Sucking the sticky sap all day, you became enslaved to the cane, and your eyes gleamed and your jaw clenched and you sweated molasses to feast the flies.

The Africans came and there was more pooling of genes. And there were more attempts by the white colonists to preserve the pretence of racial purity. In North America laws defined Quadroons and Octoroons as black: an eighth drop of black blood and you were black. It took four generations – and no backslidin' – for a black to have white descendants. In Dixie, black people had to wait for the Civil Rights marches of the Sixties before they could ride the same buses or sit on the same park bench as whites. In Brazil, the racial hierarchy wasn't coded in law, but existed despite the insistence of Brazilian authorities that Brazil was a white nation.

As European women were few and constrained in tight Catholic families, Portuguese men turned their sexual attention to African women, producing little mulatto children, who might be both the seed and the slave of the master. Africans and Indians or *mamelucos* produced *cabures*. Children descended from all three were called *mestiços*. Black men aspired to marry women with brown skin, *mameluco* women who couldn't find themselves a husband with lighter skin, so that their children would be white. In this way, Brazil became a white nation.

One of these men was Nilson's grandfather, a century or two ago.

Over nearly four centuries, an estimated 15 million Africans came to Brazil. They vastly outnumbered the Indians of the coastal regions and their European masters. But Brazil is now a white nation. In the last census in 1990, the population of 150 million described itself as 54 per cent white and 39 per cent *caboclo* (white and Indian) or mulatto (white and black). Only 5 per cent defined themselves as black.

Because slavery was abolished only a hundred years ago in

Brazil, there are many photos of slaves. This lends their plight a reality, a banality, that no number of paintings or engravings could convey. The photos show the gardens of the *fazendas*, with white and black children playing. The black children are well-dressed, playmates for the children of the owner. The men and women too seem to be dressed for the photographer's visit. Sometimes they are domestics, valets and butlers. When farm workers are shown, it is always as though the scene has been prepared. They stand stiffly in groups, in tatty shirts, straw hats and with their trousers held by rope belts, with bare feet. There are a few interiors of simple wooden huts, with hefty women standing by the ovens. There is nothing degrading or even unusual in the photos, except that the people in them belonged to someone else, they were part of an inventory, like the walls around them, listed with the livestock and machinery.

Their lives on the coffee plantations of São Paulo were probably better than those of the slaves on the sugar estates of the *Nordeste* – the *fazendas* with their grand houses made of hard, dark-brown wood to the plans of the mansions and villas of the Mediterranean – or of those who came south in the eighteenth century to Minas Gerais, the name of which means General Mines. When the gold shout was heard, adventurers and failed sugar barons came south with their slaves to pan the rivers of Minas. They employed a wood-framed construction, a kind of bench that breached the river, on which, under a long canopy, sat a row of white foremen. In front of them, waist deep in the water and without any shade, stood the slaves, panning for gold.

Twenty-Four

To reach the Amazon River, I come to Brazil via an unusual route, from Guyana, the former British colony on the northeast coast of South America. I am overjoyed to be leaving this swampy, confused country with its mountains of lost paperwork and backed-up racial enmities, to be back again in a land of easy-going lubricity.

It has taken a week to get a seat on one of Guyana's two planes, which had Perspex taped to the broken window and two goats in the back, and my relief to have left the fetid coast and reached the interior is combined with high anticipation, for I am on my way to the equatorial rain forest.

I cross the Tacutu River, which forms the border, in a small boat and hitch a ride in the back of a truck to the frontier station, twenty miles away, near the town of Bonfim. We drive at full tilt across the dry savannahs that lie south of the Roraima Mountains. It's dusk and there is a full moon rising; a large, spectral moon that dominates the mountain ridges to the north. The night is full of the beauty of an empty world. Behind the ridges of the Sierra Pacaraima is Mount Roraima, 9000 feet high, where Raleigh was convinced he would find a kingdom to plunder equal in splendour to that of the Incas, which had made the glory and the Black Legend of Spain. The huge, laughing moon poured its dreamlight into a hidden lake, in which on nights such as this the chief would bathe, emerging glowing with gold, his majesty El Dorado.

At the frontier post, a barrier across a dirt road – although there are no fences on either side – the border guards punch my name into a computer linked to the Brasilsat. In the last few months, satellites over Brazil have been sending back alarming infra-red pictures of clouds of purple smoke from the Amazon region that spreads to the south, a region so vast not even satellites can see it in its entirety.

From Bonfim, a bus takes me to Boa Vista, capital of the state of Roraima, four hours south across the savannah. It's midnight by the time I arrive. Near the bus station at the edge of the town, I find a hotel of unfaced concrete, the familiar unfinished style of the Brazilian urban periphery. The room is grey and bare except for a bed, a naked lightbulb and a fan to keep the mosquitoes away. In the bar downstairs, grizzled, sunburnt men are drinking and playing cards. On the tables in front of them are newish leather shoulder bags, stuffed with something, and evidently important enough to be kept in sight.

The next day, I take a taxi for the mile or so to the centre of the town, a public square too large to traverse after 10 a.m. because of the heat, in which groups of men seem to be stranded under the trees. Boa Vista appears to be enjoying a long siesta, lazing in the Hispanic lassitude noted by Evelyn Waugh, who came here in the Thirties and saw nothing but *vaqueiros*, Brazilian cowboys. For lunch, there is nothing but *filet mignon*, served with beans, rice and *farofa*. And for dinner, and for breakfast. At first, I assume that the rough-hewn men dining with casual-looking businessmen are cowboys. On one side of the central square is Boa Vista's best hotel. Running off it is a wide shopping street, wild-west style, in which they are just now removing the wooden posts because there are no longer any horses. Down the smaller streets are travel agents that double as moneychangers. Inside one of these, the owner is seated at a desk with a cowboy. The cowboy has opened his small leather satchel, like the ones I had seen last night, to take out a small pouch. He pours the contents of the pouch into his palm, little glittering stones, diamonds. In the open bag, I see the barrel of a gun.

'They prospect in the mountains. They come here now because the rates are good,' the owner tells me, carefully putting away his electronic scales. 'Otherwise, when rates are better there, they go north to Venezuela.'

The owner was one of the businessmen I had seen in the restaurant. At dinner, I look more closely at the small leather bags on the tables. I soon recognise the bulge of revolvers. The faces of the men are sunburnt, lined and scarred, but relaxed. Their clothes are fresh and creased. The men are not fat but eat heartily at the huge plates of steak. These are *garimpeiros*, gold prospectors who have struck rich. Though it seems too placid to be in any hurry, Boa Vista in 1978 is in the middle of a gold rush. A few hundred miles to the west, in the territory of the Yanomami, an Indian war has broken out.

From space, satellites have seen the precious dust lying at the bottom of rivers in the Yanomami territories. The shout has been heard all the way across the forest, all the way to the *Nordeste*, and in the south. Instead of heading for the shanties of São Paulo, hardy, crazier types have decided to try their luck up here in Roraima.

In the bar of the hotel on the main square, a group of *garimpeiros* are drinking whisky. They are veterans, who have been working the *garimpos* or prospecting sites for years. One of them is a North American. Rambo, the others call him. 'We're the last of the '49ers!' he jokes, swallowing from his tumbler. 'There were maybe a thousand men out there before. When I first came we used to work with pans, like in the Klondike, then we brought the dredgers up the rivers . . . Now we fly 'em in.' They run profitable set-ups, leasing their old sifting contraptions to the new arrivals and flying in supplies in return for a half-share of the profits. 'I've got fifty men out there,' says Rambo. 'They're gettin' eaten by mosquitoes now while I'm sittin' here!' The new arrivals, *caboclos* from the Amazon region and the *Nordeste*, wait to be recruited in the bars out by the airport, or, if they have the money, buy rides on the Cessnas to anywhere the pants-seat pilots want to put them down. Some have come from the Serra Pelada, the huge, open-cast mine in the state of Pará, where thousands of *garimpeiros* worked clambering up ladders and over

208

each other in the mud. Now it's been photographed by Sebastião Salgado – and the men who once extracted with their bare hands six pounds of gold a week have gone, smiling gold-toothed smiles and laced with gold chains like the men in the hotel, while those who remain scratch out a few ounces, hoping to amass enough to be able to afford to leave their *favela* in the midst of the rain forest.

The men hoot with laughter when I ask how much money they're making. 'Wanna try?' says one. 'I can put you on a plane tomorrow . . . ' They order another bottle of imported whisky. Within a few years, there will be up to 40,000 *garimpeiros* prospecting in the lands of the Yanomami. The largest indigenous nation still extant in the Americas, numbering more than 22,000, with a way of life unchanged since time began, the Yanomami have lived until now with practically no contact. The activities of the men drinking imported whisky are about to change that, bringing disease and death to the Indians and devastation to the environment. The mercury used to separate the gold dust, once introduced in the rivers, finds its way into fishes and plants, and the dredgers leave fine silt that clogs the freshwater streams, causing them to turn into stagnant, fetid pools.

Among the men are two with Indian grandparents. It was something I was to hear often from *caboclos*. To admit to an Indian parent, it seems, would be too much of a stigma. Paulo wears Ray-Ban aviators and Odonel has gold charms dangling from his felt hat. They say the Yanomami are their friends. 'We're out there in the wild like them. We used to trade with them and pay them' – with what, I wonder? – 'to carry supplies.' Odonel says they warn their men to beware of the natives, but what can they do? Paulo tells me about some *garimpeiros* who found an Indian *maloca* – the large thatched houses around which tribal families of between thirty to 100 Indians live – that was empty except for women and a few old men. They tied up the men and raped some of the women. A few days later, the Indians came for revenge. They killed two of the *garimpeiros* – 'They had arrows and knives and rifles that they get from the missionaries' – before the rest of the group could flee. The *garimpeiros* returned to the *maloca*, which the Indians were dismantling to move elsewhere, and killed four of them before they were satisfied.

'They are ignorant,' says Paulo. 'If they were my men, I would have left them out there to die. There's enough room for everybody.'

A permit is needed to prospect, but what is a piece of paper in the world's biggest forest? The *garimpeiros* easily cross from national land into regions that are marked out in a federal bureau somewhere as the reserve of the Yanomami, and supposedly protected by the army. 'Ha!' says Rambo, who turns out to be a Vietnam veteran. 'The army doesn't give a shit. Tell you what, *they* give the *garimpeiros* machine guns.' He treats me to a lesson in Brazilian military psychology. 'The *caboclos* are like the South Vietnamese. And the Indians, well, they aren't the Viet Cong exactly. They aren't even the Mohicans. But the priests are stirring them up, and the army's worried about the border, 'cause there isn't one really. I'll tell you why they're worried, 'cause the gold ain't nothing. There's uranium there, that's why. Now . . . If I could get a piece of that!'

'What would you do, Rambo?' jokes Odonel.

'I'd blow the world to kingdom come!'

The Yanomamis, who were only contacted in the Seventies, have experienced the atomic bomb. In 1990, television cameras were brought to the *malocas* to film whole villages, hundreds of Indians, prostrate with malaria, a disease they had never encountered before contact. Like the Indians who greeted Cortez, they had no resistance to such infections. And with the fevers come starvation. A nurse lifted the arm of a baby, like the stem of a wilted flower. At a dispensary in Boa Vista, sixty Yanomamis lay sick with malaria, tuberculosis and venereal diseases. The increasingly violent contacts with the *garimpeiros* were blamed. The federal government sent in medical teams. Ivanaldo Yanomami, an interpreter with the federal Indian bureau, gave evidence to a government commission.

'Many *garimpeiros* carry diseases and many Yanomami are dying. Many *garimpeiros* are criminals. They carry arms, revolvers, rifles, and the state police take the side of the *garimpeiros*.' A missionary talked of genocide. 'The lands of the Yanomami were being stolen,' he said, 'and their women raped.' The president of the *garimpeiro*

210

syndicate in Boa Vista accused foreign missionaries of being subversive agents. The bishop of Boa Vista and the visiting federal police chief were besieged in the episcopal palace by *garimpeiros* protesting their rights to exploit the gold reserve.

The following year, 1991, President Collor decreed the creation of a reserve of 94,000 square kilometres for the Yanomami, one of the 278 reserves he was obliged to create under the terms of the new constitution. For the first time in five centuries, the Indians became again masters of their territory. Despite their fears that the Indians would one day bid for succession with their valuable tin mountain of Surucucu, the generals obeyed the presidential order to bomb more than 100 airfields in the region and expel all but a few thousand *garimpeiros*.

———————

I had intended to fly down to Manaus – the former rubber capital of the Amazon, now one of the centres of Latin America's electronics industry – but decide instead to take the bus. The Mercedes bus has had the fairings removed from underneath, leaving the axles and suspension visible, for reasons that would become evident the next day.

It's 11 p.m. when we set off, hurtling along an asphalt road through the rocky savannahs, past cattle ranches separated by clumps of forest that grow thicker as we speed south through the dark. There are two buses travelling in a convoy, the newer of the two behind. Later, it will be clear how much of a joy this speed was for the drivers.

At 4 a.m., the buses pull into a station in Caracarai, on the banks of Rio Branco. The drivers sling their hammocks under the coaches and go to sleep. Those passengers with hammocks find trees and the rest of us sleep in the coaches. Most of the passengers are young men, coming or going from jobs. As I fall asleep, I can hear nearby an incessant, rolling thunder.

A few hours later, I wake to see the source of this roar, the Rio Branco. In the soft dawn light we cross the river on a wooden raft slung between guide ropes, pulled by a diesel motor on the shore.

On the opposite banks, the forest is waiting, a green wall broken only by the wooden jetty. The buses go first, empty, followed by the passengers, as a sudden current could easily sweep the fragile raft away. The river is 200 yards wide and the current strong, though we are more than 300 miles from the point where it joins the Rio Negro, in a swirling eddy of milky and dark waters, to flow another 300 miles and into the Amazon.

Once across the river, our journey begins. The road is uncovered, just a flattened heap of red dirt, pitted and holed by the rain, a constant obstacle course for the drivers, two in each bus, who work in shifts and have to pay careful attention, swerving and veering to avoid the worst of the holes. I sit at the front, fascinated, full of admiration for the drivers in their pink shirts with the company badge on the pocket. It's the hardest job I've ever seen anyone do, a feat of sustained concentration. A mistake could mean a skid and hours lost if not worse, for the banks of the red dirt mound that is the road are high. Some stretches of the road are worse than others, made treacherous and washed away to mud in parts by the rain. Even though the drivers make the journey twice a week, it's always a different journey, because the contours of the road change every day with the rains. The drivers scoff at my interest, and the passengers laugh. It's not unusual, they say, to have to push the bus for hours in the torrential rains of the wet season, when parts of the road turn into rivers of mud. This is why the fairings have been removed, to prevent the mud clogging underneath.

The reason for their phlegmatic indifference to the half-made road I take to be characteristic Brazilian pride and make-do at first, as we plough for hours through the green, uncaring forest. But the muddy red swathe, our presence on it, the bus and the people, in the midst of a huge, hot, humid ocean, soon begin to seem heroic.

Intermittently, the walls of this ocean recede either side of the road, where the forest has been burnt. Instead of the forest, there is a parched vista of twisted, dead trees, many still smoking above the scorched, ash-blackened earth. The tallest of these are the heveas, the rubber trees, whose trunks and branches survive the conflagration to be cut down and used as lumber. Everywhere, the ground is smouldering – the purple smoke seen from the satellites – and in some areas the fires are still burning. These clearings are the beginnings of ranches and farms. The contorted, charred remains of the trees, and the mounting midday heat, combine for the moment to create a hellish landscape of terrifying desolation and apparently purposeless destruction.

Along some stretches of the road, the clearings are more frequent and, gradually, different characteristics emerge, giving an instant archaeology of the Amazonian settlement of the last twenty years, for the cultivation cycle is short, requiring a tremendous effort for just a few years' reward. On some clearings, the smouldering fires have died down and clearing has begun, by horse or tractor as there are few large machines. On some, farmhouses have been built, log cabins with wooden corrals for horses and pens for pigs and goats. On these farms, there is nothing from our century, not a tractor or a sack of stockfeed. Apart from the equatorial heat, there is nothing to distinguish them from the farms of the North American pioneers of the early nineteenth century.

All journeys, observed Levi-Strauss, are journeys across time and through societies. Travelling, it's possible to see the world in different stages of development, heading towards the same destination. From the windows of the bus I can speed through American history. But these farms will never reach our century . . . Many have already been abandoned, as the land, which is essentially sand, after producing crops for a few years, will support only cattle, and the impoverished settlers lack the resources to keep herds on a viable scale, so they begin again, burning more land, or give up and move to the cities. The abandoned farmhouses are left to the ghosts of dashed hopes, gradually overgrown by a dry, desultory tangle of vines that spread from the trees that were spared for shade. Patches of scrub grow in what were temporarily fields, many of which were never cleared of their burnt stumps. And, if nothing else happens, this will be the view from the road for the next hundred years, the length of time it will take for the forest to grow back.

Highway BR 174 – the road between Boa Vista and Manaus – is part of the *Transamazônica*, the highway planned to link Caracas on the shores of the Caribbean with Rio, São Paulo and Buenos Aires to the south. It was the first trunk route in South America that didn't run east or west to the ports, to ship raw materials out of what Eduardo Galeano has called the open veins of the continent, but was supposed to link South America with itself.

Work on BR 174 commenced in the early Seventies, a torrid enterprise headed by army engineers as the result of a decision hatched in the Escola Superior da Guerra to cut a swathe through the virgin jungle. Still unfinished when the money ran out in '82, it was hugely expensive, and is now massively underused. In twenty-four hours, I saw a handful of lorries and two cars, solitary, ageing Volkswagen Beetles, going who knows where in the middle of the world's largest tropical rain forest.

The military had strategic aims in building this and other roads through the Amazon basin. They wanted to confirm Brazilian hegemony over a region that represents 40 per cent of the national territory and to facilitate the extraction of its resources. The generals also saw in this a potential solution to the chronic poverty of the *Nordeste*, encouraging the 'wild' migration of landless peasants. The labourers who built the roads were given plots of land alongside; these are now the desolate, lifeless clearings.

Suddenly, we come to a settlement, a small town of log houses and streets of red mud. There are giant yellow earth-movers parked to one side of the road and, opposite, horses tied to wooden rails outside a store. The bus pulls in for a break and I get out to buy some fruit from a wooden shack by the side of the road.

A group of teenage girls have been waiting for the bus. They are *caboclos*, Portuguese and Indian. They approach me with frank curiosity.

'Where are you from?' one of them asks.

When I tell them, they don't believe me.

'Take us with you,' they joke. 'Go on.'

As we talk, the bus leaves . . .

214

I look around in desperation. There are a few streets leading away from the main road for a few hundred yards and behind, all around, a wall of green. There is no perspective in the forest, no bearing, just the fertile, exuberant foliage. We had been rolling for five hours already, and we weren't set to arrive in Manaus until the middle of the night. For a moment, I feel as though I am genuinely stranded, not just in a town that isn't on any map, an island in the ocean, but in another time, of horses and mud. The girls laugh, seeing my alarm. Then I remember that we had been travelling in a convoy and there is another bus behind.

Relieved, I treat the girls to sodas. The town has been here five years and life in it is predictably dull. Their fathers trade goods with the farmers along the road. They want to go to Manaus. What's it like? I ask. 'Legal,' they agree. Cool. One of the girls will be going to college there. The others curl their lips as she tells me this. I realise that television has taught them how to behave, taught them the latest slang, taught them to be bored here in the depths of the rain forest. Levi-Strauss would be dismayed. It's no longer even possible to travel through time. Television has brought everybody up to date.

Nor is it possible to traverse different ages of society. The girls all wear the same T-shirts. Despite different levels of social development, all Brazil seems to wear the same T-shirts, given away by the last political caravan to pass through.

Gradually, the vistas of burnt forest cease as the bus ploughs south along the red dirt road to development, through the hot afternoon, through the undisturbed forest. We cross the Jauaperi River, inching forward on wooden boards barely wide enough for the wheels of the bus, supported by a bare, rickety structure. I try not to look at the water flowing beneath the windows, and wonder how much the drivers get paid.

The hours pass, the heat and humidity become intense, and the road doesn't get any better. There has been nothing but forest now for more than a hundred miles. The land rises and falls gently, and the road cuts through a few low ridges and crosses deep bogs. The equatorial sun dazzles, holding the tremendous dampness of the forest at bay.

What I didn't see in the forest: summer swallows swooping in the treetops, fluttering through the high, leafy canopy; gaggles of monkeys running up and down the trees, a circus of busy laughter, or swinging from branch to branch in gay defiance of any predator other than those with arrows or guns – for monkeys are easy to catch and tasty to eat. I didn't see any of the snakes that slither noiselessly through the dead leaves, or wait tangled over treacherous bogs, the boas with jaws that dislocate sufficiently wide to swallow a man, with bodies long enough to take weeks to digest such a feast. I saw none of these things, but I wasn't disappointed.

Nor did I hear anything, though I listened hard at dusk and thought I heard an owl, announcing the yellow moon. It surely was my imagination, for owls are rare and their spooky hoots filled the Indians with foreboding. I didn't hear a jaguar baying or even a parrot guffawing at the passing of the bus. It was only later, moving quietly on the rivers, that I saw and heard some of these things. And even on the rivers, the magisterial stillness reigns.

Instead, as the day began to cool, the forest gave up its secret. I could feel its overwhelming presence not through my senses, but in my lungs . . . With the sun low, the air grew cold and damp, a dampness that flooded my chest. I felt I was drowning, thousands of miles from the sea. The air seemed to turn to water, a water lighter and fresher than any other, a moisture that invaded my clothes and penetrated the pores of my skin. I was asphyxiated by the primeval, life-giving humidity.

Jorge Amado describes the forest as a sea that had never been explored, locked in its own mystery, lovely, radiant, young, like a virgin, and ardently desired. He describes the lianas, mires and prickly thorns keeping guard over age-old trunks, and wonders at the emotions that must have seized the hearts of men who cut the first trails through her, hacking at vines, sloshing through bogs and streams under the leafy canopy a hundred feet above, rapidly losing all bearings.

I grew scared as night fell on the red dirt road, a fear I hadn't felt since I was a child, a child's fear of the night. I had travelled much farther than I expected, back to the beginning of the world. I felt as though I had seen the history of the world in a day, a long,

216

hallucinatory day. Now that day was ending and even older night was beginning, the night of the forest.

We crossed the Alalau River, 200 miles north of Manaus, on one of the rough wooden bridges with only a few planks for the wheels of the bus. Three employees of the FUNAI, the federal Indian agency, were killed here in 1973, felled by the foot-long curare-tipped darts blown from seven-foot pipes with great range and accuracy. To build BR 174, the army's 6th Battalion of Civil Engineers had to traverse the territory of the Waimiri-Atroari. They were reckoned to number 6000 at the turn of the century, and there were still an estimated 3000 when the roadworks began. The FUNAI agents, including latterday half-Indian scouts who spoke their language, had been sent in after the massacre of missionaries who had also failed to convince the Waimiri-Atroari of the virtues of our roadbuilding civilisation.

In 1944, the Waimiri-Atroari had massacred a survey team from the 4th American army who came to log the geological riches of an area that would by the Eighties be the largest mining exploitation in the state of Amazonas, the biggest of the five Amazon states.

The FUNAI agents were killed in reprisal for the attempted rape of Indian women by labourers who had come across one of their villages. They gave them pornographic magazines and danced naked in front of the women. Gilberto Pinto, in charge of 'contact' with the tribe during construction, complained to the army, warning of the dangers of any encounter with them, but the army merely issued its men with guns. A year later, Pinto and six of his assistants were found dead at the attraction post on the Abonari River. The army said they had been killed by arrows, but the corpses were never seen by independent witnesses.

With the death of Pinto, the building of BR-174 went ahead unhindered. Attraction posts were established in the mineral-rich region to the west of the road and, despite the protests of the Russell tribunal in Amsterdam, the government annexed 30 per cent of the territory it had 'granted' them in 1971, to build the Pitinga mining complex. The rest of their lands were declared off-limits. By the time the plight of the Waimiri had become the theme of an International Indian Week in 1983, sponsored by the Russell tribunal, the mining complex was a veritable private city in the middle of the jungle north of Manaus, with 10,000 inhabitants and its own hydro-electric power from the Balbina dam.

In 1986, the last missionaries – liberationists who had defied the government and were organising the Waimiri to defend their lands – were expelled by the FUNAI, at the request of Indians favourable to national integration. It was a typical manipulation of the FUNAI, which is meant to act in consultation with Indians, who are put up in luxury hotels in Brasilia so they can better appreciate the benefits of integration. Two villages of 100 or so Waimiri were resettled to avoid the rising waters of the dam. They were given an indemnity by Eletronorte, plus motorboats, chainsaws, axes and televisions, with a guarantee of free servicing for twenty-five years. The televisions will help them forget that their nation now only comprises 400 people.

Twenty-Five

___

The Indians were murdered and enslaved but always held for the colonists the key to a powerful mystery. The same mystery that we in the north now want to hear them sing, perhaps for the last time: the mystery of our own alienation from nature.

The colonists wanted to mark the world, to leave a trace of their passage in it. They wanted to clear the jungle and build settlements and roads and pass on property. The Indians wanted only to pass through the world, like a snake or a bird, without disturbing it.

Fabulous birds appeared along the shoreline, birds that made no sound and no movement, watching the approach of the ships through a dense green curtain.

Glimpsed through the undergrowth along the shoreline, that's how the natives of the New World appeared at first to the sailors.

The deep red feathers about the neck of the toucan were especially prized by the Indians. Disguised as birds, they could go about the forest unperceived. Part of the jungle, they were invisible in the jungle. Or, disguised as fierce cats, wearing their skins and claws, they could stalk prey . . .

Safe in their invisible plumage, they watched the approach of the ships from behind screeds and fronds, assuming that the tall boats and the men who stood on them were part of the same immutable world as themselves, with everything in its place, each a part of the other.

The Indians had no inkling of Christian egotism. They were – or appeared to the European sailors to be – quite passive. They were easily subdued, and led to slaughter, despite the pleas of the Dominican friar Bartholomew de Las Casas, who fifty years after Columbus' voyage wrote to the king of Spain denouncing the destruction of the native populations.

Two centuries later, in 1743, when Charles de la Condamine sailed up the Amazon – then still called by one of its Indian names, the Marañon – there were no more tribes hostile to Europeans along the banks. They had all been 'descended', led to the altar – an expression which seems to acknowledge that they had fallen from grace into the hands of the friars. Having come to the missions, hundreds of thousands wasted and died, prey to epidemics or an unaccountable lassitude. But the missionaries weren't troubled. They had done their work, and could die contentedly themselves from the malarial fevers. The souls of the Indians would no longer return to the ether, to be reincarnated as an animal or a plant.

La Condamine was on his way to Quito, where he had been sent by Louis XV to measure the circumference of the world at the Equator, a project which, like the scientific triumph of the moon landings in our century, would confirm the light of reason. He regarded the Indians he met with little pity. Scrutinising their traits with the objectivity of the scientist, he concluded that in the different customs of each tribe or 'nation' was as much to distinguish one from the next as there was to distinguish the different peoples of Europe, who, he reasoned, would all seem alike to an oriental visitor. There were hundreds of tribes. And yet . . .

'I believed that I recognised in all of them the same fundamentals of character,' wrote the enlightened eighteenth-century observer. 'Insensibility is its basis. I cannot decide whether it should be honoured with the name apathy or discredited with that of stupidity. It doubtless arises from their small range of ideas, which do not extend beyond their needs.' He catalogued the evidence before him. The Indians were 'gluttons to the point of voracity, when they have something to satisfy it, but sober when obliged by necessity to be so – they can do without anything and appear to want nothing.' This was not unusual for hunter-gatherers, who, like the jaguars in the forest, would gorge when food was available and fast when it was scarce. 'Pusillanimous poltroons to excess,' he called them, 'unless carried away by drunkenness. Enemies of work, indifferent to all motives of glory, honour or gratitude.'

But he was failing to observe the native value system here, which had its own codes of hospitality and respect. Nor did it occur to him to ask why they should be interested in European concepts of valour. 'Solely concerned with the immediate object and always influenced by it; without care for the future; incapable of foresight or reflection,' enumerated La Condamine. 'They abandon themselves, if nothing hinders them, to puerile joy, which they manifest by leaps and immoderate bursts of laughter without object or design. They spend their lives without thinking and grow old without emerging from childhood, of which they retain all the defects.'

This, according to La Condamine, was true of both mission Indians and those not yet descended. It seemed perfectly wonderful to other enlightened souls back in France, however, who argued that his account was evidence of the nobility of savages. But the rational philosopher, keen to schematise nature's gestures, could find no useful scientific material here. He left the whole Indian business in the wringing hands of the clergy, where it remained until the science of anthropology, 150 years later, began to look at remaining Indian customs, at first as arguments in support of European history, and then – as anthropologists like Levi-Strauss began to scrutinise the world from the remaining tribal points-of-view – as an argument *against* European history.

And yet La Condamine was impressed by the ways of certain tribes, who cultivated turtles in pools for their soft flesh and, once settled in the missions, traded cacao for trinkets from Europe: knives, mirrors, needles, scissors, combs and other 'small furnishings'. The women crocheted coloured beads into small crotch-aprons, all they used to wear before the missionaries came to hold up

221

before them the mirror of shame, and which, underneath the simple dresses of the mission, they continued to wear. La Condamine found that the Indians, when they wanted to be, were less spendthrift than their Spanish and Portuguese neighbours. He also noted the use by the Omagua of a curious gum, which they moulded into shoes, containers, vessels for drinking and hollow balls that ricocheted with great force. This material they called *Cahout-chou*, rubber, the unique properties of which would temporarily transform the region a hundred years later.

The forest, for the Indians, is a living entity, every plant or animal in it part of the whole, as the fish is part of the river. If the cohesion of the living forest, produced by the constant exchange between these entities, is ruptured – by fires or floods, dynamite or chainsaws – then illness and catastrophe must follow.

The forest is a world of shadows. Its plant and animal denizens are shadows of light, the fierce, invigorating light of the sun. To consume a root or roast an anteater is to take a part of the light, and the light is not infinite, but must lie fallow before it is renewed – gathering energy in the night for a new day. The days and nights in the forest are long, ancient, primeval.

When the Yucuna Indians clear a *chácara*, to grow crops for a few years, it can take many lifetimes for the light to regenerate the original forest. The Indians are careful to leave the edges of the clearing wild, so that it will be impregnated again, and to plant fruit trees to attract birds who bring seeds and droppings. Thus they hand down a common wealth.

How many generations did it take for Indians to acquire the knowledge of forests that would grow back long after their death? In the jungle, the days and nights are uncountable.

Each plant or animal has its guardian, an animistic spirit that looks after prey, wild fruit or crops. Among the Tanimuca people, in the far reaches of the Amazon, the guardian of the jungle is the jaguar, according to the anthropologist Martin von Hildebrand, and the guardian of man is the jaguar man, or shaman.

He is the one who decides when and where a plant should be

gathered or an animal hunted. The spirits that guard the plants and animals can also create sickness and cause accidents.

Anyone who takes too much of any part of the collective whole for himself will become prey to the spirits. Fasting expiates the guilt of the tribe for consuming the forest. Ritual offers their apologies.

Through ritual and intoxication, the shaman communicates with the spirits, to learn of their moods – the anteater who protects animals, the tapir who guards fruits, and the snake who guards the crops. Only then can he advise on where the tribe should hunt or what they should grow. He also rules over the sexual life of the tribe and its health practices. He is the store of the tribe's common wisdom about their environment and themselves.

The animistic shadows of the jungle are long. In Brazil, they stretch all the way to modern-day Rio, where they flicker in the animal figures of the *Jogo do Bicho*, the animal lottery. But the faith that once lit them has been replaced by superstition. They are played for luck.

Nevertheless, in Brazil more so than in the United States, elements of Indian culture have been assimilated by the colonists. The Portuguese language, with a closer sonority to Indian languages than English, has soaked up the Indian names for things – the tropical animals and plants with no European equivalent – as well as the names for places that are all that remain in North America. And like the North Americans, the Brazilians have glorified, for their own glory, the people they destroyed.

José de Santa Rita Durão was the first Brazilian to glorify the Indian, in an epic poem published in 1781. It tells of the history of the colony from its discovery to the expulsion of the last of the Dutch invaders. Its title, *Caramuru*, was the name given to a shipwrecked Portuguese sailor found by Indians who made him their king. It was a somewhat rosy political allegory. Similar themes occurred in the novels of the nineteenth-century Indian Romantic José de Alencar, glorifying Indian life. An opera by Carlos Gomes based on one of these stories lent its overture to the state to serve as the national anthem.

We in the cities consider ourselves beyond the 'simplistic' beliefs of the Indians. But even in the cities we aren't safe from the fear of nature. We fear an imminent ecological catastrophe as a result of upsetting the balance of nature. We examine our skins for melanomas as we wait for science to offer a solution to the hole in the ozone layer, which science failed to notice, and the effects of which it can't predict. We huddle like children in the forest as doomsayers predict global warming, floods and famine. We buy anything in a green package and we are inclined to buy into the theory of Gaia, the Earth Goddess, propounded by Professor James Lovelock, which says, paraphrasing the Indians, that the earth is a living being and, scavenged of her forces and choked with poisons, she will soon be vomiting all over us, engulfing up our puny civilisation, and lying fallow for a few hundred millennia.

In this new song of Daniel that is the Gaian cult of eco-apocalypse – set for the numerological red zone of the turn of the millennium – there is mixed up a great deal of guilt, fear, the observance of odd dietary rules, and the glimmering of a new morality. These are the classic elements of a new creed, the religion of ecology, of which Lovelock is the first mystical prophet. Others have said the same things, of course, like Chief Sitting Bull a hundred years before, but unlike Professor Lovelock, they lacked the training to debate with the elders of the scientific temple. And, for the moment, the ecological conscience – the germ of a new belief system – lacks the rigour to respond to the complexity of modern society, for who would give up their car to save a tree? But it's noticeable that Green movements, when they organise politically, score immediate gains, usually at the expense of the last band of moral radicals, the Marxists.

In the pre-Christian religions of the Americas – the belief systems of the noble savages that the Jesuits of the missions tried in vain to 'save' – was the pattern of ecological co-existence in a world of limited resources.

It has to be faced that the two ways are not compatible. 'The traditional economy of the Indians is almost the exact opposite of the market economy, in which a person's status increases with his wealth and possessions,' writes the ecologist Peter Bunyard.

224

For the Indians, someone who accumulates wealth is poor indeed, because he must have no one with whom to share.

Towards the end of his life, the psychologist Carl Jung went to Africa, gathering material for what would eventually become his theory of the collective unconscious. He encountered the Masai tribesmen and learnt of the vanished Bushmen of the Kalahari. In Africa, he found wonder and mystery. Jung came to his theories of the common impulses that lie in the human psyche from the observation that as the churches were emptying, his waiting room was filling up. He ascribed this to a common need, what he called a God-shaped hole. He felt that modern man was cut off from his natural self, that he suffers from what Africans describe as a loss of soul.

It would be tragic to find, once they have gone the way of the Kalahari Bushmen, that the Indians of the Amazon forest held some spiritual key, that they had a word for our modern metropolitan sense of loss and displacement, a solution to crime and traffic jams, just as they knew the medicinal secrets of plants.

Twenty-Six

Ailton Krenak is a small man with silky dark hair and a lucid, calm gaze, the leader of the Union of Indian Nations.

A few years ago, he called together the shamen of the Indian tribes of Brazil for a magical ceremony. His aim was to penetrate the dreams of Brazilian politicians and fix in their subconscious a respect for the Amazon and its indigenous peoples.

On another occasion, he was invited to the chamber of deputies, and arrived in a suit and tie, but with his face blackened, an Indian preparation for a funeral.

He lives in the city, but says: 'Cities are a cancer, a leprosy on the face of the earth, and they are a phenomenon of the twentieth century. People who are planning them are worms. And the people who run the media are criminals because they are selling the idea of the paradise city, and it's a lie. Cities are full of violence; against people, against children. It's a mad-house. People want a car, an apartment, a salary, they're searching for something all the time, but not life. And the green parts of the city are the biggest lie of all.'

He says this without anger, without despair, without impatience, as though explaining it to a curious child.

We are sitting in a garden, surrounded by the city, by apartment blocks and telecommunications towers. A flock of green parrots swoops down, rare in the city, chased by a swarm of army helicopters traversing low above our heads.

'But what do you say to these people?' I gesture at the apartments, dumbfounded.

Krenak speaks slowly . . .

'I've been asked the same question in other circumstances. In London, I was told, "We're here in a city with a high quality of life, apparently, planes and cars, and we feel paralysed. We live in a fish tank. How can we change it?"

'I said the cities are not a problem, they're just an expression. The people who come to the cities don't know where they're going, don't know where they come from. They're huddling together but they aren't looking for something together. They are linked to each other but they cultivate individualism. They don't know what the others are thinking. They don't know when children are born, when they reach puberty, when they die.

'People in the forest organise their lives around birth, growth and death and everything is a party, a feast; a feast for planting, for growing and changing one's state, for working, for ripening, for culling. Everything is a feast. Not searching for a plane or a car; looking for joy. When we came into the world, we had the joy of being in a beautiful place full of surprises. To pass your life here is a wonderful gift. It's not a separation, it's a passage from one state to the other, and it remains in memory.

'I carry in me a memory that goes back many, many years, to the birth of my grandfather. The memory of creation is transmitted by the generations. It's not something that was, it's something that is. It's a permanent event. I'm with my ancestors now – and with my children's children.'

The Indians are soft. Their sweet, gentle disposition inspired the raptures of the Jesuits. Ailton's handshake is like holding water. But he has a steady, unblinking gaze that holds me and examines me as he speaks.

He is in his thirties, and has benefited from a measure of respect won by an earlier generation of Indian leaders. Mario Juruna became famous in the Eighties for using a tape recorder to record the outlandish promises and entreaties of the officers of the FUNAI, the federal Indian bureau. Juruna later became a federal deputy, and wrote a book denouncing the practices of the FUNAI, which had been purged of pro-Indian elements by the military, and specialised in setting Indian leaders against each other to preserve its authority to sublet their lands and lead a fat life on the pretext of protecting them.

Juruna learned and used the methods of the colonists and their institutions. Ailton has resorted to the methods of his forebears. He grew up on a reserve where Indians of different tribes, with different customs, were mixed indiscriminately. He himself is descended from two tribes, the Xavante, to which Juruna also belonged, and the Krenak-Aores. He has a Brazilian wife, the granddaughter of Italian immigrants, and lives in a house in the suburbs of São Paulo, on a plot of land that should ordinarily be the site of an elegant villa, like the ones opposite. Instead, perched on the brow of the small hill is an airy, empty building, one of the oldest houses in the state of São Paulo, the floor of which was once the floor of an Indian *maloca*. The river that once ran nearby has become a sewer. The house has been transformed into a small museum. Krenak calls it the Forest People's embassy.

Photos lining the walls show the activities of the Centre of Indian Research, a farm in the state Goias run by Ailton's organisation. It's described as a centre for the study of applied biology and botany. 'Not in the European sense,' says Krenak, 'but how to handle it.' There is a photo of the first graduation group. Carlos Krenak, Bruno Tikuna, Almir Sumi, Abrão and Geraldo Yanomami. The first names are their Brazilian ones; they have a native first name which they don't reveal to outsiders, and the second names are those of their tribes, the extended families from which they descend. Brazilians too are often known by a single name, as their Portuguese surnames are often long and cumbersome.

Ailton was born in an Indian camp, grew up there, and attended school and university. Returning to the camp, he formed a movement, the Union of Indian Nations, that won research grants and subventions from the Catholic University and the Federal University of Goias, and a large bursary from the Onassis Foundation, which paid for the Centre of Indian Research.

Outside, there is a plaque that says, *The Centre for Indian Research is not a place, it's a road that leads back to the memory of the creation of the world. It tells of stories and traditions that we knew long ago, as we knew before the new that is the work of scientists and researchers . . .* The Centre is dedicated to *guarding the memory of plants, animals and stars.*

They are studying native agriculture to find ways to make use of their knowledge of the plants and animals of Brazil, native plants like *calopogonia, macuna, preta, guandu, vagem* – all of them types of bean – and fruits like the *mamão* and tomato. They have been extracting oil from *barú* and *jatobá* nuts. There are fisheries and livestock pens full of boars and rats. 'The aim,' says Krenak, 'is to mix technologies, Indian and Western. All our experiences for the three years of the institute's existence have been noted down in a chaotic way. Now they're being formed into a data bank.' The results – like a flour that can be obtained from grated *jatobá* – are being communicated to the tribes. Rich in protein, the *jatobá* falls to the ground and is eaten by birds and animals. Most of it is lost. 'Indians used it only as a medicine, a cure for stomach ache.' And then there is *barú*, a seed like chocolate, something else that was thrown away.

I ask him who he feels these discoveries belong to.

'When we created the Centre, we didn't have any ideas about the ownership of these things,' he says. Now he thinks that the Indian population should be compensated for the use of their knowledge. 'We made the Research Centre to know what we had, because all these American and international companies were exploiting these things and the Indians got nothing.' He quotes a government figure, estimating Brazil is losing $8 billion a year. 'Brazil is trying to get an agreement signed to get the First World to pay when it uses the fruits of the Amazon. But the rich countries won't compromise and the poor countries have no room to manoeuvre. The US and Japan don't want to stop growing and the poor countries have no choice. The US won't stop destroying the ozone layer but they want us to stop destroying the forest . . . '

This is what Krenak thinks of Collor's much publicised expulsion of the prospectors from the newly established Yanomami territories: 'He sends fireworks here and there – but so what? How are you going to educate people to respect those frontiers? Brazil,' he says, not without humour, 'is a camping site: *seringueiros, fazendeiros, banqueiros, garimpeiros, bandeirantes, operários, empresários, índios, metalurgicos, usineiros!*'

He takes me for a walk around the garden, identifying the native trees, including a jaboticabeira, a tree whose fruit grows on its trunk under generous dark-green foliage. The delicious fruit of the jaboticabeira is a myth for Brazilian kids. If there is a house with one, all the kids will go there.

'There's a kind of *bush phobia* in Brazilians,' he continues. 'They want to destroy the forest, because there's so much; they want to tear it out. To build Brasilia, they destroyed the *cerrado* and then built the city. Then they called in landscapers to plant new trees instead of using the ones that were there. The Brazilians are not going to make good ecologists. They live in this beautiful world and they want to transform it.'

Ailton has observed here the first and greatest condition of the American colonies; the need to conquer, settle and build, to defy the oppression of the open, naked spaces that would otherwise overwhelm them.

Bush phobia. 'People who are born in the bush are viewed by people in the city as backward. It's before television . . . It comes from the last century, when the rich sent their children to Europe and they came back with a European model of the world, of art and architecture. There are Swiss houses in the Avenue Paulista!'

To Ailton, it seems not merely a quirk of style, but an act of supreme absurdity to build in the equatorial hills a house suitable for the Alps.

'They didn't know how to use the energy of the sun, because they ran away from the sun. They used hats and shades to hide from the sun,' he says, echoing the sermons of Father Antonio Vieira 300 years earlier. 'The enormous agricultural potential shows how original, unusual solutions could be born in Brazil: architecture based on Indian forms, medicine based on herbal knowledge, similar to oriental medicine, employing meditation, acupuncture. Why didn't they use it? In medicine, biology, architecture, engineering, Brazil has lost so much already . . . '

Imagine if the Europeans had managed to obliterate oriental medicine in the same way. Where would knowledge of acupuncture come from now? Would we have to wait for science to reformulate it, or to find another species like ourselves in outer space – the only place we are ever likely to find one again to repeat the shock of 1492 – and hope that they hadn't also destroyed such things?

'The sons of whites don't think of Brazil as their home but as a *fazenda*,' says Krenak ruefully. 'Niemeyer filled Brazil with concrete. Nobody can stay there on a hot day. Brasilia is a place with no water, they had to *create* lakes. Instead of using *buriti* – straw – they used fibreglass, a petroleum by-product. The guy who studied in Europe was ashamed of straw because he thought it was a black, peasant material.

'Brazilian culture is a prosthetic culture, grafted onto Brazil . . .'

The head of a mining syndicate once asked Krenak about the forest, the Indian lands. 'Why don't you let us in? We'll extract the gold and the diamonds together. Your people will benefit. We'll help to preserve the environment, it'll be all over.'

'Do you have a mother?' Krenak asked him.

'Yes.'

'The earth is my mother. How would you feel if I took her eyes out, extracted her kidneys?'

The man was furious. 'Are you threatening me?'

TV cameras rolled . . .

'*He* was threatening me!'

In the garden, there are banana palms: fat, flamboyant little bushes that came from Africa, full of bulging fruit on stems too heavy to carry more than one at a time. There are Brazilian pines, *pinheiros*, tall as firs but blighted by pollution. Ailton focuses on the buds that sprout on a fallen tree. 'When the tree is sick it sends

231

all its energy to the bark, to protect itself. That's why it grew weak inside and the wind could blow it over.' The gales and torrents that have racked São Paulo this year and last are not normal. A few years ago, they caused dramatic floods in Rio. These are the furies of a sky bloated with toxins it can't absorb. 'The earth is sick and when you are sick your body can't function,' says Ailton. He is acquainted with the theory of Gaia, and thinks there is nothing particularly new in the idea of a conscious planetary entity.

'The earth is my mother.'

Ailton talks of urban apocalypse, but appears serenely untroubled himself.

'The great problem is going to come when you have nostalgia for nature and the cities are so big that you can no longer *find* nature. There's no nature left.'

I ask if he has a solution.

'There is no simple answer. I was in the University of São Paulo and a geographer asked how he could help the people of the forest. I said the best way would be to stay here. Find a balance here. Stay and help the people of the city.

'Brazilian people go to the bathroom and look to the horizon, they don't know where their shit goes. The sacred sense of water has been lost. People with money buy bottled water. Others drink their own shit, and when they put chlorine in they drink that instead, destroying their intestinal bacteria . . .

'If the water is dead, the spirit is dead. Even just splashing it in your face . . . '

The woes of the urban-dweller do not preoccupy the modern Indian leader.

'Indigenous people are all around the world. It's a quiet people but it accounts for two-thirds of the world. I look and I see more that is traditional. Take away Europe, the US and Japan and where else do you see anyone that counts the time like that, crazy people, accelerated?

'The Third World is another way of saying people who are outside modern civilisation. Modern civilisation is a group of enterprises that try to dominate people because they need trained people to fulfil their planning. It's a temporary arrangement brought about by those people.

'For a long time it was also an ideological arrangement: right and left. Happily this ideology is being dropped. What'll be left after that is people who will again have a chance to live without frontiers, without control.'

He identifies the fear of the urban dweller, the fear of loneliness: people crowded in an elevator, going up, up together but afraid of each other.

'Western civilisation is a detour,' he says flatly, adding that it 'has happened in Indian tribes too. We have stories about people taking this detour – but they were white people . . . '

Ailton wears a necklace with the teeth of a monkey around his neck, over a black T-shirt and a jean jacket. I ask what the necklace signifies. He smiles. 'The Christians arrived with crosses around their necks that signified Christ's crucifixion.' He breaks a few leaves from the branch of a *pinheiro* and rubs them in his palms, then he presses his palms against my temples and massages them. 'It doesn't signify anything, it just is.'

As we talked, a storm built, the afternoon storm that gathers, filling the streets of the city, the insides of buses and buildings, with electrostatic tension, sending jagged pangs through the temples. These headaches everyone complains of. They take aspirins, figure they must be tired or photophobic or something. The headaches are symptomatic of the gathering clouds, low clouds that lurk behind the apartment blocks, voluptuous and dense. The air becomes suddenly cool, more muggy still.

Breezes lift the edges of papers. The clouds grow, sharp white at the outside and dirty grey inside. The blue of the sky turns to white, till all is white, hazy. All this happens in half an hour. There is a charged stillness that makes the skin shiver, a palpable depression provoking lassitude and nausea. When the rains come it is with sexual release. Some afternoons the rains barely fall, at other times they shower furiously, a spasm.

And it happens every afternoon, an inevitable tension and release, expected and welcome at least for the freshness that will come afterwards, the renewed scents of the flowers. Then the thunder explodes like a cannon, a sound whose source is everywhere, all around at once. And the rain falls at once, like a wave of water crashing down. Krenak predicts apocalyptic tides in the coming years. Already from the skies fall hailstones as big as tennis balls that crash down and smash car windows.

It was never like this before. The summers were hot and humid, the storms building over days and days. Now they come every day, the convulsions of an angry sky. Clouds that sit like fat malevolent goblins, filling the space between the ground and a point high above the earth, too high and too hot to contemplate. But at their centre they are deathly cold, and carry blocks of ice as big as a house.

Twenty-Seven

—————

La Condamine brought to Europe bowls made of it; the king of Portugal had waterproof clothes made of it in 1780; soles of shoes made of it were exported to the US in the nineteenth century, where Charles Goodyear found a way to make the resin keep its softness without becoming brittle. The stakes were raised in 1890, when John Dunlop invented the pneumatic tyre, and later, Michelin adapted it for the automobile.

Because of rubber, peasants came from the *Nordeste* to die in the swamps of an emerald hell, Indian tribes were kidnapped by the *people eaters* to labour in the plantations, while Booth Line ships came to Belem on the Atlantic coast and plied the river to Manaus, bringing European stones to pave the streets, girls to walk them, linen freshly washed in Europe – because the waters of the Amazon were too dirty – and even orchestras and opera stars. In 1896, the curtain rose for the first time at an opera house in the middle of the jungle, and Caruso sang *La Gioconda.*

The opera house, which is smaller than any in Europe but still a marvel, has now been partly restored, a tourist attraction and vestige of Amazon Baroque, the era of King Rubber in Manaus.

A line of Caterpillar diggers caked in red dirt baked orange by the

235

sun, with wheels as big as houses, announce that we are arriving in the city in the heart of the jungle. Chevy pick-ups pass on the road and the wooden shanties begin as we approach the city from the north; Brazilian ribbon development, the same outside every city, with here the emerald forest for a backdrop.

Instead of wood recuperated from building sites, however, these shanties employ the raw materials of the forest, cut down by hand, shaped into rough planks and nailed into two-storey houses. The shacks are built on stilts, the open ground below serving as shelter for chickens and horses. When the rains come, the occupants can see the waters sluicing under the floorboards, leaving the house fresh at least. The roofs are made of the inevitable tin to hold off the tropical downpour. There is cassiterite – tin ore – in abundance, enough to last for centuries, to cover the jungle in tin shacks, in the nearby mine of Pitinga. Giant floating dredgers churn up the silt, spewing 2 million hectares of mud, a sea of mud, to be turned one day into fisheries.

Brazil hopes to rival Malaysia in tin production, revenge for the Malaysian trees that spoiled the Brazilian monopoly in this vital twentieth-century commodity. The botanist Wickham smuggled saplings from Belem, claiming they were orchids, and took them to Kew Gardens in London, where they grew strong enough to be transferred to the British colony and grow in neat, orderly lines, confirming the order of the world.

There are some splashes of colour in the shanties, the beginnings of a gay tropical style, like the modest houses of the *Nordeste*. But any colour is soon faded by the sun, washed by rain and ground by dust. Purple turns to a weak blue and magenta shutters become a dull pink. Sheets and underwear sit like coloured birds on the washing lines on the balconies. There are flowers on some porches. Under the balconies lie piles of logs on which children scrabble.

The population of Manaus has quadrupled in twenty years, and the creation of a free-port, a stroke of inspiration for a city a thousand miles from the ocean, has made it relatively prosperous. Foreign electronics giants have come here to benefit from the tax advantages, making the former rubber city the improbable electronic goods capital of Latin America. There are more than 400 businesses. There are skyscrapers twenty storeys high, and dozens more over ten storeys high, a startling counterpoint of man-made vertigo against the broad jungle horizon. From the top floors of the skyscrapers, the view north is that of any other city: factories and residential suburbs on the low ground, villas and *favelas* on the hills. To the south, across the Amazon, the ocean of green forest begins again.

Inspired by the unexpected sight of the skyscrapers, I try to picture the kind of architecture that would be appropriate to the smouldering ruin of the jungle. Steel and glass defies all sense, but triumphs by virtues of height and air-conditioning. White stucco would be the most elegant against the green trees, an architecture of fluid curves, as imagined by Niemeyer, sloping with the contours of the hills. But what building could bear the heat and humidity, or the silence? The Indians have an answer, building huge houses, the *malocas*, mini-malls made of bamboo and straw, with a wide raised floor and a gently sloping roof. The rain washes rather than persecutes these buildings, leaving them fresh and agreeable. They're open to the breeze, the mosquitoes and the public gaze. But the Indians have no need for privacy. If they want solitude, they have only to go a few hundred yards away.

I picture a radiant city, floating in the sky, above the green carpet and winding rivers; or an eco-friendly city hollowed out under the canopy of leaves, a wooden Venice, like the water-borne cities of Asia. The Brazilians have always looked at the wrong models, at the European and, now, North American blueprints. The canopy could be supported by the trunks of the giant *saumauma*, four yards in diameter and fifty yards high, with bark that resembles the skin of an elephant, ribbed and dark; or the *várzea* that rise like pylons, incontestable pieces of natural engineering. Indians dress their *maloca* at the feet of this great spirit to ask for protection from storms, for the *várzea* is not troubled by anything. Not even fires and chainsaws. *Fazendeiros* don't credit such beliefs but say they are too much bother to uproot, and leave the burnt husks for horses to walk around.

The fish market at Manaus, an iron structure designed by Gustave

Eiffel and manufactured in England, is another vestige of the era of the rubber barons. A rectangular pavilion with a louvred roof running the length to catch the breeze and suck out the smells of the fish, it sits with one end high on stilts over the river, for the river is low at present, its banks covered in garbage, the garbage covered with massive black vultures, loitering implacably, fighting with children to pick the dump clean. Riverboats and steamers sit below in the water, amid the small fishing boats. In the lagoons and inlets that stretch along the coast are flat-bottomed river boats and wharves, some of them the old rubber processing plants, now fallen idle.

Further along, by the port, there are huge container ships. When the haze builds it's hard to see the opposite shore. The Amazon is three miles wide at Manaus, and deep enough to berth the ocean-going freighters that come and go from an ocean a thousand miles away.

For six months of the year, the city is deluged with rain, a warm rain from heavy grey skies that floods the roads, built for this reason with a high camber and deep storm drains in the old town. The rains are announced by winds that arrive with a sudden thunderclap. The grey waters of the great river, apparently placid, hide swirling eddies of dangerous currents.

On a Sunday afternoon, I join hundreds of people going to the beach, to swim in the Amazon. The water is opaque and rust-coloured from the red dirt, but clean and refreshing. Nobody seems much concerned about piranhas, which are rare near the city, and more likely to be found up distant creeks.

Relatively affluent for Brazil, its street markets full of cheap electronic goods, Manaus is the most decadent of cities, which existed for a moment and then had no reason to exist, so one had to be found. Tourism is touted as the base of the next economic cycle, and already there are regular flights from the international airport to the US and Germany. But this reckons without the ability of the forest to inspire and then mock the grandest of designs, like those of the industrialist Daniel K. Ludwig, who built a giant paper mill

238

in Japan and towed it to the Amazon, losing a billion dollars. The mill was bought by Brazilian investors and now turns a profit.

Brazilians dream of exploiting the wealth of the Amazon. To the southeast, 700 miles away in the state of Pará, is the city of Itaituba, centre of a mining region five times the size of Belgium, with a 'pleasure zone' of thirty-two nightclubs, many offering underage prostitutes, Indian girls sold by their fathers for a few bottles of *cachaça*, or the kidnapped children of *caboclo* peasants. The public and the federal authorities are scandalised, but there are just four policemen in Itaituba.

Even this pales next to the planned industrial inferno of the Carajas project, the greatest iron ore deposit in the world, enough, it is said, to last for five hundred years, located in a range of hills at the southeastern rim of the forest. The exploitation of this region will make the Valley of Death near São Paulo look merely quaint. With the finance of northern banks – including many in Europe, which will be a major client for the steel – twenty-eight foundries are to be built. Four are already operational and three more are under construction. The banks have conditioned their financing to studies on environmental consequences, and these studies appear to have okayed the destruction over the next twenty-five years of a forest area the size of Great Britain to provide cheap fuel for the furnaces to smelt the ore. The banks were presumably reassured by Article Seven of the new constitution, which obliges mining companies to repair the damage they cause to the environment, noble but impracticable. The banks have commissioned no studies into the consequences in terms of human misery either: economic slavery, disease, work accidents and child prostitution. Nor have their depositors in the north, who think the social ills of the Victorian era a thing of the past, asked for anything more than a sound return on the money lent. By sacrificing its trees as well as its people – more than a third of whom are virtually starving anyway – Brazil will escape the colonial stigma of being an exporter of raw materials, selling bulk metals instead for a few dollars more to repay foreign debts.

From the West comes another threat to the forest. After commissioning the inevitable environmental study, which now lies in a drawer somewhere, the World Bank has extended finance for surfacing BR 364, linking Cruzeiro do Sul in the state of Acre with Pucallpa in Peru and opening a route to the Pacific awaited with impatience by the Japanese, whose appreciation of the virtues of good tropical hardwoods has already led to the destruction of large parts of the forests of Southeast Asia. For a while, a rumour circulated that the Japanese, the world's largest creditor, might swap the debts of Brazil, the Third World's largest debtor, for mineral and forestry reserves. But this was just the Japanese ambassador thinking aloud. The Brazilians rejected the idea. Exploitation of the Amazon has only just begun. Recently, oil deposits have been found under the sandy soil, and Brazil is determined to be master of the oeuvre, even if it means that, having used foreign finance, they end up, like Bolivia when Potosi was finally exhausted, owing more than they earned.

———

The *Governador* likes to hunt alligators. He is short, chubby and wears black-leather elevator-heeled boots. The hides of the alligators make fine boots and bags. The *Governador* stalks the alligators from his launch, up quiet creeks, combining trips with speeches to his far-flung rural voters.

They are relatively few, but the *Governador* counts on their support. Three times, he has been elected governor of Amazonas, the largest state in the Amazon region. 'I wasn't elected by the trees,' he says. 'I was elected by the people!'

Gilberto Mestrinho is the governor of Amazonas. And the alligators are nasty, wary creatures, who lurk in swamps under the cover of a federal ban on hunting them. The *Governador* accuses the government of hypocrisy. Alligators are hunted in the US, in Africa and elsewhere. Why can't they be hunted in Brazil? The sport would bring tourists. It would help to develop the Amazon region. He accuses the international environmental movement, which is putting pressure on the government, of hypocrisy. There is no ban on cars, he argues, which cause the greatest damage to the environment.

His voters are not great car users. But they like to eat alligator from time to time: a great delicacy in the Amazon. I tried some, despite the ban. It has the rich flavour of tuna and the meaty texture of game.

And his voters contribute in their way to the destruction of the environment, employed to clear the forest for development, churning the red dirt for minerals. Some of them even work for relatives of the *Governador*, who own the mining company Gold Amazon, which covets guess which mineral. Those who don't vote for the *Governador* accuse him of having a vested interest.

The environmental movement is the guise of other vested interests, retorts the *Governador*, that pretend to want to halt mining activity but really want to control it. They don't want to see Brazil develop. They don't want to see competition from Brazilian Amazonian alligator skins, timber or minerals. If gold were properly extracted it would affect huge interests in South Africa or the Soviet Union, so environmental groups defend the inviolability of the Amazon and influence the orientation of governments and congress.

Gold has been found on the Yanomami reserves, and the *Governador*, whose grandmother was Indian, would like to see it mined by foreign companies, with a royalty for the Indians. In any case, he doesn't understand why they need such a vast reserve: 9.3 million hectares. He says there are far fewer Yanomami than the government thinks: 3000 or so. And, after the invasion of the *garimpeiros* in recent years, this may be true. He would like to see the reserves shrunk. 'Even if they drove Jeeps and flew planes they'd spend their whole lives getting to know the reserve, it's so big!'

Reducing the Yanomami reserve is one of the proposals in the Amazon Code formulated by the *Governador*, a charter he intends to put to congress. For this, he is looking for the support of the governors of the eight other states that comprise the Amazon. Governor Edmundo Pinto of Acre would like to see Amazon development too, but he is not convinced. He says Mestrinho's code risks turning the region into 'a chainsaw empire'. His objection will be overcome when he is found dead in a luxury hotel room in São Paulo. The motive for his murder is unclear.

241

Mestrinho argues that the federal government should stop protecting alligators, 'who invade our villages and eat our children!'

The *Governador* has embarked on a populist crusade, defending the Amazon against Brasilia and the foreigners. Brasilia never cared about the jungle until the West saw the fires raging on their satellite maps in 1987. Now the government shrewdly sees in world concern at the fate of the forest that it has a new bargaining chip at the World Bank table. Even before the wealth of the forest can be exploited, it can serve as collateral. The government is examining its options, which entails gelling, for the moment, the exploitation of the forest.

'I'm against this business of the forest being untouchable,' says the sixty-three-year-old instigator of the Amazon Code. Ecologists, he claims, 'are creating the conditions for man's expulsion from the Amazon. He can't exploit the forest, he can't fish, he can't hunt and he can't mine. What's he going to do? Something is wrong here.' He grows angry at the interference: 'I don't say anything about the way the North Americans treat their Indians, or the way the Italians treat gypsies. They never asked me before they dropped the atom bomb or sprayed Agent Orange over South Vietnam!'

The *Governador* has been invited to address an Amazonian conference that is being held in São Paulo. He is the first speaker, and he thanks the environmentalists who have come from all over the world for inviting the governor of the largest Amazonian state, prefacing his remarks by saying, 'I'm not an enemy of ecology.' But he accuses the ecologists of ignorance and meddling . . .

He began in the summer of 1991 to look for support for his Amazon Code, which would allow controlled exploitation of the forest. Mining interests would be allowed to operate much more widely, providing they respected environmental safeguards. Approval for operations and responsibility for control would be transferred from federal to state authorities. The *Governador* would be able to open up the Amazon as he saw fit. He points to his own record of conservation, claiming his state is one that has least damaged the forest.

Tania Munoz, president of IBAMA, the federal environmental agency, and one of President Collor's Green appointees, says the code is 'lamentable and opportune'. The newspaper *O Globo* attacked it as 'a collection of absurdities'. But this snub by the intelligentsia of the south simply gives more force to supporters of Mestrinho's Amazon revolt.

The *Governador* is no stranger to controversy. As a congressman in 1964, he was impeached for alleged corruption, but nothing was proven. Gold Amazon was suspected of involvement in the deaths of seventy-two Tukano Indians in 1986, the worst Indian massacre for decades, but nothing was proven. His critics say that behind his Amazon Code lie mining companies that contribute to his campaign funds, and that he has taken up the flag of commercial interest for his own interest, but of this there is again no proof. Mestrinho denies any links with mining companies. It's obvious where his true interests lie.

'I wasn't elected by the trees,' he says. 'I was elected by the people.'

His adversaries say he was re-elected after distributing 5000 chain-saws to the *posseiros*, the pathetic, impoverished smallholders of Amazonas. He denies this too, 'But if I had, what would be wrong with giving decent tools to these miserable people? Northerners would like our people to use only axes, and remain bogged down in poverty. Well, it's we who will decide about the development of the Amazon!'

This kind of rhetoric goes down well with the generals ... 'There is a long history of attempted foreign invasion in the north of Brazil,' says General Thaumaturgo Sotero Vaz, chief of the army in the state of Pará. 'The Dutch, the French, the English have tried, and we have always repelled them. And now it starts again. This time, they are disguised as ecologists. But we will once more send these scoundrels back!' According to the general, the international community, under the pretext of saving the planet, wants to steal Brazil's green treasure, a patrimony lodged deep in the army's *esprit de corps*.

One of the highest military distinctions in Brazil is the Amazon Survival Award, the recognition of prodigious feats of endurance and self-reliance. Until now, the military has been able to justify its budget, which it effectively voted itself, by the argument of the red

243

menace. At the end of the Eighties, in the Escola Superior da Guerra in Rio, the political academy of Brazil, a new theory began to circulate, in which the spectre of the Communist International was replaced by the danger of the NGOs, Non Governmental Organisations seeking control of the forest and its resources in the name of environmental or humanitarian causes, under the aegis of the USA, via the UN; the menace of the Green International.

It's not the first time Amazon nationalism has been voiced. In 1968, the then governor of Amazonas, Artur César Reis, was warning of covetous international eyes on the Amazon, a region whose 'resources are ample enough to sustain Brazil for centuries'. He said the government should be ready to resort to '*manu-militari*' to expel 'the missionaries and the pseudo-scientific survey missions'. He was apoplexed at a federal offer to accept the migration of 250,000 Arabs from the West Bank after the recent war between Israel and Egypt.

Among those who support the *Governador* today are Senator Albano Franceo, president of the National Confederation of Industry. He scoffs at the claims made for the environmental value of the forest. 'The Amazon forest is old and decrepit. The level of photosynthesis has greatly declined. One could cut it down and build dams and it wouldn't make much difference. We know today that 95 per cent of the world's oxygen is produced by the oceans.'

The *Governador* accuses the Northerners of being ecological fanatics, more concerned with plants than people.

'We mustn't mock the concern of the world,' protests Tania Munhoz at Mestrinho and his supporters. 'We could very well reconcile development with respect for ecosystems. It's a necessity even. And we must certainly be ready to negotiate a hard bargain with the developed countries, but the so-called internationalisation of the Amazon that you pretend so much to fear has been a fact for a long time. You know as well as I do that multinationals already control the greatest number of mines, industries and farming and forestry projects. And with your blessing, *senhores*!'

Gilberto Mestrinho is encouraged that Brazil is becoming interested in the Amazon region.

'Until the Sixties, the region was of interest only to Humboldt and Hitler, who had plans for the settlement of the Amazon. When the US proposed to flood the Amazon, where were the environmentalists?

'Now anything we do in the Amazon is harmful. Why? Because with satellites we discovered the greatest mineralogical bounty in the world. Then the Amazon became untouchable. Because the exploitation of the Amazon would have harmed international interests!

'In Brazil we began to believe that the forest is being destroyed. It was preached that we would no longer have trees in the states of Acre and Amazonas. But that hasn't happened, because the satellites don't distinguish between mist and smoke. Nonetheless the world became very emotional. We couldn't remove a single tree because the weather in Sweden would be affected. The idea spread that we would be harming the climate worldwide. But the forest is extremely dense and dark, it has a natural process of renewal.'

He holds up a pie-chart of the world lumber market. 'South America, which has half of the world's forest, doesn't take part in this market. The First World doesn't want to share anything, just a lot of rhetoric and hypocrisy. Anyone in the Amazon knows we can exploit the lumber. If we cut down a tree at eighty centimetres it will grow again. For many years, the railways were powered by lumber and can anyone find the source of this lumber now? Lumber exploitation at six hundred and thirty dollars per acre offers a better yield than agriculture but again we're thwarted by environmentalists hiding economic interests.

'As for the *garimpeiros*, mining all over the world is harmful because it is not an organised activity. The miner has become a bandit. We have to organise and teach the miners, teach them not to use mercury. The devastation is not as bad as it sounds, and it's confined to a few regions. But for this the ecologists raise a fury, these same people who do nothing to stop the sale of mercury! No, they sell us all the mercury we want.

'When it was seen that there were enormously valuable gold reserves in the Roraima region, the environmentalists got on their feet, to create a reserve for the Yanomami. My grandmother was an Indian, I grew up with Indian people. I know what they want

245

... Why do they need such a large area, too big for them ever to know? Because a Swede says we have to preserve them!

'We *can* have sustainable development. We have to use native experience. Timbers, animals, fauna and so on, we need to update our knowledge. But first we have to demystify the Amazon. The burning was not what people think it was. Biodiversity could be maintained by just 28 per cent of the forest. And we would have to flood only 3 per cent to generate all the energy that Brazil uses today.'

He proposes a legal framework by sector: tourism, lumber, mining, transportation. 'We need a framework for entrepreneurs. We must discuss the Amazon without emotion. Of the original forest, only 1.2 per cent has been affected. If we had scientific help we could exploit it properly but we don't get it, because economic interests don't want the competition. It suits them that the Amazon goes on being the beautiful gift of God . . .

'The developed world destroyed its environment for comfort and well-being. One third of the agricultural support of the EEC, which prevents our farmers from exporting, would pay for the cleaning up of the industrial pollution in Europe. Instead, they turn to us . . .

'You keep your hunger, your misery, your poor people, they tell us, but preserve your trees so we can come one day and enjoy them. I can't put up with this!'

Twenty-Eight

The *Governador* has a point. This is acknowledged even by his opponents, like Professor Orlando Valverde, seventy-five-year-old president of the National Campaign for the Defence and Development of the Amazon, the very first pro-Amazon group, formed in the Sixties to fight the Hudson Institute project to flood the entire region for hydroelectric power to drive the whole of America.

'I enjoyed his lecture,' says the professor, 'and I believe he's not an enemy of ecology but it's wrong to say that nobody protested at the project for the Great Amazon Lake. We fought that and several of our members ended up in jail as a result. The Brazilian environmental movement grew from that.'

The author of five books on the Amazon, the professor went to work in the Sixties on the Brasilia-Belem road, part of the *Transamazônica* project. 'I was captivated by the forest. You realise how little you know. It was really exciting. I made a tremendous sacrifice, but I'm glad,' he reflects. 'All my children are engineers, you know, even the girls.'

Professor Valverde agrees with Mestrinho that the Amazon is not untouchable. 'But he refers to natural renewal, and it's just not possible when great areas are deforested. We agree that you must value the experience of the natives. But we don't agree that

247

28 per cent is sufficient to preserve biodiversity. Where the species are located, nobody knows. If you don't know which part to preserve, what do you do?'

He displays a veteran impatience with Mestrinho's nationalistic cant. 'I agree with his comments about pollution from the First World, but we have allies there too, not only enemies. The interests are spread throughout the world, not just to make money.' And he scoffs at the statistics quoted by Mestrinho minimising the damage so far, saying that about 8 per cent has been 'cut clear, has gone, though a NASA survey says as much as 25 per cent has been partly ruined.'

He points out that Mestrinho's remarks about the Yanomami reserve have to be put in context. The reserve represents just 1 per cent of Brazilian territory, whereas the Venezuelans have granted the Yanomamis, who know nothing of the borders between the two countries, a reserve of equal size, representing nearly 10 per cent of Venezuelan territory. He adds that in 1991, the Inuit were given one fifth of Canadian territory, plus $26 billion.

'The Yanomami are not nomads, they are gatherers. They depend on a very large area. Their agriculture is a system of shifting cultivation, they work a plot for two or three years and they make sure to encourage secondary growth to regenerate the primary forest.'

He doesn't agree with swapping debt for conservation, 'because they would get it cheap. The foreign banks knew that the military was corrupt. Brazil was poor' – he shakes his head – 'then it became miserable.'

'Who are the enemies now?' I ask.

'Mestrinho is the enemy! I don't know all of them, fortunately.' He means the big eyes on the Amazon. 'I don't want to know them. I am a decent man.'

The nationalistic, anti-north cry of 'Hands off my forest, I'll cut it down if I want' can be heard all the way to the *favelas*, and in the hallways of universities where foreign professors find themselves harangued at the mention of ecology.

With the shanties filling uncontrollably, violence growing daily, and corruption – Collor's personal crusade before he was accused of being the most corrupt of all presidents – still rampant, the 'internationalisation' of the Amazon offers a convenient diversion. The Amazon remains a myth for Brazilians, with its vast riches awaiting the poor peasant.

The first instinct at the haemorrhage of the open veins of Latin America has always been protectionism. It's against the law to export the least weed from Brazil without a licence, which didn't stop Sir Henry Wickham stealing the secret of rubber from the Indians. Not a cent was ever returned to them from the wheels on which the modern world rolls.

The second reaction is barter. Collor – with few credible strategies left – talks of exchanging Brazil's enormous foreign debt off against the setting aside of large areas of the forest. It's an idea that might appeal to ecologists but it leaves bankers wondering what their return will be other than a vague 'green dividend' for the publicity-conscious among them. The great champion of this idea has been the governor of the state of Pará, Jader Barbalho, who has even worked out some figures, putting at $130 million, coincidentally the debt of the state of Para, the cost of an eco-freeze on a million hectares for twenty years. His plans call for selling to foreign companies not minerals but eco-tourism. The idea has received serious interest from Germany.

The fires consume an average of six million hectares a year from the largest forest in the world, 500 million hectares. They are lit by *fazendeiros* looking to enlarge their cattle ranches or smallholders trying to scratch a living from soil that falls fallow in two or three years.

At the bureau of the federal environment agency in Brasilia, every day at midday, two satellites transmit their photos. According to Celsio Schenkel, Director of Ecosystems, the fires have dimmed from 14,000 square kilometres burned in 1990 to 8000 square kilometres in 1991. The fires started by smallholders are growing fast, but they represent only a small percentage. The fires started by the large landowners have greatly diminished. But this is not the result of some sudden attack of environmental guilt.

Large-scale deforestation is costly and with the global recession they haven't the means to invest.

José Lutzenberger, Secretary for State for the Environment until he told foreigners not to bother sending money as it would only be stolen, is one of the doomsayers, influenced by Gaian doctrines of James Lovelock, whose books he translated in Brazil. Lutzenberger wants all hands off the Amazon. He has suggested that it will suffice to destroy one third of the jungle for the process of deforestation to become irreversible. Of the uncanny mix of deep humidity and searing heat, only the heat would be left. Nobody can say what effect the transformation of an area the size of Western Europe into a desert would have on the global climate.

Nobody knows for sure what the role of the Amazon is in the world ecosystem. Even conservationists admit that the rain forest is not, as was once thought, the lungs of the world, but probably an enormous regulator of temperature and humidity. It's also a huge plant and animal reserve the details of which are known perhaps only to the Indians. It was only thanks to years of work with the Indians by its scientists that the German firm Bayer was able to profit from the pharmaceutical uses of the venom of the Jajaraca snake, notably against hypertension.

The forest has become the chic concern of comfortable environmentalists, comfortable in their cars, their warm houses, their nuclear-powered world. Development aid has become a fashion business. The least Amazonian project can gather funding easily, but relief projects for the *Nordeste*, the *sertão* where twice as many live, suffering much greater hardship from the recurring drought, flounder.

And quite out of fashion, like the *Nordeste*, is any aid to some of the largest shanty towns in the world: those of Rio de Janeiro and São Paulo, where the latest flocks of poor migrants can't even find a place in the *favelas*.

'It's easy to talk about ecology when you aren't hungry,' says the governor of the state of São Paulo, and nobody, environmentalist or nationalist, can disagree.

250

Twenty-Nine

At the bus station in São Paulo, where Nilson has come to meet his sister Meris, the people shuffle, dragging bags and cases. One family has arrived with heavy cardboard boxes, wrapped in newspaper and tied with string, that they drag to a waiting car. The boxes are full of cocoa pulp that they're going to turn into confectionery.

There is a TV crew waiting for suspected cases of cholera on the green and yellow Itapemirim line buses from the *Nordeste*. They are there to follow up a story in the newspapers that morning about the disease spreading southwards. By four o'clock, the TV crew is heading back to the studio with nothing to edit. There is no point in waiting, because if someone staggered from the bus after three days' travel and collapsed in a heap with 40 degrees of fever and chronic diarrhoea, it would be too late to make the evening news. This is what happened after the TV crew left. The unfortunate person sweated and perhaps died, remaining a statistic and not a case history. Such is the existential problem of catastrophe in a world where they let the camera crews through ahead of the paramedics.

To halt the spread of the epidemic to Rio and São Paulo, medical teams have been checking the buses, asking passengers if they feel OK, or if they have the symptoms of fever, vomiting and diarrhoea that bring death in less than forty-eight hours, a quick, delirious death from extreme dehydration.

Nilson doesn't know this, because he can't read the newspaper. He could, if he had the time, but he worked for twelve hours the day before. He had set off at 6 a.m., arriving by 8 at Tony's. Then he went with the others in the back of a truck carrying potted palms and bathroom towels to an office building downtown. They arrived at 9 and the day began, cleaning offices. He worked for twelve hours. They finished at 9 p.m. and it took him nearly three hours to get home.

First he took the subway. Then he had to wait for the bus. While he waited, he ate a cheeseburger at the counter in the bus station. It was all he had eaten since the morning, when Tony had given them coffee and some cake. So he was tired, and all he saw on the TV when he got home was a country duo, a *Dupla Caipira*, singing about how sweet life used to be. Nilson had fallen asleep long before the song ended.

Tony had given him the afternoon off to meet his sister. First he had to rush to see the woman he worked for, Marly, who had promised to lend him some money against his wages to pay the deposit on a room that he was going to share with Meris. The rent would be higher at the new place, but Nilson has found a new job now and Meris will be working too.

Nilson will soon be quitting Tony. He has found a job as a door clerk in a building for $170 a month. He found the job through an agency. A friend who works with Tony applied, but couldn't read or write. So he told Nilson about the job. Nilson will be working the night shift, from 7 p.m. to 7 a.m. He is lucky to have found the job, as he must move out of the room he is in and get another so Meris will be able to stay with him. He will have to pay the rent for a room himself instead of sharing it, until Meris can find work. Tony says things are not going so great at the moment, but he's promised to see what he can do.

In the new job, Nilson will have to be wary. Doormen and guards are the targets of robbers who attack them to get their guns. Nilson won't have a gun. If he was armed, he would have to have a licence. But the robbers don't know that.

The central bus station of the city of São Paulo is the disembarkation point for a pitiful human tide. It's a bus station on the scale of the American continent, so big you can't see the other end of the hall where people sit or sleep, waiting for their connections. The first time Nilson came here, he was getting off the bus, like seven million others before him. He felt small and afraid. He thought someone was going to steal his bag. He couldn't see his elder sister Deborah, who had said she would be there to meet him. She had sent him the ticket and had promised to be there, and he felt a rising panic as he saw how big the station was. It was bigger than the station in Rio de Janeiro, where he had got off to buy a soft drink at the counter and indulge in the fact that he was in Rio for the first time, like a tourist. He observed the Cariocans, loud and swaggering. He had never before seen so many people with sneakers and sunglasses. If anyone caught his gaze he gave them a shy thumbs-up, and they returned the gesture! Rio was big, but São Paulo was bigger. It was faster and colder. This was the impression he had from the streets as the bus headed in, and in the three years he had been here, this impression was confirmed. In the winter, Nilson wore a jacket for the first time. São Paulo was newer, and the people busier. And he couldn't smell the ocean, as he could even in Rio. He was far from the coast. When he was out on the fishing boats, he sometimes felt that he never wanted to come back to the shore, so complete was the world, and so sure and valid his place in it, on the boat doing what he knew well. Now he sometimes feared he would never see the ocean again.

Nilson is looking, searching for Meris. He watches a family leaving the bus, a woman with four children. The children are frail and weak and their clothes are dirty. They have the soft, hungry eyes that Nilson knows from the farm workers lost in the town of São Luis. The youngest of the children is a mere baby, perhaps a few weeks or months old, trembling on the shoulder of her mother. The woman is skinny – the whole family is starving, Nilson knows – but she is well-dressed, wearing a fresh white blouse and neatly pressed slacks that she has kept throughout the trip for her arrival.

Hunger and pride. They've been driven by hunger and pride

to leave their shacks and move south, on the remorseless road to the city, part of the massive rural exodus. The children are thin and ill-fed. Their walk is feeble, their look dizzy and tired. Their backs are bowed, their hips are sunken, but the mother is *smiling*. She has made it, she has got here, where there are factories and municipal houses. She is proud, and she believes everything will be alright now. She just has to find a home and a job. The baby is asleep on her shoulder, unaware of the new and dreadful world that awaits.

In the recently built bus terminal, vast concrete halls under a concrete canopy that already leaks water here and there onto orange plastic seats, children scream and run and a Japanese girl is engaged in a long passionate kiss with her Portuguese boyfriend. Her tongue explores his mouth with teenage abandon. She shifts her legs but, trapped in the seat next to her, he turns his hips.

On the windows of the ticket offices is a sign reminding customers of the new federal rules. Children aged twelve to sixteen must have valid papers to travel alone. A list follows: birth certificate, etc. Under twelve, they must be accompanied by a legal guardian, parent, or adult family member. The measure is designed to stop the stream of orphans into the big cities, the *pixotes*. So they hang around the bus stations trying to steal rides, not sure if they have arrived somewhere or if they have yet to leave.

Nilson takes his sister home on the subway. Meris' eyes are bright. She hangs on to the straps and watches the tunnel walls rushing by. It's the first time she has ever been on a train, let alone one that hurtles along underground, and bravado quickly overcomes her fear. She sees the people sitting in the car with bored, weary looks. How can they be so unimpressed, she wonders. Right away, she decides that this is the correct expression, and sets herself to mastering it. She lifts her chin and sucks her cheeks. As the sleek, clean, cool metal car pulls into the third station – which is the Centro – she sees the clothes of the people on the platform, the jeans and shirts, the dresses and the bags they all carry, and decides that this is paradise. This is where she wants to be.

254

'You're gonna work at the same company as me,' Nilson tells her. He has everything fixed up. 'You're going to be a cleaner, like me.'

'I don't want to be a cleaner,' Meris protests. 'I want to be a maid.'

'You have to. Anyway, a maid is a cleaner.'

'Oh,' says Meris.

She knows that the people in the carriage, even the ones with brown skin like her, are not cleaners. She looked at their hands, which were smooth, and their knees, which were covered by stockings. These women worked in shops, she decided. They were the women who waited behind counters, who sat in the diners at midday with men in shirts and ties.

Then she thought about her baby. She felt sad, wise and foolish at the same time. Her baby was three weeks old. She had heard her crying all the way here, felt her breasts aching and felt the cotton damp in her bra.

'What about Carlos,' asks Nilson, 'is he looking after her?'

She screwed up her face. Guys only want to make babies, they don't want to look after them. 'Mama is looking after her.'

Sad, wise and foolish. She had wanted him to be the first, because otherwise it would have been someone else and she was frightened of that. They only did it four times before he stopped coming to the house. Then she found she was pregnant. No one knew until it was almost ready. They thought she was getting fat at first. When her sixteenth birthday came, she decided to tell Quiani, who told Marinete, who told her mother. Making babies is easy. She just lay down, and there was the baby, covered in blood and crying, a sound so soft her heart broke. Her mother took her new grandchild and wondered if she had the courage to leave it somewhere. Then she sat down and cried with the baby, and one of her sisters took the infant, cleaned it, and gave it back to Meris. That was three weeks ago. Now here she was, in paradise, so excited she gasped, especially when she saw how elegant and assured the men looked. They had to be better than Carlos, she decided.

Nilson saw that she had started to sob.

'Meris,' he said. He put his arm over her shoulder and tried to avoid the stares of the other passengers. He needn't have, for they all knew at once what had happened. They knew about Nilson's father, and about Meris' baby. They could tell by looking at the faces of Nilson and Meris. If it hadn't happened to them, or to someone in their family, they had heard it from their maid or their cleaner. There were seven million stories like those of Nilson and Meris in São Paulo. The tears they elicited were poured into the cement that held the bricks. They're what built the city, what keeps it running.

At the next stop, they got off and sat in the park. It was early evening and the park was full of people. Meris had never seen so many people. She was gratified to discover that the world was so big, and made up her mind to lose herself in it, to become someone new.

Thirty

They paved paradise, and put up a memorial to Latin America,
near the Barra Funda and the *favelas* of the Viaduto Pompéia, in
the middle of a sea of undulating concrete, cool concrete conceived
by Niemeyer to be without right angles, in a flatland between the
railway and the residential suburbs, the empty lots and the shopping
centres . . .

In the middle is a statue, a cubist concrete hand, ten feet tall,
palm open to the sky, bleeding. The bloodstain forms the shape of
Latin America. Across the road is the Latin American parliament.

'We got permission from Niemeyer to plant palm trees,' Maureen
Bisilliat tells me, with an air of triumph. 'Get some trees in here, in
the middle of all this concrete!'

The memorial is 'a space of meeting and identity for all where we
can come daily to face our history and look for the elements capable
of revealing our future,' according to Governor Orestes Quercia.

Latin America is an enigma in its own eyes, according to Eduardo
Galeano.

The memorial is an empty space of unfaced concrete, buildings
like buried cylinders and curved, cantilevered hangars of cool concrete. When the rains come, they leave glistening pools. Steam rises
from the concrete as the sun returns.

257

In one part of the memorial is the *Pavilhão da Criatividade*, a long scroll of concrete like a twenty-foot high wave breaking on a curved shoreline. Behind the glass wall that runs the length of one side is a collection of pieces of folk art from across Latin America, pieces full of vivacity, humour, abandon; clashes of colour and sensibility, religions and cultures; everything produced by hands that inherited, held in memory the form of what they were going to make. Pieces of a brightness and sensuality that belongs to children. Here is more magic we have lost – or find only in airport gift shops, synthetic imitations to which Maureen Bisilliat, who assembled the collection, refers with sorrow.

She takes me on a tour of the museum.

From Ecuador there are velvet robes; ceramics painted with ziggurat animal patterns, like the backs of turtles, by the Canelo Indians; a wooden statue of Mama Negra, a man in drag who milks a giant cow in the fertility feasts of Cotopaxi. From Peru there are crazy-coloured costumes with silver embroidery and some made of coins sewn together used in a dance that satirised the conquistadores; a triptych of clay tableaux show the exodus of the inhabitants of Ayacucho, which began with the happy rural life of yesterday, endured political upheavals overflown by a blood-spattered helicopter, and ended in the backyards of Lima, where they have come to escape the guerrilla war with the Sendero Luminoso.

Clay figurines of religious processions are common everywhere; brightly painted, with flat innocent eyes, they contain all the optimism of Latin America, and something of the despair. I am profoundly touched by these contemporary relics of an innocent age; naive pieces like the crosses are decorated with shells, dice, confectionery, flowers, stones, small skulls and enamel badges, Christ a face in a chocolate television set. The attitudes are caricatural, caught and frozen at the wrong moment, puncturing official dignity, the spirit of *Carnaval*.

From Guatemala, a conquistador wears a braided jacket, parrot feathers and a monkey face in the Festa da Conquista; the weave and the colours of the sashes worn by peasants indicate status in a code that dates from the pre-Columbian era; there are amulets

258

dedicated to the cult of San Simon, or Judas Iscariot, adopted and venerated for his ability to calm evil spirits.

From Mexico there are skulls and skeletons made of sugar, to give to children on the Day of the Dead, the urban fiesta that permits the dead to come back to life, to remind the living of what is to come; there are cloaked skeletons riding red nags – night mares – or astride a green mantis. The grinning skeletons that inhabit the effigies paraded on the Day of the Dead in the suburbs of Mexico City mock the pretensions of the persons who normally fill these clothes.

From Brazil, carnival garb: hats in the shape of houses, palaces and churches, made out of beads, threads, wire and glass, like the body prosthetics of the carnival costumes. There is an Amazon bestiary carved in hardwoods: Roxinho for the *onça*, a *tamanduá* in Macauba, painted parrots and cranes; cockades large as a horse's yoke made of blue and red plumes fashioned by the Caiapó and Carajá Indians and a necklace made of jaguar's claws.

There is the regalia for the Bumba-meu-boi, a dance of Iberian-African machismo – part bullfight, part Bundu – a dervish in bulls' heads or tribal head-dresses; and a miniature parade of clay figures, all the personalities of the *Bumba-meu-boi da ilha* festival that takes place each year in São Luis, Maranhao. The African Gods were crafty. They hid in the Catholic saints to survive. But the Bumba-meu-boi was different, a cargo cult that found its way out in the bullring, a ritual fight expressed through tauromachy.

The thousands of pieces were all collected by Maureen Bisilliat over a period of two months in the mid-Eighties. Her budget, for purchases, air tickets and hotels for herself and her late husband, was $180,000. The folk history of Latin America. A ridiculous Third World bargain.

'It was a kind of a mythical trip,' she says. 'We had the feeling we were flying like condors over the continent. Usually, to make a museum like this takes years.'

Being in the museum was like being inside a story by Marquez, where it rains for six years without cease and without explanation, where the past is the present.

259

A brisk woman with croaky voice and a nicotine blink, she was born in Surrey, England. Her mother was a painter and her father a diplomat from Argentina. 'I once tried to become British when I was eighteen,' she says ruefully. She has lived in England, Denmark, Colombia. Her father was posted to Washington when the war broke out. Maureen was seven.

After the war, she studied art in Paris and then took up photography. She spent five years documenting the Xingú. 'It was enough, I felt I had become involved without losing objectivity.' She captured them proud and naked, brimming with inner composure, staring into the eyes of the North without panic for once, in all their animal glory.

Of the folk crafts she has just shown me she says:

'It's still alive and evolving. They adopted synthetic colours but with great beauty. Peru exports to Scandinavia. You have this coming and going and if you don't it dies off. Balsa rafts are now made of isopore. They started using the polystyrene.

'But things that are pseudo have no place. Airport has no place but if people use synthetics that's OK.' By airport she means the stools made of softwood rather than hardwood. 'No, it has to be hard!'

Her view of craftwork is of something not to be fenced off, not something you can't touch, like the rain forest.

'All you ever see is images of paradise and devastation . . . My feeling is the obvious feeling – that you have to be careful about it. The topsoil erodes and the rivers get clogged up. The Amazon is big. The part I know is the Xingú park.'

Her photos of the Xingú are the equal of Leni Riefenstahl's pictures of the Masai. She was part of the team that worked in 1968 on a milestone issue of *Realidade*, the Brazilian *Life*, devoted to the Amazon. Thirty reporters and photographers went out, following the army engineers, the road gangs and the migrants, after the decision to open up.

'We went to check the health conditions on the River Purus, towards Acre. Tragic. Families had lost many children to Black Fever . . .

'The word *preserve*: on the one side it's very positive. On the other side it's an illusion. What I know is craft work. *They have* the secret of their forms. So if the involvement as in *desinvolvimento* – development – is done with a conscious reasoning . . . People who work with the rubber, tappers, they have to protect the trees. If you work with, you live off, but if you extract, that's destruction . . . It's like the airport crafts, made en masse.'

Why has she stayed in Brazil?

'Brazil is very vital. There is a tremendous vitality,' she coughs.

Thirty-One

I lie on the hotel bed listening to the sounds outside, the noises of animals: a deep, low grumbling from the cats, gusts of hysterical laughter from bright-coloured birds, monkeys chattering and squealing.

I am in the middle of the rain forest; from the window I can see the murky red-brown waters of the Amazon, meandering through a green carpet. The birds and animals are native species, but they don't live in the forest. They are kept in a zoo in the hotel grounds to provide the atmosphere missing from the surroundings. Near the hotel are public beaches with bars and restaurants and pleasant suburban villas.

Marly had promised to meet me here in Manaus, and then we would go to the jungle, to see if we liked it there, living in a tree-house like Tarzan and Jane. Then she said it was looking hard for her to get away. She had to see her family, she had outstanding commitments related to her new job and, I surmised, a new boyfriend. We talked a lot on the phone, spent the time allotted to us – our time, as she called it, being a fatalist – on crackly, fading connections; we left our passion in a cable on the ocean floor.

Lying on the bed, on the phone to Marly, I am distracted by

the sounds of the animals, Brazil parodying itself for my benefit. I realise that what I like about her is what I like about Brazil, the mix of folly and seriousness; her pride and independence, and her wish to be strong and original. She was a daughter of Yansan, who wanted to build waterworks and housing, someone who believed in magic and science.

By the time we meet again in São Paulo, I will be reconciled to the knowledge that she doesn't need me. I'll say something about being an emotional imperialist, taking advantage of her feelings, and she will give her enigmatic, orchid smile.

We talk on the phone to avoid saying what we have to say. I tell her about the road to Manaus and the skyscraper city in the jungle with its streets full of stalls selling electronic toys. I tell her about the zoo that she would love, it's so corny, so sincere. And about the hotel full of wealthy Brazilians on vacation who come back in the afternoons with their arms full of radio-cassettes, CD-players, cameras and TVs. Then the men just sit around the pool drinking, arguing and getting fat while the women catch up with the *telenovelas* in the TV lounge. They aren't interested in the river cruises. These are full of German tourists. The Brazilians just want to shop.

She says that she can see her country becoming more and more like the United States. And this makes her sad. 'Brazil never used to be a country obsessed with money. Now people are unhappy.'

It's because of the TV, I tell her.

'Yes. Before, they didn't know what they didn't have. Now they know.'

I realise simply that I have been seduced by innocence and folly. I think I could have come ashore in Brazil at any time over the last five centuries and it would have been the same. I glimpsed this, and finally understood it, in the collection of folk art at the *Memoriale*, and I adored it in Marly, dark and tan and young and lovely.

The prodigious magic I discovered was a brush with sensual enchantment in a world ruled by coincidence and laughter; the encounter with sublime, instinctual forces far older than the New World, but nearer there to a gaudy, crazy surface.

263

These forces had lured me back to Brazil, where I was surprised to still find alive, if on the run, a figure of my faded idealism in Rio's Robin Hood. But Escadinha was more like Lampiao, the bandit leader of the *Nordeste* who went about with dollar bills pinned to his hat, than he was like Che. In any case, new verses have been added to the long ballad of Latin American bandit revolutionaries, telling of Abimael Guzman, the mad, murderous Maoist on a quest for bloody absolution. His Shining Path guerrillas served both the interests of the drug cartels in destabilising the region, and the Peruvian government as a pretext for militarisation against the left. Caught in the crossfire between those who claim to defend them, peasants fled the Andean hills to huddle in shacks on the edge of the cities, on the edge of the 21st century.

To understand Escadinha, I had to witness the fate of peasants in Brazil, the latest arrivals in the big city, hanging on to the doors of trains, pressing for space in the elevator in which everyone is your enemy; the pathetic destinies of millions swept up in an ever-quickening rural exodus; people who think that a TV is all the history they will need.

Marly tells me that Nilson, the *Nordestino* she employed to clean her apartment, has started drinking. He turns up less regularly. He complains about his sister, who goes out dancing with men while he works. She says he talks about how long it has been since he saw the sea, his father, and he starts to sob. 'He cries like a child. Then he starts to clean the floor. I don't know what to do.'

The jungle has stopped burning, but the city is still growing.

In the half-made world of Brazil, in the mockeries of laws and institutions, was a carnival reflection of my world; as if from high-sounding principles – the right to vote, to education, to justice – a real country can be born. In the rain forest, Indians carve radios out of wood, and listen for music. But Brazil is not like other countries. Everyone wears a plastic watch in Brazil, even future presidents.

Collor's friends supported his liberal democratic ideals; they wanted to see Brazilian people thrive and move forward, and to prosper along with them. Afterwards, some of them came to see Collor's campaign treasurer, Paulo Cesar Farias, who hung around the corridors, suggesting policy, discussing government contracts. It's how America got built.

The anti-Collor campaign was a replay of the one to get rid of the military government that had opened the way for his election. After the vote in favour of his destitution, the deputies stood up and sang the national anthem. The vote was broadcast live on TV. Many towns set up public screens and unions announced strikes that day so their members could march as the deputies sang.

Like all villains, Collor was also a scapegoat, sacrificed to reinforce Brazil's image of itself as a proper functioning state, and to expiate the ills he hadn't been able to cure. His impeachment was really an exorcism. In the carnival democracy, this ritual aspect was blatant: the black and green daubings across the faces of protestors; the cry of *Fora Collor*, Collor out! From the steps of a public library opposite his home, with its new swimming pool paid for by Farias, the former president denounced the 'crooked oligarchies who didn't want to see my reforms go through'. Collor himself had come from a provincial oligarchy. His anti-corruption drive meant only a changing of the guard. He was so impressed with foreign goods that he got himself a French attorney to lead his team of Brazilian lawyers. It didn't help. Carnival democracy turned the world upside down. A corrupt American president got impeached.

Across the railway tracks from the *Memoriale*, I had watched the bulldozers taking the shacks away under the freeway. Jori was flying a kite she had made with string and paper, flying it high above the freeway, the bulldozers and the police vans, high above the garbage and the debris. The little girl had made the kite from paper she had found in the garbage, paper on which were architectural drawings. When Jori's kite came down near me, I picked it up to give to her, reminded of the Little One sucking her pacifier, the shy gaze in her eyes. The drawings were plans for a nearby shopping mall, to be called the Eldorado Mall.

In the Eldorado Mall, there is a place called America, a restaurant with a ceiling painted a deep, bright blue, and small, white clouds, a perfect American sky, like the sky in the Cathedral of the Poor, or the skies in the old baroque churches, painted by the Little Cripple.

265

In America, the cheeseburgers are plump and juicy, and the salads are called Yuppies. The *caboclos* are still the servants. Small, smiling brown people, the descendants of Amerindians; descended from an idyll to which we dream of ascending.

She smiles and thanks me for my order, and I wonder if it's the smile of the conquered, or that of the conqueror.